This book is dedicated to everyone who gives a '36-hour day' to the care of a person with a dementing illness.

THE 36-HOUR DAY

Caring at Home
for Confused Elderly People

NANCY L. MACE
PETER V. RABINS, M.D.

with
BEVERLY CASTLETON
CHRISTOPHER CLOKE
EVELYN McEWEN

HODDER AND STOUGHTON
LONDON SYDNEY AUCKLAND TORONTO

in conjunction with

AGE CONCERN ENGLAND

British Library Cataloguing in Publication Data

Castleton, Beverly
The 36-hour day: a family guide to caring for persons with Alzheimer's disease, related dementing illness and memory loss in later life.
1. Presenile dementia—Patients—Home care
2. Senile dementia—Patients—Home care
I. Title II. Cloke, Christopher III. McEwen, Evelyn
IV. Mace, Nancy L. V. Age Concern England
649.8 RC521

ISBN 0 340 37012 2

Original USA edition

UK edition (with adaptations)

Typeset in Linotron 202 Baskerville by
Rowland Phototypesetting Limited, Bury St Edmunds, Suffolk

Printed and bound in Great Britain for
Hodder and Stoughton Educational,
a division of Hodder and Stoughton Limited
Mill Road, Dunton Green, Sevenoaks, Kent, TN13 2YD
by Richard Clay (The Chaucer Press) Limited, Bungay, Suffolk

Contents

Foreword

A great many people are involved in the care of elderly patients with dementia, from the doctor and nurse who manage the illness but who can remain detached from the problem, to the sufferer and the care-giving relation, from whom the problem never goes away. The doctor is preoccupied with whether or not he has made the correct diagnosis, undertaken the necessary investigations and prescribed the safest and most effective treatment. The nurse worries how the patient eats, drinks, and sleeps; when and how she uses the toilet; whether she is going to wander away. Meanwhile the patient may be preoccupied with her bowels or with waiting for her long-deceased husband to return from work to eat the meal she has prepared for him. The patient's daughter (and I make no apology for casting both patient and carer in the feminine role, because this is as it is in the majority of cases) is preoccupied with how much longer the patient will exhaust and torment her with outrageous behaviour, and how much longer she will be able to bear it; with what is going to happen next; with what caused it all; with whether she will suffer from the same thing herself in her own old age.

The doctor, nurse, social worker and health visitor endeavour to become aware of the preoccupations of patients, colleagues and relatives, just as relatives want to know what is pre-occupying the doctors. But in many cases the gap remains unbridged. And indeed it is a formidable task to understand, let alone to explain how an intelligent and considerate person, in charge of her own life and sensitive to the needs of others, becomes an irresponsible, dangerous, unfeeling automaton. Also, what happens to a devoted carer who finds herself trapped within four walls with a crazed, unpredictable caricature of a person once loved, now pitied for what she has lost and resented for what she has done to others.

If it is possible for a book to explain these horrifying and bewildering processes in terms that a lay person can understand, this one does so. Its striking title, *The 36-Hour Day*, emphasises that the true victim of this disease is the carer; her many tasks mean that she has not enough hours in the day for the patient's needs let alone for her own. The professional skill of doctors and nurses can do much to mitigate the manifestations of the disease, and even in a few cases to eradicate it. But their work finishes and they go home at night to tranquillity, while the carer battles on bewildered and unenlightened.

This book has now been made available to British readers on the initiative of Age Concern England. The considerable work of 'translating' the terminology and the references to services to fit the British scene has been skilfully executed by Dr Beverly Castleton, with the assistance of the staff of Age Concern England. It is to be hoped that at least one of the 36 hours of the carer's day, and one of the 24 hours of the 'professional's' day, can be set aside for reading this book and referring to it, because it contains much wisdom, sound sense, good advice and practical assistance which can help carers and professionals to understand one another's preoccupations. A more tolerable life for the carer entails better care for the patient and less pressure on doctors and nurses. We should all be grateful for this book.

Professor Bernard Isaacs
Department of Geriatric Medicine
University of Birmingham

Preface

Although this book was written for the families of people with dementing illnesses, we recognise that other people, including those suffering from these conditions, may read this book. We welcome this. We hope that the use of such words as *patient* and *brain-injured person* will not discourage those who have these illnesses. These words were chosen because we want to emphasise that the people who suffer from these conditions are ill, not 'just old'. We hope the tone of the book conveys that we think of you as individuals and people and never as objects.

This book is not intended to provide medical or legal advice. The services of a competent professional should be obtained when legal, medical, or other specific advice is needed.

At present not all professionals are knowledgeable about dementia. We frequently refer to trained personnel who can help you, but we recognise that you may have difficulty finding the help you need. You, the care giver, will need to utilise both professional resources and your own good judgment. This book cannot address the particulars of your situation, but is intended only as a general guide.

In addition we recognise that criteria for allocating services are often locally determined and the provision and availability of such services as home helps, Meals-on-Wheels, day centres, district nursing and community psychiatric nursing vary from area to area. Charging policies may also differ from one local authority to another.

We use examples of family situations to illustrate our discussion. These examples are not descriptions of real families or patients. They are based upon experiences, feelings, and solutions that families and patients have discussed with us. Names and other identifying information have been changed.

Both men and women suffer from these diseases. To simplify reading, we will use the masculine pronouns *he* and *his* and the feminine pronouns *she* and *hers* in alternate chapters.

How the translation came about

When I was first asked by Hodder and Stoughton to comment on *The 36-Hour Day* I said that I thought that it was a superb book, combining practical advice with detailed specific examples of how to cope with a family member impaired by dementia. I also commented on how much more useful the book would be if some of the sections could be rewritten to ensure that all the text was relevant to a British audience.

I, effectively, talked myself into the mammoth, but rewarding task of 'translating' the book. How could I refuse, knowing the desperate need for this book which gives such a wealth of positive guidance to the carers of demented people. Thankfully, it was a task which I did not have to complete alone for soon I was joined by Chris Cloke and Evelyn McEwen from Age Concern England.

Inevitably, Chapters 15 and 16 have had to be extensively rewritten but we have endeavoured to make all the changes sensitive and true to the original intent of the text.

The benefits of having a British version of this excellent book we are convinced will be considerable.

Beverly Castleton

Acknowledgments

So many people have given of their time, experience, and wisdom that it is not possible to name them all. We wish to thank all those known and anonymous who have contributed ideas and information.

The T. Rowe and Eleanor Price Foundation, through the establishment of the T. Rowe and Eleanor Price Teaching Service in the Department of Psychiatry and Behavioral Sciences at The Johns Hopkins University School of Medicine, has brought together a team of people to learn about and teach the care of persons with a dementing illness. Paul R. McHugh, M.D., director and psychiatrist in chief of the Department of Psychiatry and Behavioral Sciences, has made the study of the dementias and their impact on families and patients a major focus of the department. Many of the ideas presented here are his. He has also read the entire manuscript, contributed to its form and content, and advised us throughout its development. Marshal F. Folstein, M.D., director of the Division of General Hospital Psychiatry, has taught us much about the care of patients and their families and has been a source of many of the ideas presented in this book. Ernest M. Gruenberg, M.D., Ph.D., and Morton Kramer, Sc.D., have added to our understanding of the social impact of dementia.

Our colleagues have made significant contributions to the content of the book. Jeanne M. Floyd, R.N., developed many of the management techniques we discuss and has worked closely with us in making specific suggestions about care. Together with the nursing staff of the psychogeriatric unit of the Phipps Clinic and Head Nurse Eva Ridder, R.N., she has developed and tested many new ideas. Janet Abrams Bachur, A.C.S.W., wrote sections of the material on finding resources and selecting a nursing home. She also read much of the manuscript and contributed to it her extensive knowledge of resources and family therapy. Sue R. Hardy, O.T.R., has researched, developed, and tested much of the material on occupational and physical therapy. Jeanne, Janet, and Sue helped compile the reading list.

Mary Jane Lucas, R.N., shared with us her extensive knowledge of patients and families who suffer from these illnesses. Her group therapy with spouses of patients suffering from dementia has shaped our general knowledge of families' emotional reactions and our specific ideas about group work with family members. Jerome D. Frank, M.D., Ph.D., read and commented on the section of the manuscript which discusses emotions.

Most important among those who have taught us are our patients and their families. From them we have learned of problems, solutions, and, most important, the strength, courage, and love with which families and patients face the dementing illnesses. Many members of the Alzheimer's Disease Association of Maryland (ADAM) and the Alzheimer's Disease and Related Disorders Association (ADRDA) have read the manuscript, contributed to it, and taken the time to call, write, and share solutions to problems they have faced. It is not possible to name each of them, but we especially wish to thank Glenn I. Kirkland, Mary LaRue, Bobbie Glaze, John J. Mitchell, Joan and Douglas Luebehusen, and Col. W. H. Van Atta for their contributions. The ADRDA, through the personal cooperation of Jerome H. Stone, president, and other professional staff, has given unstinting advice and support in the development of this book.

Hazel E. Carroll, R.N., director of nursing at the Keswick Home, Baltimore, Md., Ruth Lovett, R.N., former assistant director of nursing at Greater Baltimore Medical Center, and Osa Jackson, Ph.D., R.P.T., assistant professor in the Physical Therapy Department of the University of Maryland School of Medicine, have generously shared with us their knowledge and skill in patient care. Robert Katzman, M.D., chairman of the Department of Neurology at the Albert Einstein College School of Medicine, and Miriam Aronson, Ph.D., assistant professor in the departments of Psychiatry and Neurology of the Albert Einstein College School of Medicine, have read the manuscript. Their insights and comments have been most helpful.

We are grateful to the many people who have advised us in areas outside our expertise. Phyllis J. Erlich, Esq., drafted and reviewed the section on legal matters and contributed to the section on financial concerns. Frederick T. DeKuyper, assistant general counsel of The Johns Hopkins University, also read and commented on the chapter on financial and legal matters.

Matthew Tayback, Sc.D., director of the Maryland State Office on Aging, and Susan Coller, director of training and educational development of the Maryland State Office on Aging, provided information about federal and state offices on aging. Nancy P. Whitlock, of the Medical Assistance Policy Administration of the Maryland Department of Health and Mental Hygiene, and Sheridan Gladhill, Richard Strauss, William Coons, and Robert Augustine, of the Health Care Financing Administration, guided us through the complexities of Medicare and Medicaid policy. Gene VandeKieft, C.I.C., of Rice and Associates, Inc., advised us about insurance. Domenic J. LaPonzina, public affairs officer of the Baltimore District of the Internal Revenue Service, assisted us with tax law. Oliver P. Boyer, Jr., of the Jarrettsville Federal Savings and Loan Association, suggested many of the places to look for financial assets.

Maggie Rider, our secretary, cheered us on, kept the office running smoothly while we wrote and rewrote the manuscript, and provided suggestions about the book's content. Bonnie Strauss and Violet E. Goodman helped with important administrative assistance, and a team of typists saw us through many revisions. We especially appreciate the advice and guidance of our editor, Anders Richter, and the staff of The Johns Hopkins University Press who coordinated and expedited publication.

Family and friends are a special blessing as a book develops. They live with a manuscript on the dining room table, they think up possible titles on their vacation, they encourage, cheer, and endure. They have read the manuscript and shared their vision and their ideas. Our special thanks go to Karen Rabins, Hank Kalapaca, Randy Lang, Catherine Lang, Mr and Mrs F. R. Lawson, Eugene Peterson, and Edna Bradford.

Acknowledgments for the UK edition

Age Concern England would wish to thank the Disabled Living Foundation for their help in sections relating to disability, particularly Chapters 4 and 5. Dr Castleton would like to thank Professor Tom Arie for his advice and encouragement.

1 Dementia

For two or three years Mary had known that her memory was failing. First she had trouble remembering the names of her friends' children, and one year she completely forgot the strawberry jam she had made. She compensated by writing things down. After all, she told herself, she was getting older. But then she would find herself groping for a word she had always known, and she worried that she was getting senile.

Recently, when she was talking with a group of friends, Mary would realise that she had forgotten more than just an occasional name—she lost the thread of the conversation altogether. She compensated for this too: she always made an appropriate answer, even if she secretly felt confused. No one noticed, unless perhaps her daughter-in-law, who said to her best friend, 'I think Mother's memory is going.' It worried Mary—sometimes depressed her—but she always denied that anything was wrong. There was no one to whom she could say, 'I am losing my mind. It is literally slipping away as I watch.' Besides, she didn't want to think about it, didn't want to think about getting old, and, most important, she didn't want to be treated as if she were senile. She was still enjoying life and able to manage.

Then in the winter Mary became ill. At first she thought it was only a cold. She saw a doctor, who gave her some pills, and asked her what she expected at her age, which annoyed her. She rapidly got much worse. She went to bed, afraid, weak, and very, very tired. Mary's daughter-in-law got a telephone call from Mary's neighbour. Together they found the old woman semiconscious, feverish, and mumbling incoherently.

During the first few days in the hospital Mary had only an intermittent, foggy notion of what was happening. The doctors told her family that she had pneumonia, and that her kidneys were working poorly. All the resources of a modern hospital were mobilised to fight the infection.

Mary was in a strange place, and nothing was familiar. People, all strangers, came and went. They told her where she was, but she forgot. In strange surroundings she could no longer compensate for her forgetfulness, and the delirium caused by the acute illness aggravated her confusion. She thought her husband came to see her: a handsome young man in his war uniform. Then when her son came, she was surprised that they would come together. Her son kept saying, 'But Mum, Dad has been dead for twenty years.' But she knew he wasn't, because he had just been there. Then when she complained to her daughter-in-law that she never came, she thought the girl lied when she said, 'But Mother, I was just here this morning.' In truth, she could not remember the morning.

People came and poked and pushed, and shoved things in and out and over her. They stuck needles into her and they wanted her to breathe through a mask over her mouth and nose. She did not understand and they could not explain that the inhalations she received through the mask would improve her breathing. The mask became part of her nightmare. She could not remember where she was. When she had to go to the toilet, they put cotsides on her bed and refused to let her go, so that she cried and wet herself.

Gradually, Mary got better. The infection cleared and the dizziness passed. Only during the acute phase of her illness did she imagine things, but after the fever and infection had passed, the confusion and forgetfulness seemed more severe than before. Although the illness had probably not affected the gradual course of her memory loss, it had weakened her considerably and taken her out of the familiar setting in which she had been able to function. Most significantly, the illness had focused attention on the seriousness of her situation. Now her family realised she could no longer live alone.

The people around Mary talked and talked. No doubt they explained their plans, but she forgot. When she was finally released from the hospital, they took her to her son's house. They were happy about something that day, and led her into a room. Here at last were some of her things, but not all. She thought perhaps the rest of her things had been stolen while she was sick. They kept saying they had told her where her things were, but she couldn't remember what they said.

This is where they said she lived now, in her son's house—except that long ago she had made up her mind that she would never live with her children. She wanted to live at home. At home she could find things. At home she could manage—she believed—as she always had. At home, perhaps, she could discover what had become of a lifetime of possessions. This was not her home: her independence was gone, her things were gone, and Mary felt an enormous sense of loss. Mary could not remember her son's loving explanation—that she couldn't manage alone and that bringing her to live in his home was the best arrangement he could work out for her.

Often, Mary was afraid, a nameless, shapeless fear. Her impaired mind could not put a name or an explanation to her fear. People came, memories came, and then they slipped away. She could not tell what was reality and what was memory of people past. The bathroom was not where it was yesterday. Dressing became an insurmountable ordeal. Her hands forgot how to button buttons. Belts hung inexplicably about her, and she could not think how to manage them or why they hung there.

Mary gradually lost the ability to make sense out of what her eyes and ears told her. Noises and confusion made her feel panicky. She couldn't understand, they couldn't explain, and often panic overwhelmed her. She worried about her things: a chair, and the china that had belonged to her mother. They said they had told her over and over again, but she could not remember where her things had gone. Perhaps someone had stolen them. She had lost so much. What things she still had, she hid, but then she forgot where she hid them.

'I cannot get her to have a bath,' her daughter-in-law said in despair. 'She smells. How can I send her to the day centre if she won't have a bath?' For Mary the bath became an experience of terror. It was a mystery. From day to day she could not remember how to manage the water: sometimes it all ran away, sometimes it kept rising and rising, so that she could not stop it. The bath involved remembering so many things. It meant remembering how to undress, how to find the bathroom, how to wash. Mary's fingers had forgotten how to undo a zip; her feet had forgotten how to step into the bath. There were so many things for an injured mind to think about that panic overcame her.

How do any of us react to trouble? We might try to get away from the situation for a while, and think it out. One person may go out for a beer; another may weed the garden or go for a walk. Sometimes we react with anger. We fight back against those who cause, or at least participate in, our situation. Or we become discouraged for a while, until nature heals us or the trouble goes away.

Mary's old ways of coping with trouble remained. Often when she felt nervous, she thought of going for a walk. She would pause on the doorstep, look out, drift out, and walk away—away from the trouble. Yet the trouble remained and now it was worse, for Mary would be lost, nothing would be familiar: the house had disappeared, the street was not the one she knew—or was it one from her childhood, or where they lived when the boys were growing up? The terror would wash over her, clutching at her heart. Mary would walk faster.

Sometimes Mary would react with anger. It was an anger she herself did not understand. But her things were gone, her life seemed gone. The compartments of her mind sprang open and fell shut, or vanished altogether. Who would not be angry? Someone had taken her things, the treasures of a lifetime. Was it her daughter-in-law, or her own mother-in-law, or a sister resented in childhood? She accused her daughter-in-law but quickly forgot the suspicion. Her daughter-in-law, coping with an overwhelming situation, was unable to forget.

Many of us remember the day we began secondary school. We lay awake the night before, afraid of getting lost and not finding the classrooms the next day in a strange building. Every day was like that for Mary. Her family began sending her to an adult day centre. Every day a driver came to pick her up, and every day her daughter-in-law came to get her, but from day to day Mary could not remember that she would be taken home. The rooms were not dependable. Sometimes Mary could not find them. Sometimes she went in the men's toilet. Sometimes she did not know whether they would come to get her in the evening.

Many of Mary's social skills remained, so she was able to chat and laugh with the other people in the day centre. As Mary relaxed in the centre she enjoyed the time she spent there with other people, although she could never remember what she did there well enough to tell her daughter-in-law.

Mary loved music; music seemed to be imbedded in a part of her mind that she retained long after much else was lost. She loved to sing old, familiar songs. She loved to sing at the day centre. Even though her daughter-in-law could not sing well, Mary did not remember that, and the two women discovered that they enjoyed singing together.

The time finally came when the physical and emotional burden of caring for Mary became too much for her family and she went to live in a nursing home. After the initial days of confusion and panic passed, Mary felt secure in her small, sunny bedroom. She could not remember the schedule for the day but the reliability of the routine comforted her. Some days it seemed as if she were still at the day centre, sometimes she was not sure. She was glad the toilet was close by where she could see it and did not have to remember where it was.

Mary was glad when her family came to visit. Sometimes she remembered their names, more often she did not. She never remembered that they had come last week and so she regularly scolded them for abandoning her. They could never think of much to say but they put their arms around her frail body, held her hand, and sat silently or sang old songs. She was glad when they didn't try to remind her of what she had just said or that they had come last week, or ask her if she remembered this person or that one. She liked it best when they just held her and loved her.

Someone in your family has been diagnosed as having a dementia. This could be Alzheimer's disease, multi-infarct dementia, or one of several other diseases. Perhaps you are not sure yet which condition it is. Whatever the name of the disease, a person close to you has lost some of his intellectual ability—the ability to think and remember. He may become increasingly forgetful. His personality may appear to change, or he may become depressed, moody, or withdrawn.

Many, although not all, of the disorders that cause these symptoms in adults are chronic and irreversible. When a diagnosis of an irreversible dementia is made, the patient and his family face the task of learning to live with this illness. Whether you decide to care for the person at home or to have him cared for in a nursing home or hospital, you will find yourself facing new problems and coping with your feelings about having someone close to you develop an incapacitating illness.

This book is designed to help you with that adjustment and with the tasks of day-to-day management of a chronically ill family member. We have found that there are questions many families ask. This material can help you begin to find answers, but it is not a substitute for the help of your doctor and other professionals.

What is dementia?

You may have discovered that many names have been given to the symptoms of memory loss and loss of thinking and reasoning capacity in adults. This is the result of different descriptions and definitions in older medical books. Commonly used terms include 'organic brain syndrome', 'senility', 'hardening of the arteries' or 'chronic brain syndrome'. Your doctor may say 'Alzheimer's disease', 'multi-infarct disease', 'senile dementia' or 'presenile dementia'. In this book we will refer to these conditions as *dementia*.

Doctors use the word *dementia* in a specific way. It means a loss or impairment of mental powers. It comes from two Latin words, which mean *away* and *mind*. Dementia does not mean insane. It has been chosen by the medical profession as the least offensive and most accurate term to describe this group of illnesses. *Dementia* describes a group of symptoms and is not the name of a disease or diseases that cause the symptoms.

There are two major conditions that result in the symptoms of mental confusion, memory loss, disorientation, intellectual impairment, or similar problems. These two conditions may look similar to the casual observer and can be confused. (They will be discussed in more detail in Chapter 17.) The first condition, *delirium*, comprises a group of symptoms in which the person is less alert than normal. He is often drowsy but may fluctuate between drowsiness and restlessness. Like the impaired person, he is also confused, disoriented, or forgetful. These conditions have also been called 'acute confusional states' or 'reversible confusional states.' Delirium can be caused by illnesses such as pneumonia or kidney infection, malnutrition, or reactions to medications.

With the second condition, *dementia*, there is impaired intellectual functioning in a person who is clearly awake. The symptoms of dementia can be caused by several different diseases. Some of these diseases are treatable, others are not. Thyroid disease, for example, may cause a dementia that can be reversed with correction of the thyroid abnormality. In Chapter 17, we have summarised some of the diseases that can cause dementia.

Alzheimer's disease appears to be the most frequent cause of irreversible dementia in adults. The intellectual impairment progresses gradually from forgetfulness to total disability. Structural changes in the brain are visible in post-mortems of people who suffered from Alzheimer's disease. The cause of the illness is not known, and at present doctors know of no way to stop or cure it. However, much can be done to make the patient comfortable and help the family feel in control of the situation.

Multi-infarct dementia is believed to be the second most common cause of irreversible dementia. This is a series of strokes within the brain. Sometimes the strokes may be so tiny that neither you nor the afflicted person is aware of any change, but all together they can destroy enough bits of brain tissue to affect memory and other intellectual functions. This condition used to be called 'hardening of the arteries', but post-mortem studies have shown that it is stroke damage rather than inadequate circulation that causes the problem. In some cases treatment can reduce the possibility of further damage.

Alzheimer's disease and multi-infarct dementia sometimes occur together. The diagnosis and characteristics of these diseases are discussed in detail in Chapter 17.

People who have dementing illness may also have other illnesses, and their dementia may make them more vulnerable to other health problems. Other illnesses or reactions to medications often cause delirium in people with dementing illnesses. The delirium can make the person's mental functions and behaviour worse. It is vital to his general health and to make his care easier to detect and treat other illnesses promptly. It is important to have a GP who is sympathetic and who will respond quickly to this need.

Depression is common in older people, and can be the cause of memory loss, confusion, or other changes in mental function. Dementia caused by depression is reversible. The depressed person's memory frequently gets better when the depression is treated. Although depression can also occur in a person with an irreversible dementia, depression should always be treated.

Several other uncommon conditions cause dementia. These will be discussed in Chapter 17.

The dementing diseases know no social or racial lines: the rich and the poor, the wise and the simple alike become victims. There is no reason to be ashamed or embarrassed because a family member has a dementing illness. Many brilliant and famous people have suffered from dementing illnesses. Although dementias associated with the final stage of syphilis were common in the past, this is very rare today. There is no other known link between dementia and venereal disease.

Severe memory loss is *never* a normal part of growing older. According to the best studies available, 5 per cent of older people suffer from a severe intellectual impairment and a similar number may suffer from milder impairments. The diseases become more prevalent in people who survive into their 80s and 90s, but about 80 per cent of those who live into very old age never experience a significant memory loss or other symptoms of dementia. A slight forgetfulness is common as we age but usually is not enough to interfere with our lives. Most of us know elderly people who are active and in full command of their intellect in their 70s, 80s, or 90s. Margaret Mead, Pablo Picasso, Arturo Toscanini, and Duke Ellington were all still active in their careers when they died: all were past 75; Picasso was 91.

As more people in our population live into later life, it becomes crucial that we learn more about dementia. The total of significantly affected sufferers in the United Kingdom is estimated to be about ¾ of a million.

The person with a dementing illness

The person suffering from a dementing illness has difficulty remembering things, although he may be skilful at concealing this. His ability to understand, reason, and use good judgment may be impaired. The onset and the course of the condition depend upon which disease caused the condition and upon other factors, some of which are unknown to researchers. Sometimes the onset of the trouble is sudden: looking back, you may say, 'After a certain time, Dad was never himself.' Sometimes the onset is gradual: family members may not notice at first that something is wrong. Sometimes the afflicted person himself may be the first to notice. The person with a mild dementia is often able to describe his problem clearly: 'Things just go out of my mind.' 'I start to explain and then I just can't find the words.'

People respond to their problems in different ways. Some people become skilful at concealing the difficulty. Some keep lists to jog their memory. Some vehemently deny that anything is wrong or blame their problems on others. Some people become depressed or irritable when they realise that their memory is failing. Others remain outwardly cheerful. Usually, the person with a mild to moderate dementia is able to continue to do most of the things he has always done. Like a person with any other disease, he is able to participate in his treatment, in family decisions, and in planning for the future.

Early memory problems are sometimes mistaken for stress, depression, or even mental illness. This misdiagnosis creates an added burden for the person and the family.

A wife recalls the onset of her husband's dementing illness, not in terms of his forgetfulness but in terms of his mood and attitude:
'I didn't know anything was wrong. I didn't want to see it. Charles was quieter than usual; he seemed depressed, but he blamed it on people at work. Then his boss told him he was being transferred—a demotion, really—to a smaller branch office. They didn't tell me anything. They suggested we take a holiday. So we did. We went to Scotland. But Charles didn't get any better. He was depressed and irritable. After he took the new job, he couldn't manage that either; he blamed it on the younger men. He was so irritable, I wondered what was wrong between us after so many years. We went to a marriage guidance counsellor and that only made things worse. I knew he was forgetful but I thought that it was caused by stress.'

Her husband said at the time, 'I knew something was wrong. I could feel myself getting uptight over little things. People thought I knew things about the plant that I—I couldn't remember. The counsellor said it was stress. I thought it was something else, something terrible. I was scared.'

Some people experience changes in personality. Many of the qualities that a person has always had may remain: he may always have been sweet and lovable and may remain so, or he may always have been a difficult person to live with and may become more so. Other people may change dramatically, from amiable to demanding or from energetic to apathetic. They may become passive, dependent and listless, or they may become restless, easily upset and irritable. Sometimes they become demanding, fearful, or depressed.

A daughter says, 'Mother was always the cheerful, outgoing person in the family. We knew she was becoming forgetful but the worst thing is that she doesn't want to do anything anymore. She doesn't do her hair, she doesn't keep the house tidy, she absolutely won't go out.'

Often little things enormously upset people with memory problems. Tasks that were previously simple may now be too difficult for a person and he may react to this by becoming upset, angry, or depressed.

From another family: 'The worst thing about Dad is his temper. He used to be easy-going. Now he is always shouting over the least little thing. Last night he told our ten year old son that Alaska is not a state. He was shouting and arguing and stalked out of the room. Then when I asked him to have a bath we had a real fight. He insisted he had already had a bath.'

It is important for those around him to remember that much of the person's behaviour is beyond his control: for example, he may not be able to keep his anger in check or to stop pacing the floor. The changes that occur are not the result of an unpleasant personality grown old; they are the result of damage to the brain and are usually beyond the control of the patient.

In those illnesses in which the dementia is progressive, the person's memory will gradually become worse, and his troubles cannot be concealed. He may become unable to recall what day it is or where he is. He may be unable to do simple tasks such as dressing, and may not be able to put words together coherently. As the dementia progresses, it becomes clear that the damage to the brain affects many functions, including memory, motor functions (coordination, writing, walking), and speaking. The person may have difficulty finding the right name for familiar things and he may become clumsy or walk with a shuffle. The sick person's abilities may fluctuate from day to day or even from hour to hour. This makes it harder for families to know what to expect.

Some people with dementing illnesses have hallucinations (hearing, seeing, or smelling things that are not real). This experience is real to the person experiencing it and can be frightening to family members. Some people become suspicious of others; they may hide things or accuse people of stealing from them. Often they simply mislay things and forget where they put them, and in their confusion think someone has stolen them.

A son recalls: 'Mum is so paranoid. She hides her purse. She hides her money, she hides her jewelry. Then she accuses my wife of stealing it. Now she is accusing us of stealing the silverware. The hard part is that she doesn't seem *to be ill. It's hard to believe she isn't doing this deliberately.'*

In the final stages of a progressive dementing illness, so much of the brain has been affected that the person is often confined to bed, unable to control urination and unable to express himself. In the last stages of the illness the patient may require skilled nursing care.

It is important to remember that not all these symptoms will occur in the same person. Your family member may never experience some of these symptoms or may experience others we have not mentioned. The course of the disease and the prognosis vary with the specific disorder and with the individual person.

Where do you go from here?

You know or suspect that someone close to you has a dementing illness. Where do you go from here? You will need to take stock of your current situation and then identify what needs to be done to help the impaired person and to make the burdens on yourself bearable. There are many questions you must ask. This book will get you started with the answers.

The first thing you need to know is the cause of the disease and its prognosis. Each disease that causes dementia is different. You may have been given different diagnoses and different explanations of the disease, or you may not know what is wrong with the person. However, you must have a diagnosis and some information about the course of the disease before you or the doctor can respond appropriately to day-to-day problems or plan for the future. It is usually better to know what to expect. Your understanding of the illness can help to dispel fears and worries, and it will help you to plan how best you can help the person with a dementing disease. Chapter 2 describes how a diagnostic assessment is done.

Even when the disease itself cannot be stopped, *much can be done to improve the quality of life for the afflicted person and for the family*. Chapters 3 to 9 list many of the problems that families face in caring for a person with a dementing illness and offer suggestions for managing them.

Dementing illnesses vary with the specific diseases and with the individual who is afflicted. You may never face many of the problems discussed in this chapter. You may find it most helpful to skip through these chapters and read those sections that apply to you.

The key to coping is common sense and ingenuity. Sometimes a family is too close to the problem to see clearly a way of managing. At other times there is no one more ingenious at solving a difficult problem than the family members themselves. Many of the ideas offered here were developed by family members who have called or written to share them with others. These ideas will get you started.

At some point you may find that you will need additional help in caring for an impaired person. Chapter 10 discusses the kinds of help that may be available and how to locate them.

You and the impaired person are part of a family that needs to work together to cope with this illness. Chapter 11 discusses families and the problems that can arise in families. Chapter 12 discusses your feelings and the effects this illness may have on you. Caring for yourself is important for both you and the confused person who is dependent on you, and is discussed in Chapter 13.

Chapter 14 is written for young people who know someone with a dementing illness. Perhaps, as a parent, you will want to read this section also and plan a time to discuss it with your son or daughter. The entire book is written in such a way that a young person will be able to understand any other sections he may want to read.

Chapter 15 discusses legal and financial matters. Although it may be painful to plan ahead, it is most important to do so. Perhaps now is the time to get started with things you may have been avoiding.

A time may come when the impaired person cannot live alone. Chapter 16 discusses nursing homes and other living arrangements.

Chapter 17 discusses the diseases that cause dementia and explains how they differ from other brain disorders. However, it is written to give you a general understanding of terms and conditions, not as a tool for diagnosis.

Chapter 18 briefly reviews the research into Alzheimer's disease and multi-infarct dementia. The reading list in Appendix 1 refers you to other, more detailed information on research.

You may want to use this handbook to inform others about the diseases that cause dementia. The dementing illnesses affect large numbers of people, but their effects on families and their potential management are sometimes poorly understood by professionals and by the general community. Education does not always have to come from the professional person. You, the family, can effectively inform others. Share what you know about dementia with your GP, nursing home staff, and others. Basic education on a personal level will help to bring dementia out into the open and into the light of research. This will result in improved care, improved emotional and financial support, and research to seek cures or preventive measures. Use what you know and use this handbook. You will increase the understanding of those around you, and you will reach families who have been struggling in isolation.

Caring for a person with a dementing illness is not easy. We hope the information in this book will help you, but we know that simple solutions are not yet at hand.

Often the text of this book discusses problems. However, it is important to remember that confused people and their families do still experience joy and happiness. Since dementing illnesses develop slowly, they often leave intact the impaired person's ability to enjoy life and to enjoy other people. When things go badly, remind yourself that no matter how bad the person's memory is, or how strange his behaviour, he is still a unique and special human being. We can continue to love a person even after he has changed drastically, and even when we are deeply troubled by his present state.

2 Getting medical help for the impaired person

This book is written for you, the family. It is based on the assumption that you and the sick person are receiving professional medical care. The family and the medical professionals are partners in the care of the impaired person. Neither should be providing care alone. This book is not meant to be a substitute for professional skills. However, we recognise that, at the time of writing, families may have difficulty finding the kind of medical care they need. Misconceptions about dementia do exist among professionals. Not all doctors or other professionals have the time, interest, or skills to diagnose or care for a person with a dementing illness. As the public becomes better informed about the dementing illnesses this will become a thing of the past

What should you expect from your doctor and other professionals? The first thing is an accurate diagnosis. Once a diagnosis has been made, you will need the continuing help of a doctor and perhaps other professionals to manage the dementing illness, to treat concurrent illnesses, and to help you find the resources you need. This chapter is written as a guide to help you find the best possible medical care in your community.

In the course of a dementing illness you may need the special skills of a doctor, a social worker, or a nurse. Each is a highly trained professional whose skills complement those of the others. They can work together first to assess the impaired person and then to help you with continuing care. They may use the skills of other professionals as well.

The assessment of the person with a suspected dementia

It is important that a thorough assessment be made when a person suffers from difficulty in thinking, remembering, or learning or shows changes in personality. A complete assessment tells you and the doctors several things:

1 the exact nature of the person's illness,
2 whether or not the condition can be reversed or treated,
3 the nature and extent of the disability,
4 the areas in which the person can still function successfully,
5 whether the person has other health problems that need treatment and that might be making her mental problems worse,
6 the social and psychological needs and resources of the sick person and the family or care giver, and
7 the changes you can expect in the future.

Procedures vary depending on your GP or which hospital consultant is approached. However, a good assessment includes a medical and neurological examination, an assessment of the person's social support, and an evaluation of her remaining abilities.

The assessment may begin with a careful examination by a consultant. He will take a *detailed history* from someone who knows the person well and from the ill person if possible. This tells the doctor how the person has changed, tells him what symptoms the person has had, and gives him information about other medical conditions. The doctor will also give the person a *physical examination*, which may reveal other health problems. A *neurological examination* (asking the person to balance with her eyes closed, tapping her ankles or knees with a rubber hammer, and other tests) may reveal changes in the functioning of the nerve cells of the brain or spine.

The doctor will also do a *mental state examination*, in which he asks the person questions about the time, date, and place where she is. Other questions test her ability to remember, to concentrate, to do abstract reasoning, to do simple calculations, and to copy simple designs. Each of these reveals problems of function in different parts of the brain. When he does this test, he will take into consideration the person's education and the fact that the person may be nervous.

The doctor will order *laboratory tests*, including a number of blood tests. The *FBC* (full blood count) detects anaemia and evidence of infection, either of which malfunctions can cause or complicate a dementing illness. *Biochemistry tests* check for liver and kidney problems, diabetes, and a number of other conditions. Vitamin B12 level tests and folate level tests check for vitamin deficiencies, which might cause dementia. *Thyroid studies* assess the function of the thyroid gland. Thyroid problems are among the more common reversible causes of dementia. The *VDRL test* can indicate a syphilis infection (syphilis was a common cause of dementia before the discovery of penicillin), but a positive VDRL test does not necessarily indicate that the person has ever had syphilis. The blood tests usually involved inserting one needle, which is no more unpleasant than a pin prick.

The *lumbar puncture (LP)* is done to rule out infection in the central nervous system (for example, tuberculosis) and it may reveal other abnormalities. It is usually done after a local anaesthetic has been injected into the back and has few complications. This investigation is rarely done as often there is no reason to suspect these conditions.

The *EEG* (electroencephalograph) records the electrical activity present in the brain, involving little wires attached to the head with a pastelike material. It is painless but may confuse the forgetful person. It aids in the diagnosis of delirium and can offer evidence of abnormal brain functioning, but occasionally it is normal in a demented person.

The *CAT scan* (computerized axial tomogram) is a sophisticated X-ray that produces a picture of the brain. (Ordinary skull X-rays show primarily the bones, and do not show the brain itself.) Changes compatible with Alzheimer's disease may be visible on a CAT scan, but this diagnosis should not be made on the basis of a CAT scan alone. The CAT scan can find evidence of stroke, multi-infarct dementia, tumours, changes in the flow of the fluid that surrounds the brain, and collections of blood which can put pressure on the brain.

The CAT scan involves lying on a table and placing one's head in an object that looks like a very large hair dryer. It is painless but may confuse an already impaired person. If so, a mild sedative can be prescribed to help the person relax. It is not performed on all patients, but is ordered when the doctor needs it.

The history, physical and neurological examinations, and laboratory tests will identify or rule out each of the known causes of dementia. Other assessments in addition to the medical assessment are done to understand the person's abilities and help you to plan for the future.

A *psychiatric and psychosocial evaluation* is based on interviews with the person and her family. This provides the basis for the development of a specific plan for the care of the individual, and may involve the doctor, nurse and/or the social worker. It includes helping the family assess their own emotional, physical, and financial resources, the home in which the person lives, the community resources, and the patient's ability to accept or participate in plans.

An *occupational therapy* assessment helps to determine how much the person is able to do for herself and what can be done to help her compensate for her limitations. It is carried out by an occupational therapist. These therapists are important members of the team. Their skills are sometimes overlooked because in the past they were consulted only in cases where there was the potential for physical rehabilitation. However, they are able also to identify the things that the person can still do, and to devise ways to help the person remain as independent as possible. Part of this assessment is an *ADL* (activities of daily living) assessment. The person is observed in a controlled situation to see if she can manage money, prepare a simple meal, dress herself, and perform other routine tasks. It is noted whether she can do part of these tasks. These therapists are familiar with a variety of appliances that can help some people.

Neuropsychological testing (also called cerebral function testing or psychometric testing) may be done to determine in which areas of mental function the person is impaired and in which she is still independent. This testing takes several hours. The tests assess such things as memory, reasoning, coordination, writing, and the ability to express oneself and understand instructions. The testing psychologist or occupational therapist will be experienced in making people feel relaxed and will take into consideration differences in education and interests.

The final part of the assessment is *your discussion with the doctor* and perhaps with other members of the assessment team. At this time the doctor will explain his findings to you and to the patient if she is able to understand at least part of what is happening.

At this time the doctor should give you a specific diagnosis (he may explain that he cannot be certain) and a general idea of the person's prognosis (again, he may not be able to tell you exactly what to expect). The findings of other tests, such as the ADL, the psychological tests, and the social history, will also be explained to you. You should be able to ask questions and come away with an understanding of the findings of the assessment. The doctor may make recommendations such as the use of medications or health services or he may refer you to a social worker who can advise you about health services. You, he, and the afflicted person may identify specific problems and set up a plan to cope with them.

A complete assessment may take more than one day. It usually takes several days for the laboratories to report their findings to the doctor and for him to put all this information together into a report.

Assessments may be done either with the patient admitted to the hospital or on an outpatient basis. Several factors, including especially the general health of the patient, affect the decision to do an inpatient or an outpatient assessment.

Sometimes family members and occasionally professionals advise against 'putting a confused person through the "ordeal" of an assessment.' We feel that every person with problems in memory and thinking should be fully assessed. An assessment is not an unpleasant ordeal. Staff accustomed to working with demented people are usually gentle and kind. It is important that they make the person as comfortable as possible so that they will be able to measure her best performance.

As we have said, there are many reasons why a person might develop the symptoms of dementia. Some of these are treatable. If a treatable problem is not found because an assessment is not done, the afflicted person and her family may suffer unnecessarily for years. Certain diseases can be treated if they are found promptly, but can cause irreversible damage if they are neglected.

Even if it is found that a person has an irreversible dementia, the assessment will give you information about how best to care for the impaired person and how best to manage her symptoms. It gives you a basis upon which to plan for the future and, finally, it is important that you know that you have done all that you can for her.

How an assessment is arranged

In some areas it can be difficult to find someone who is interested in doing a thorough assessment of a person with a suspected dementia. This is changing. Your GP may do the assessment or may refer you to a hospital specialist who may be either a neurologist, psychiatrist, psychogeriatrician or geriatrician.

How do you decide whether an accurate diagnosis has been made for someone in your family? In the final analysis, you must settle on a doctor whom you trust and who you feel has done all he can, and then rely on his judgment. This is much easier when you understand something about the terminology, the diagnostic procedures, and what is known about the dementias. If you have been given differing diagnoses, discuss this frankly with the doctor. It is important that you feel certain that an accurate diagnosis has been made.

You may hear about people with similar symptoms who are 'miraculously' cured, or you may hear statements like 'senility can be cured'. Considerable confusion has arisen because some of the causes of dementia are reversible and because dementia and delirium are sometimes confused. There are some unscrupulous individuals who offer bogus 'cures' for these tragic illnesses. An accurate diagnosis and a doctor you trust can assure you that all that can be done is being done. You can also be kept informed about the progress of legitimate research through the Alzheimer's Disease Society and from the major research institutes.

Medical treatment and management of dementia

Dementing illnesses are diseases that require continuing medical attention. The availability of professional services varies. You, the care-giver, will provide much of the co-ordination of care. However, there are times when you will also need the help of professionals.

The doctor

You will need a doctor who will prescribe and adjust medications, answer your questions, and treat other, concurrent illnesses. The doctor who provides continuing care will not usually be the specialist providing the initial assessment of the person. He may be your family doctor or a member of a geriatric or psychogeriatric unit such as a clinical assistant in charge of a day hospital. This doctor can refer the patient to a neurologist, psychiatrist or geriatrician if necessary. The doctor who provides continuing care must:

1. be willing and able to spend the necessary time with you and the sick person;
2. be knowledgeable about dementing illnesses and the special susceptibility of impaired patients to other diseases, medications, and delirium;
3. be easily accessible;
4. be able to make referrals to occupational therapists, physiotherapists, social workers, and other professionals.

Many GPs are able and willing to provide such care, but unfortunately there will be doctors who do not meet these criteria and you may decide to change your GP. Should you change your address then you are entitled to simply sign on with another practice. However, if there is no change of address and you want to obtain a different family doctor in the same area, you must first write to your original GP asking his permission for you to be released from his list of patients. You should then write to the new practice outlining your reasons for wanting to change and stating that you have the permission of your GP to effect such a change. The new practice is not obliged to accept you on to its list, but usually do so if your case for changing is reasonable.

The nurse

In addition to the knowledge and experience of a doctor, you may need the skills of a nurse. Health visitors, district nurses and community psychiatric nurses (CPN) together with GPs are part of the Primary Health Care Team working from the surgery or health centre. In most areas now the community nursing team includes CPNs who can usually take referrals from a GP. In some districts the CPNs are hospital based and may only take referrals from psychiatrists and psychogeriatricians.

The nurse may be the person whom you can reach most easily and who can co-ordinate the work that you, the doctor, and others do to provide the best possible care. She may be the person who understands the difficulties of caring for a person at home. She can observe the person for changes in her health status which need to be reported to the doctor and she can give you support and counselling. After talking with you, she can identify and help to solve many of the problems you face. She can teach you how to provide practical care for the person (coping with catastrophic reactions, giving baths, helping with eating problems, managing a wheelchair). She can teach you how and when to give medicine and how to know whether it is working correctly. The nurse comes to your home to assess the patient and offer suggestions for simplifying the person's environment and minimising the effort you need to expend.

The district nurse may also be helpful to you if the patient is frail and needs considerable help with dressing, bathing and transferring or if she is bed bound. There may well be a Twilight Nursing Service often used as a 'putting to bed' service and this can be invaluable when caring for the impaired person. A Terminal Care Service for those dying at home may be available.

The nurse will be able to give advice on coping with incontinence and will have access to a supply of nursing aids such as commodes, incontinence appliances and disposable pads which she can arrange to have delivered to your home. There may be specialist advice available in your district from an incontinence adviser and a stoma care therapist.

The community occupational therapist may be asked to advise on aids and can organise stair rails, toilet rails and raised toilet seats to be fitted. She can supply feeding aids. The domiciliary physiotherapist may also be available to help.

There are private nursing agencies which can provide services not available locally under the NHS, but this is, of course, an expensive alternative.

The social worker

Social workers have a unique combination of skills: they know the resources and services in your community and they are skilled in assessing your situation and needs and matching these with available services. They are professionals whose skills in helping you find resources can be invaluable. They can also provide practical counselling and help you and your family think through plans and solve disagreements over care.

Your GP will be able to refer you to a community social worker, or if the sick person is in hospital, the hospital social worker may be able to help you.

All Local Authorities have a Social Services Department; to locate such departments look in your local telephone directory or call in at your local Citizens Advice Bureau. Anyone with a problem or query can seek help from a social worker in their local office without necessarily having to be referred by a doctor. The duty social worker will probably be able to give you immediate advice or will refer you to the appropriate agency to deal with your problem.

3 Characteristic problems of dementia

In chapters 3 to 9 we will discuss many of the problems that families may encounter in caring for a person with a dementing illness. Although as yet nothing can be done to cure some dementing illnesses, it is important to remember that *much can be done to make life easier for you and the person with a dementing illness*. The suggestions we offer come from our clinical experience and from the experiences that family members have shared with us.

Each individual and each family are different. You may never experience many of these problems. The problems you will face are influenced by the nature of the specific disease, by your personality, by the ill person's personality, and, often, by other factors, such as where you live. We do not want you to read through this section as if it were a list of what lies ahead of you. It is a comprehensive list of where difficulties lie for you to use as a reference when a specific problem arises.

The very nature of brain injuries can make them difficult to live with. The brain is a vast, complex, mysterious organ. It is the source of our thoughts, our emotions, and our personality. Injury to the brain can cause changes in emotions, personality, and the ability to reason. Most dementing illnesses do their damage gradually, so the effects are not seen suddenly, unlike the effects of a major stroke or head injury. Consequently, the behaviour of a person with a dementing illness often seems puzzling in contrast to behaviours due to other illnesses. It is not always evident that many of the visible symptoms (changes in personality, for example) are the result of a disease. Because the person often looks well, people may interpret his behaviour as 'odd' or 'crazy' and may not be as understanding of your problems as they would be if he had another, more familiar disease. Increased community education is helping to change this.

Some general suggestions

Be informed. The more you know about the nature of dementing illness, the more effective you will be in devising strategies to manage behaviour problems.

Share your concerns with the patient. When a person is only mildly to moderately impaired, he can take part in managing his problem. You may be able to share with each other your grief and worries. Together you may be able to devise memory aids that will help him remain independent. Mildly impaired people may benefit from counselling that can help them accept and adjust to their limitations.

Try to solve your most frustrating problems one at a time. Families tell us that the day-to-day problems often seem to be the most insurmountable. Getting mother to have her bath or getting supper prepared, eaten, and cleaned up can become daily ordeals. *If you are at the end of your tether, single out one thing that you can change to make life easier, and work on that.* Sometimes changing small things makes a big difference.

Get enough rest. One of the dilemmas families often face is that the care-giver may not get enough rest or may not have the opportunity to get away from his care-giving responsibilities. This can make the care-giver less patient and less able to tolerate irritating behaviour. If things are getting out of hand, ask yourself if this is what is happening to you. If so, you may want to focus on finding ways to get more rest or more frequent breaks from your care-giving responsibilities. We recognise that this is difficult to arrange. We will discuss this in Chapter 10.

Use your common sense and imagination; they are your best tools. Adaptation is the key to success. If a thing cannot be done one way, ask yourself if it must be done at all. For example, if a person can eat successfully with his fingers but cannot use a fork and spoon appropriately, don't fight the problem; serve as many finger foods as possible. Accept changes. If the person insists on sleeping with his hat on, this is not harmful; go along with it.

Maintain a sense of humour; it will get you through many crises. The ill person is still a person. He needs and enjoys a good laugh too. Sharing your experiences with other families will help you. Surprisingly, these groups of families often find their shared experiences both sad and funny.

Try to establish an environment that allows as much freedom as possible but also offers the structure that confused people often need. Establish a regular, predictable, simple routine for meals, medication, exercising, bedtime, and other activities. Do things the same way and at the same time each day. If you establish regular routines, the person may gradually learn what to expect. Change routines only when they aren't working. Keep the person's surroundings reliable and simple. Leave furniture in the same place. Put away clutter.

Remember to talk *to* the confused person. Speak calmly and gently. Make a point of telling him what you are doing and why. Let him have a part in deciding things as much as possible. Avoid talking *about* him in front of him, and remind others to do this also.

Have an identity bracelet made for the confused person. Include on it the nature of his disease (e.g. 'memory impaired') and your telephone number. This is one of the single most important things you can do. Many confused people get lost or wander away at one time or another and an identity bracelet can save you hours of frantic worry.

Keep the impaired person active but not upset. Families often ask if retraining, reality orientation, reminiscence therapy or keeping active will slow down or stop the course of the disease. Likewise, they may ask if being idle hastens the course of the disease. Some people with dementing illnesses become depressed, listless, or apathetic. Families often wonder whether encouraging such a person to do things will help him to function better.

The relationship of activity to the course of dementing illness is not clear. Research continues in this area. Activity helps to maintain physical well-being and may help to prevent other illnesses and infections. Being active helps the ill person to continue to feel that he is involved in the family and that his life has meaning.

It is clear that people with dementing illnesses cannot learn as well as before because brain tissue has been damaged or destroyed. It would be unrealistic to expect them to learn new skills. However, some individuals can learn simple tasks or facts if they are repeated often enough. Some impaired people who feel lost in a new place eventually 'learn' their way around.

At the same time, too much stimulation, activity, or pressure to learn may upset the confused person, may upset you, and may accomplish nothing. The key to this is balance:

1 Accept that lost skills are gone for good (the woman who has lost the ability to cook will not learn to prepare a meal), *but* know that repeatedly and gently giving information within the person's abilities will help him function more comfortably (the person going into a strange day care setting will benefit from frequent reminders of where he is).
2 Realise that even small amounts of excitement—visitors, laughter, changes—can upset the confused person, *but* plan interesting, stimulating things within his capabilities—a walk, visiting one old friend.
3 Look for ways to simplify activities so that a person can continue to be involved within the limits of his abilities (the woman who can no longer prepare a whole meal may still be able to peel the potatoes).
4 Look for things the person is still able to do and focus on them. A person's intellectual abilities are not all lost at once. Both of you will benefit from carefully assessing what he can still do and making the best use of those abilities. For example,

Mrs Baldwin often cannot remember the words for things she wants to say but she can make her meaning clear with gestures. Her daughter helps her by saying 'Point to what you want.'

Memory problems

People with dementing illnesses forget things quickly. For the person with a memory impairment, life may be like constantly coming into the middle of a film performance: one has no idea what happened just before what is happening now. People with dementing illnesses may say they will call a friend and forget to do so, may start to prepare a meal and forget to turn the cooker off, may forget what time it is or where they are. This forgetfulness of recent events can seem puzzling when the person seems to be able to remember clearly events long past. There are some specific suggestions for memory aids throughout this book. You may think of others that will help you.

Forgetful people may remember events long past more clearly than recent events or they may remember some things and not others. This has to do with the way the brain stores and receives information; *it is not something the person does deliberately*. The success of memory aids depends on the severity of the dementia. A mildly demented person may devise reminders for himself, while a severely impaired person will only become more frustrated by his inability to use the aid. People who are able to read can do simple tasks if you write out instructions. Writing down names and often used phone numbers also helps. If you are going out, write down where you are going. If you will be out at a mealtime, leave a written reminder to eat.

Have clocks and calendars in view to help the confused person remember what time it is. Mark off the days as they pass. It is often helpful to put a simple list of the day's activities where the person can easily see it. A regular daily routine is much less confusing than frequent changes.

Leave familiar objects (photographs, magazines, TV, radio) in their usual places where the person can see them easily. A tidy, uncluttered house will be less confusing to an impaired person and misplaced items will be easier to find. Some families have found that putting labels on things helps. Labelling drawers 'Mary's stockings', 'Mary's nightgowns' may help.

Remember, however, that with progressive dementing illnesses the person will eventually be unable to read or will not be able to make sense of what he reads. He may be able to read the words but unable to act on them. Some families then use pictures instead of written messages. For example, it may help to put a picture of a toilet on the bathroom door if the person is in an unfamiliar place or has trouble remembering where the bathroom is.

People are often more confused at night and may get lost going to the bathroom. Strips of reflector tape on the wall from the bedroom to the bathroom are useful. Night lights will help him see where he is.

Pictures of family members and close friends may assist the more confused person to remind himself of who these people are. If you are visiting someone in hospital or in a nursing home, you might try taking along a family photograph album. Looking at the photographs may stir bits of pleasant memory in the confused mind.

Overreacting or catastrophic reactions

Even though Miss Ramirez had told her sister over and over again that today was the day to visit the doctor, her sister would not get in the car until she was dragged in, screaming, by two neighbours. All the way to the doctor's surgery she shouted for help and when she got there she tried to run away.

Mr Lewis suddenly burst into tears as he tried to tie his shoelaces. He threw the shoes in the wastebasket and locked himself, sobbing, in the bathroom.

Mrs Coleman described several incidents similar to this one, where her husband had mislaid his glasses.

'You threw out my glasses,' he told her.

'I didn't touch your glasses,' she answered.

'That's what you always say,' he responded. 'How do you explain that they are gone?'

'You do this to me every time you lose your glasses.'

'I did not lose them. You threw them out.'

Reflecting back, Mrs Coleman knew that her husband had changed. In the past he would have merely asked her if she knew where his glasses were instead of accusing her and starting an argument.

People with brain diseases often become excessively upset and may experience rapidly changing moods. Strange situations, confusion, groups of people, noises, being asked several questions at once, or being asked to do a task that is difficult for them can precipitate these reactions. The person may weep, blush, or become agitated, angry, or stubborn. He may strike out at those trying to help him. He may cover his distress by denying what he is doing or by accusing other people of things.

When a situation overwhelms the limited thinking capacity of a brain-injured person, he may overreact. Normal people sometimes do this when they are bombarded with more things at one time than they can manage. Impaired people have the same reaction to simpler, everyday experiences. For example,

Every evening Mrs Hamilton gets upset and refuses to have a bath. When her daughter insists, she argues and shouts. This makes the rest of the family tense. The whole routine is dreaded by everyone.

Having a bath actually means that Mrs Hamilton must think about several things at once: undressing, unbuttoning, finding the bathroom, turning on taps, and climbing into the bath. At the same time she feels insecure without clothes on and she feels she has lost her privacy and independence. This is overwhelming for a person who cannot remember doing the thing before, who can't remember how to do all these tasks, and whose mind cannot process all these activities at once. One way to react to this is to refuse to have a bath.

We use the term *catastrophic reaction* to describe this behaviour. (The word *catastrophic* is used in a special sense; it does not mean that these situations are necessarily very dramatic or violent.) *Often a catastrophic reaction does not look like behaviour caused by a brain illness. The behaviour may look as if the person is merely being obstinate, critical, or overemotional.* It may seem inappropriate to get so upset over such a little thing.

Catastrophic reactions are upsetting and exhausting for you and for the confused person. They are especially upsetting when it seems as if the person you are trying to help is being stubborn or critical. The person may get so upset that he refuses necessary care. Learning how to avoid or lessen catastrophic reactions is a major key to easier management of them.

Sometimes catastrophic reactions and forgetfulness is the first abnormal behaviour family members see when they begin to realise that something is wrong. The mildly impaired person may benefit by being reassured that his panic is not unusual and that you understand his fear.

The things that help to prevent or reduce catastrophic reactions depend on the individual, on you, and on the extent of his limitations. You will gradually learn how to avoid or limit these reactions. *First, you must fully accept that this behaviour is not just stubbornness or nastiness but a response the person with a dementing illness cannot help*. If you are in doubt, give strong consideration to the possibility that the behaviour is beyond the control of the impaired person.

Aids that remind the confused person about what is going on, such as following familiar routines, leaving things in familiar places, and written instructions (for people who can manage them), help to reduce catastrophic reactions. Because catastrophic reactions are precipitated by having to think of several things at once, simplify what the confused person has to think about. Take things one step at a time, and give instructions or information one step at a time. For example, when you help a person have a bath, tell the person one thing at a time. Say, 'I'm going to unbutton your blouse,' and then reassure her, 'It's all right.' Say, 'Now I'm going to slip your blouse off. That's fine. You're a big help. Now step into the bath. I will hold your arm.'

Give the confused person time to respond. He may react slowly and become upset if you rush him. Wait for him. If a person is having frequent catastrophic reactions, try to reduce the confusion around him. This might mean having fewer people in the room, having less noise, turning off the TV, or reducing the clutter in the room. The key is to simplify, to reduce the number of signals the impaired, disoriented brain must sort out.

Plan things the impaired person can realistically do. If strange places upset him, you may not want to take him on a trip. If he gets tired or upset quickly, plan shorter visits with friends.

You can avert some catastrophic reactions by simplifying the task facing the impaired person. Mr Quinn's family recognised that tying shoelaces had become too difficult for him but that he needed to remain as independent as possible. Buying him slip-on shoes solved the problem. Mrs Coleman's husband often lost things because he forgot where he put them. She found it helpful to ignore his accusations and help him find his glasses. Knowing that accusing her was his way of reacting to his forgetfulness made it easier for her to accept the insult.

When the person does become upset or resistant, remain calm and remove him from the situation in a quiet, unhurried way. Often the emotional storm will be over as quickly as it began and the confused person usually will be relieved that the upset is over. His short memory may work to your advantage: he may quickly forget the trouble.

Try not to express your frustration or anger to the confused person. Your frustration will further upset him when he cannot understand your reaction. Speak calmly. Take things one step at a time. Move slowly and quietly. Remember that the person is *not* being obstinate or doing this intentionally. Avoid trying to reason or argue with an upset individual; this only adds to his confusion and increases his overreaction.

Gently holding a person's hand or patting him may help calm him. Some people respond to being slowly rocked. Try putting your arms around him and rocking back and forth. Some people will be soothed by this but others may feel that your arms are restraining them and will become more upset. Physically restraining a person often adds to his panic. Restrain a person only if it is absolutely essential and if nothing else works.

You may lose your temper with a person who is having catastrophic reactions or is unable to do what seems like a simple task. If you do lose your temper, it usually will make the person's behaviour worse. Occasionally losing your temper is not a calamity; take a deep breath and try to approach the problem calmly. The person will probably forget your anger much more quickly than you will.

The most important thing, with this and other situations, is not to let yourself get frustrated and discouraged, but to try to examine thoughtfully what is happening. Try to identify exactly what is upsetting the confused person, and consider how you can change that.

Problems with speech and communication

You may have problems understanding or communicating verbally with the impaired person. There are two kinds of problems of communication: the problems a person with a dementing illness has in expressing himself to others, and the problems he has in understanding what people say to him.

Problems the impaired person has in making himself understood

The nature of communication problems and whether or not they will get worse depend on the specific disease. Do not assume that things will get worse.

Some people have only occasional difficulty finding words. They may have trouble remembering the names of familiar objects or people. They may substitute a word that sounds similar, such as saying 'tee' for 'tie' or 'wrong' for 'ring.' They may substitute a word with a similar meaning, such as saying 'wedding' for 'ring' or 'music thing' for 'piano'. They may describe the object they cannot name, such as 'it's a thing that goes around' for 'ring' or 'it's to dress up' for 'bowtie'. Such problems usually do not interfere with your ability to understand what the person means.

Some people have difficulty communicating their thoughts.

Mr Jones was trying to say that he had never had a neurological examination before. He said, 'I really have not, not really, ever have been done, I have never . . .'

In some language problems the person cannot communicate the whole thought but he can express a few of the words in the thought.

Mr Mason wanted to say that he was worried about missing his transport home. He could only say, 'Bus, home.'

Sometimes people are able to ramble on quite fluently, and it seems as if they are talking a lot. They will often string together commonly used phrases, so what they say at first seems to make sense, but upon reflection the listener may not be sure he understood the thought being expressed.

Mrs Simmons said, 'If I tell you something, I might stop in the middle and . . . I'll be sure about what I've done, . . . said, . . . sometimes I stop right in the middle and I can't get on with . . . from . . . that. In past records . . . I can be so much more sure of the . . . After I get my bearings again I can just go on as if nothing happened. We thought it was high time to start remembering. I just love to . . . have to . . . talk.'

In these examples, it is possible to understand what the person is saying if we know the context.

When the limitations in ability to communicate frustrate the confused person and frustrate you, they can lead to a series of catastrophic reactions. For example, the impaired person may burst into tears or stamp out of the room when no one understands him.

Sometimes a person is able to conceal language problems. When a doctor asks a person if he knows the word for a wristwatch (a common question used to evaluate language problems), the patient may say, 'Of course I do. Why do you ask?' 'I don't want to talk about it. Why are you bothering me?' when he cannot think of the word.

In severe language problems, the person may remember only a few key words, such as 'No', which he may use whether or not he means it. Eventually the person may be unable to speak. He may repeat a phrase, cry out intermittently, or mumble unintelligible phrases. In some language problems there seems to be no meaning in the jumbled words the person produces. Family members and care givers often grieve when this happens and they can no longer communicate verbally with a loved one. We sense that language is the most human of mental skills. In some families the person continues to be a friend and companion—although a forgetful one—for a long time, but when he is unable to communicate anymore, the family feels they have lost that companionship. You may worry that the person will be ill or in pain and unable to tell you.

How you help the impaired person communicate depends on the kind of difficulty he is having. If he has been diagnosed as having had a stroke that interferes with language function, he should be seen by a speech therapist as soon as he has recovered from the acute phase of his illness. Much can be done to rehabilitate stroke victims.

If the person is having difficulty finding the right word, it is usually less frustrating for him to have you supply the word for him than it is to let him search and struggle for the word. When he uses the wrong word and you know what he means, it may be helpful to supply the correct word. However, if doing so upsets him, it may be best to ignore it. When you don't know what he means, ask him to describe it or point to it. For example, the nurse did not know what Mrs Kealey meant when she said, 'I like your wrong.' If the nurse had said, 'What?' Mrs Kealey might have become frustrated in trying to express herself. Instead, the nurse asked, 'Describe a wrong.' Mrs Kealey said, 'It's a thing that goes around.' 'Point to it,' said the nurse. Mrs Kealey did and the nurse responded, 'Oh, yes, my ring.'

When a person is having trouble expressing an idea, you may be able to guess what they want to say. *Ask* them if you are guessing correctly. You might guess wrongly and if you act on an erroneous guess you will add to the confused person's frustration. Say, 'Are you worried about catching the bus home?' or 'Are you saying you have never had an examination like this before?'

When you cannot communicate in other ways, you can often guess what a person is trying to tell you. Remember that his feeling is usually accurate, although it may be exaggerated or not appropriate to the actual situation, but that his explanation of why he feels a certain way may be confused. If Mr Mason says, 'Bus, home,' and you say, 'You aren't going on the bus,' you will not have responded to his feelings. If you correctly guess that he is worried about going home, you can reassure him by saying, 'Your daughter is coming for you at 3 o'clock.'

If a person can still say a few words, or shake or nod his head, you will need to ask him simplified questions about his needs. Say, 'Are you in pain?' 'Does this hurt?' Point to a body part rather than name it.

When a person cannot communicate, you must establish a regular routine of checking his comfort. Make sure that clothing is comfortable, that the room is warm, that there are no rashes or sores on his skin, that he is taken to the toilet at regular intervals, and that he is not hungry or sleepy.

Problems the impaired person has in understanding others

Often people with brain impairments have difficulty comprehending or understanding what you and others tell them. This is a problem that families sometimes misinterpret as uncooperative behaviour. For example, you may say, 'Mother, I am going to the shops. I will be back in half an hour. Do you understand?' Your mother may say, 'Oh yes, I understand,' when in fact she does not understand at all and will get upset as soon as you are out of sight.

People with dementing illnesses also quickly forget what they did understand. When you give them a careful explanation, they may forget the first part of the explanation before you get to the rest of it.

People with dementing illnesses may have trouble understanding written information even when they can still read the letters or words. For example, to determine exactly what a person can still do, we may hand him a newspaper and ask him to read the headline, which he may be able to do correctly. Then when we hand him the written instructions, 'close your eyes', he will not close his eyes, although he may correctly read the words aloud.

At home you may put a note on the kitchen table which says, 'Your lunch is in the fridge on a plate.' You know the person can read the note but he doesn't eat his lunch. This can be infuriating until you consider that reading and understanding are two different skills, one of which may be lost without the loss of the other. It is not safe to assume that a person can understand and act upon messages he can hear or read. You will need to observe him to know whether he *does* act upon them.

The person who can understand what he is told in person may not be able to comprehend what he is told over the telephone. When a person with a dementing illness does not understand what you told him, the problem is not inattentiveness or willfulness, but an inability of the malfunctioning brain to make sense out of the words it hears.

There are several ways to improve your verbal communication with a person who has a dementing illness:

1 Make sure he does hear you. Hearing acuity declines in later life and many older people have a hearing deficiency.
2 Lower the tone (pitch) of your voice. A raised pitch is a nonverbal signal that one is upset. A lower pitch also is easier for the hearing impaired to hear.
3 Eliminate distracting noises or activities. Both because of the possible hearing deficiency and because of the impaired person's inability to sort things out, he may be unable to understand you when there are other noises or distractions around him.
4 Use short words and short, simple sentences. Avoid complex sentences. Instead of saying, 'I think I'll take the car to the garage now instead of in the morning because in the morning I will get caught in the traffic,' just say, 'I'm going to take the car to the garage now.'
5 Ask only *one* simple question at a time. If you repeat the question, repeat it exactly. Avoid questions like this, 'Do you want an apple or pie for dessert or do you want to have dessert later?' Complex choices may overload the person's decision-making ability.

6 Ask the person to do one task at a time, not several. He may not be able to remember several tasks or may be unable to make sense out of your message. Most of the things we ask a person to do—have a bath, get ready for bed, put on a coat so we can go to the shops—involve several tasks. The impaired person may not be able to sort out these tasks. We help him by breaking down each project into individual steps and asking the person to do one step at a time.
7 Speak slowly, and wait for the person to respond. The impaired person's response may be much slower than what seems natural to us. Wait.

You can improve communication with the person and your understanding of his needs without the usual forms of conversation. People communicate through both what they say and the way they move their face, eyes, hands, and bodies. Everyone uses this nonverbal system of communication without thinking about it. For example, we say, 'He looks angry', 'You can tell by the way they look at each other that they are in love', 'You can tell by the way he walks who's boss', 'I know you aren't listening to me', etc. These are all things we are communicating without words. Brain-impaired people can remain sensitive to these nonverbal messages when they cannot understand language well, and they often remain able to express themselves nonverbally.

For example, if you are tired, you may send nonverbal messages that upset the impaired person. Then he may get agitated, which will upset you. Your hands, face, and eyes will reveal your distress, which further agitates the confused person. If you are unaware of the significance of body language, you may wonder what happened to get him upset. In fact, we all do this all the time. For example, 'No, I am not upset,' you tell a spouse. 'But I know you are,' he replies. He can tell by the set of your shoulders that you are upset.

If you are living with a person suffering from dementia, you have already learned to identify many of the nonverbal clues that he sends to make his needs known. Here are some additional ways to communicate nonverbally:

1 Remain pleasant, calm, and supportive. (Even if you feel upset, your body language will help to keep the confused person calm.)
2 Smile, take the person's hand, put an arm around his waist, or in some other physical way express affection.
3 Look directly at him. *Look* to see if the person is paying attention to you. If he uses body language to signal that he is not paying attention, try again in a few minutes.
4 Use other signals besides words: point, touch, hand the person things. Demonstrate an action or describe it with your hands (for example, brushing teeth). Sometimes if you get him started he will be able to continue the task.
5 Avoid assuming complex reasons for the person's behaviour. Because

the person's brain can no longer process information properly, he experiences the world around and within differently from the way you see things. Since nonverbal communication depends on a completely different set of skills from verbal communication, you may be better able to understand him by considering what it *feels* like he is saying rather than what you *think* he is saying, either through actions or words.

Even when a person is severely confused and unable to communicate, he or she still needs and enjoys affection. Holding hands, hugging, or just sitting companionably together is an important way to continue to communicate. The physical care that you give a severely impaired person communicates to him your concern and that he is protected.

Loss of coordination

Because dementing illnesses affect many parts of the brain, the person with a dementia may lose the ability to make his hands and fingers do certain familiar tasks. He may understand what he wants to do, and although his hands and fingers are not stiff or weak, the message just does not get through from the mind to the fingers. Doctors use the word *apraxia* to describe this. An early sign of apraxia is a change in the person's handwriting. Another, later indication is a change in the way a person walks. Apraxias may progress gradually or change abruptly, depending on the disease. For example, at first a person may seem only slightly unsteady when walking but he may gradually change to a slow, shuffling gait.

It can be difficult for the person not trained to assess dementing illnesses to separate problems of memory (can the person remember what he is supposed to do?) from problems of apraxia (can the person not make his muscles do what they are supposed to do?). Both problems occur when the brain is damaged by the disease. It is not always necessary to distinguish between them in order to help the person manage as independently as possible.

When apraxia begins to affect walking, the person may be slightly unsteady. You must watch for this and provide either a handrail or someone to hold on to when the person is using stairs and stepping up onto or down off a curb.

Losses of coordination and manual skills may lead to problems in daily living such as bathing, managing buttons or zips, dressing, pouring a glass of water, and eating. Dialling a telephone requires good coordination, and a person who does not appear to have any motor impairment may in fact be unable to dial a telephone to call for help. A pushbutton telephone may help, but it may also be difficult for the confused person to learn the new skill of using a pushbutton phone.

Some of the things a person has difficulty with may have to be given up.

Others can be modified so that the impaired person can remain partially independent. When you modify a task, the key is to simplify, rather than change, the task. Because of his intellectual impairment, the person with a dementing illness may be unable to learn a new, simpler task. Consider the nature of each task. Ask yourself if it can be done in a simpler way. For example, shoes that slip on are easier than shoes with laces. Soup is easier to drink out of a mug than to spoon from a bowl. Finger foods are more easily managed than things that must be cut with knife and fork. Can the person do part of the task if you do the difficult part? You may already have discovered that the person can dress himself if you help with buttons or fasteners.

A person may feel tense, embarrassed, or worried about his clumsiness. He may try to conceal his increasing disability by refusing to participate in activities. For example,

Mrs Fisher had always enjoyed knitting. When she abruptly gave up this hobby her daughter could not understand what had happened. Mrs Fisher said only that she no longer liked to knit. In fact, her increasing apraxia was making knitting impossible, and she was ashamed of her awkwardness.

A relaxed atmosphere often helps make the person's clumsiness less apparent. It is not unusual for a person to have more difficulty with a task when he is feeling tense.

Sometimes a person can do something one time and not another time. This may be a characteristic of the brain impairment and not laziness. Being hurried, being watched, being upset, or being tired can affect a person's ability to do things—just as it does to a normal person. Having a brain disease makes these natural fluctuations more dramatic. Sometimes people can do one task with no problem, such as zipping up trousers, and be unable to do another similar task, such as zipping up a jacket. It may seem that the person is being difficult, but the reason may actually be that one task is impossible because it is different in some way.

Sometimes a person can do a task if you break it down into a series of smaller tasks and tell him to do each step. For example, brushing your teeth involves picking up the toothbrush, putting the toothpaste on it, putting the toothbrush in your mouth, brushing, rinsing, etc. Gently remind the person of each step. It may help to demonstrate. You may have to repeat each step several times. Sometimes it helps to put a familiar tool, such as a spoon or comb, into the person's hand and gently start his arm moving in the right direction. Beginning the motion seems to help the brain remember the task.

An occupational therapist is trained to assess the motor skills the person has retained and how he may make the best use of them. The information gained from the assessment done by the occupational therapist can help you give the confused person the help he needs without taking away his independence.

In the later stages of some of the dementing diseases, extensive loss of muscle control occurs and the person may bump into things and fall down. This will be discussed in Chapter 5.

People with dementing illnesses may have other diseases as well that interfere with their ability to do daily tasks. Part of the problem may be in the muscles or joints and another part of the problem in the impaired brain. Such complicating conditions include tremors (shaking), muscle weakness, joint or bone diseases such as arthritis, or stiffness caused by medications.

There are many techniques and devices to help people with physical limitations remain independent. When you consider such techniques or devices, remember that most of them require the ability to learn to do something a new way or to learn to use a new gadget. People with dementing illnesses may not be able to learn the new skills needed.

Some people have tremors. These are shaking movements of the hands or body. These can make many activities difficult for a person, but an occupational therapist or physiotherapist may be able to show you how to minimise the effects of tremors.

Some people with neurological conditions, especially Parkinson's disease, have difficulty starting a movement or may get 'stuck' in the middle of a movement. This can be frustrating for both of you. If this is a problem, here are some helpful hints:

1 If the person becomes 'glued' to the floor while walking, tell him to walk toward a goal or object. This may help him get going again.
2 It may be easier to get out of a chair that has armrests. Raise the sitting person's centre of gravity by raising the chair seat two to four inches. A firm seat is needed. Use a firm cushion or a higher chair such as a dining room chair. Avoid low chairs with soft cushions. Instruct the person to move forward to the edge of the chair and spread his feet about one foot apart to give a wider base to stand on. Ask the person to put his hands on the armrests and then to rock back and forth to gain momentum. On the count of three, tell him to get up quickly. Ensure he takes time to get his balance before he begins to walk.
3 Sitting down in a chair may be easier to do when the person puts his hands on the arm rests, bends forward as far as possible, and sits down slowly.

Muscle weakness or stiffness may occur when a person does not move around much. Exercise is important for memory-impaired people.

Occasionally a person who is taking one of the major tranquillisers or neuroleptic drugs will get stiff and rigid or may become restless. These may be side effects of the medication. They can be very uncomfortable. Notify your doctor. He can change the dosage or give another medication to overcome this effect.

Loss of sense of time

The uncanny ability normal individuals have for judging the passage of time is one of the first losses of a dementia patient. He may repeatedly ask you what time it is, feel that you have left him for hours when you are out of sight for a few minutes, or want to leave a place as soon as he has arrived. It is not hard to understand this behaviour when you consider that in order to know how much time has passed, one must be able to remember what one has done with the immediate past. The person who forgets quickly has no way to measure the passage of time.

In addition to this defect of memory, it appears that dementing diseases can affect the internal clock that keeps the rest of us on a reasonably regular schedule of sleeping, waking, and eating. It will be helpful to you to recognise that this behaviour is not deliberate (although it can be irritating). It is the result of the loss of brain function.

The ability to read a clock may be lost early in the course of the disease. Even when a person can look at the clock and say, 'It is 3.15,' he may be unable to make sense out of this information.

Not being able to keep track of time can worry the forgetful person. Many of us, throughout our lives, are dependent upon a regular time schedule. Not knowing the time can make a person worry that he will be late, be forgotten, miss the bus, overstay his welcome, miss lunch, or miss his transport home. The confused person may not know just what he is worried about, but a general feeling of anxiety may make him ask you what time it is. And, of course, as soon as you answer him, he will forget the whole conversation, and ask again.

Sometimes a person feels that you have deserted him when you have been gone only briefly. This is because he cannot remember. Sometimes setting a timer or an old-fashioned hourglass will help these people wait more patiently for your return. Perhaps you can think of other ways to reduce this behaviour. For example,

> *When Mr and Mrs Jenkins went to dinner at their son's house, Mr Jenkins would almost immediately put his hat and coat on and insist that it was time to go home. When he could be persuaded to stay for the meal, he insisted on leaving immediately afterwards. His son thought he was just being rude.*

Things went more smoothly when the family understood that this was because the unfamiliar house, the added confusion, and Mr Jenkins's lost sense of time upset him. The family thought back over Mr Jenkins's life and hit upon an old social habit that helped them. In earlier years, he had enjoyed watching the football match after Sunday dinner. Now his son turned on the TV as soon as Mr Jenkins finished eating. Since this was an old habit, Mr Jenkins would stay for about an hour, giving his wife time to chat, before he got restless for home.

4 Problems in independent living

As a person begins to develop a dementing illness, she may begin to have difficulty managing independently. You may suspect that she is mismanaging her money, worry that she should not be driving, or wonder if she should be living alone. People with dementing illnesses often appear to be managing well, and they may insist that they are fine and that you are interfering. It can be difficult to know when you should take over and how much you should take over. It can also be painful to take away these outward symbols of a person's independence, or the confused person may adamantly refuse to move, to stop driving, or to relinquish her financial responsibilities.

Part of the reason that making these changes is so difficult is because they symbolise giving up independence and responsibility and therefore all of the family members may have strong feelings about them. (We will discuss these role changes in Chapter 11.) Making necessary changes will be easier when you understand the feelings involved.

The first step in deciding whether the time has come to make changes in a person's independence is to get a proper medical assessment. This will tell you what the person is still able to do and what she is no longer able to do, and it will give you the authority to insist upon necessary changes. For a medical assessment first contact your GP and ask if your dependant may see a specialist who may be a neurologist, a geriatrician, a psychiatrist or a psychogeriatrician. When a professional assessment is not immediately available, you and your family must analyse each task as thoroughly and objectively as possible, and decide whether the person can still do specific tasks *completely*, *safely*, and *without becoming upset*.

A dementing illness brings about many kinds of losses. It means losing control over one's daily activities, losing independence, losing skills, and losing the ability to do those things that make one feel useful or important. A dementing illness limits the possibilities the future can hold. While others can look forward to things getting better, the ill person must gradually realise that her future is limited. Perhaps the most terrible loss of all is the loss of memory. Losing one's memories means losing one's day-to-day connections with others and with one's past. The far past may seem like the present. Without a memory of today or an understanding that the past is past, the future ceases to have meaning.

As losses accumulate in anyone's life, it is natural for him or her to cling even more tightly to the things that remain. Understandably, a confused person might respond to such changes with resistance, denial, or anger. The confused person's need for familiar surroundings and the determination of most people not to be a burden on anyone make it understandable that the disabled person will not want to give up these things. To accept that, she would have to face the extent and finality of her illness, which she may not be able to do.

In addition, the person may be unable to make complete sense out of what is going on. If she is not able to assess her own limitations, it may seem to her as if things are being unfairly taken away from her and that her family is 'taking over'. By recognising how she may feel, you may be able to find ways to help her make the necessary changes and still feel that she is in control of her life.

When a person must give up a job

The time when the person must give up a job depends on the kind of job she has and whether she must drive as part of her job. Sometimes an employer will tell you or the impaired person that she must retire. Some employers will be willing to maintain a person in a job that is not too demanding. Sometimes the family must make this decision. You may realise that this time has come.

If the person must give up her job, there are two areas that you must consider: the emotional and psychological adjustments involved in such a major change, and the financial changes that will be involved. A person's job is a key part of her sense of who she is. It helps her to feel that she is a valued member of society. The impaired person may resist giving up her job or may deny that anything is wrong. Her adjustment to retirement may be a painful and distressing time. If these things happen your family doctor or a social worker may be able to help.

It is important that you consider the financial future of the impaired person. (This will be discussed in Chapter 15.) Retirement can create special problems. Individuals who are forced to retire early because of a dementing illness should be entitled to the same retirement and disability benefits as a person with any other disabling *disease*. In some cases, disability benefits have been denied on the erroneous grounds that 'senility' is not a disease and the impaired person has been forced to resign or take an early retirement. This can substantially reduce her income. If this happens, you may want to obtain legal advice.

The demented person, although she may have good skills remaining, may be unable to learn a new job. If she is denied benefits for this reason, you may want to seek legal advice.

When a person can no longer manage money

The impaired person may be unable to balance her cheque book, she may be unable to calculate the correct change, or she may become irresponsible with her money. Occasionally, when a person can no longer manage her money, she may become nasty and accuse others of stealing from her.

Said Mr Roberts, 'My wife has kept the books for the family business for years. I knew something was wrong when my accountant came to me and told me the books were in a terrible mess.'

Mr Rogers said, 'My wife was giving money to the neighbours, hiding it in the waste basket, and losing her purse. So I took her purse—and her money—away from her. Then she was always saying I stole her money.'

Since money often represents independence, sometimes people are unwilling to give up control of their finances.

You may be able to take over the household accounts by simply correcting the person's efforts. If you have to take the person's cheque book away against her wishes it may help to write down a memo such as, 'My son John now takes care of my cheque book', and put this note where the confused person can refer to it to refresh her memory.

It can be upsetting when a person accuses others of stealing, but this is easier to understand when you think about human nature. We have been taught all our life to be careful with money and when money disappears most of us wonder if it was stolen. As a person's brain becomes less able to remember what is really happening, it is not surprising that she becomes anxious and suspicious that her money is being stolen. Avoid getting into arguments about it, since they may upset her more.

Some families find that giving the forgetful person a small amount of spending money (perhaps small change or a pound coin) helps. If it is lost or given away, it is only a minimal amount. Sometimes a person needs to know that she has a little bit of cash on hand, and this is a way around conflicts about money. One peculiarity of the dementing diseases is that a person sometimes loses the ability to calculate the correct change before she loses the knowledge that she needs money.

Mrs Hutchinson had always been fiercely independent about her money, so Mr Hutchinson gave her a purse with some change in it. He put her name and address in it in case she lost her purse. She insisted on paying her hairdresser by cheque long after she could not responsibly manage a cheque book. So Mr Hutchinson gave her some cheques stamped VOID by the bank. Each week she gives one to the hairdresser. Mr. Hutchinson privately arranged with the hairdresser that these would be accepted and that he would pay the bills.

This may seem extreme. It may also seem unfair to dupe the confused person this way. In reality this allows a sick woman to continue to feel independent and it allows her tired and burdened husband to manage the finances and keep the peace.

The Disablement Income Group and the Disability Alliance can help sort out the finance and benefits a person is entitled to. Money matters can cause serious problems, especially when the person is also suspicious or when other members of the family disagree. (It may be helpful here to read Chapters 8 and 11.) Your ingenuity can be a great help to you in making money matters less distressing.

When a person can no longer drive safely

The time may come when you realise that your parent or spouse can no longer drive safely. While some people will recognise their limits, others may be unwilling to give up driving.

For most experienced drivers, driving is a skill so well learned that it is partly 'automatic'. A person can go back and forth to work every day with her mind on other things—perhaps dictating or listening to music. It does not take much concentration to drive, but if the traffic pattern should suddenly change, she can rely on the mind to focus on the road immediately and respond swiftly to a crisis. Because driving is a well-learned skill, a confused person can still *appear* to be driving well when she is not really safe. Driving requires a highly complex interaction of eyes, brain, and muscle, and the ability to solve complicated problems quickly. A person who is still apparently driving safely may have lost the ability to respond appropriately to an unexpected problem on the road. She may be relying entirely on the habits of driving and may be unable to change quickly from a habitual response to a new response when the situation demands it.

Often people make the decision themselves to stop driving when they feel that they 'aren't as sharp as they used to be.' But if they do not, you have a responsibility to them and to others to assess carefully whether or not the person's driving is dangerous, and to intervene when it is. This may be one of the first situations in which you take a decision out of the hands of the impaired person. You may feel hesitant to do this, but you will probably be relieved once you have stopped a forgetful person from driving. To decide whether the time has come, look at the skills that a person needs to drive safely and evaluate whether the confused person still has these skills—both in the car and in other situations:

1. *Good vision:* A person must have good vision, or vision corrected with glasses, and be able to see clearly, both in front and out of the corners of her eyes (peripheral vision) so that she sees things coming toward her from the sides.
2. *Good hearing:* A person must be able to hear well or have her hearing corrected with a hearing aid, so that she is alert to the sounds of approaching cars, horns, and so forth.
3. *Quick reaction time:* A driver must be able to react quickly—to turn, to brake, and to avoid accidents. Older people's reaction time, when it is formally tested, is slightly slower than that of young people, but in well older people it is usually not slow enough to interfere with driving. However, if you see that a person reacts slowly or inappropriately to sudden changes around the house, this should alert you to the possibility of the same limitations when she is driving.

4 *Ability to make decisions:* A driver must be able to make quick, *appropriate* decisions rapidly and *calmly*. The ability to make a correct decision when a child darts in front of the car, a horn honks, and a lorry is approaching all at once necessitates being able to solve complicated, unfamiliar problems quickly and without panicking. People with a dementing illness often rely on habitual responses that may not be the correct responses in a driving situation. Some people also get confused and upset when several things happen at once. You will see these problems, if they are occurring, around the house as well as in the car.
5 *Good coordination:* Eyes, hands, and feet must all still work together well to handle a car safely. If a person is getting clumsy, or if her way of walking has changed, it should alert you that she may also have trouble getting her foot on the brake.
6 *Alertness to what is going on around her:* A driver must be alert to all that is going on without becoming upset or confused. If a person is 'missing things' that happen around her, she may no longer be a safe driver.

Sometimes driving behaviours alert you to problems. Forgetful people may get lost on routes that would not have confused them previously. Being lost can distract the driver and further interfere with her ability to react quickly. Sometimes driving too slowly is a clue that the driver is uncertain of her skills—but this does not mean that every cautious driver is an impaired driver.

Confused people may become angry or aggressive when they drive or they may inappropriately believe that other drivers are 'out to get them'. This is dangerous. Occasionally a person with a dementing illness is also drinking too much. Even small amounts of alcohol impair the driving ability of people with a brain injury. This is a dangerous combination, and you must intervene.

If you are concerned about a person's driving ability, you might first approach the problem by discussing it frankly with her. Even though a person is cognitively impaired she is still able to participate in decisions that involve her. How you initiate such a discussion may affect her response. People with brain impairments are sometimes less able to tolerate criticism than when they were well, so you will want to use tact in such a discussion. If you say, 'Your driving is terrible, you are getting lost, and you're just not safe,' a person may feel she has to defend herself and may argue with you. Instead, by gently saying, 'You are getting absent-minded about traffic lights,' you may be able to give a person an 'easy way out'. Giving up driving can mean admitting one's increasing limitations. Look for ways to help the person save face and maintain her self-image at the same time that you react to the need for safety. Try offering alternatives: 'I'll drive today and you can look at the scenery.' As a last resort some families have disconnected the battery or starter wire and told the impaired person that the car could not be repaired.

Sometimes a person will absolutely refuse to give up driving, despite your tact. It may help to enlist the support of the doctor or a family solicitor. Often a person will cooperate with the instructions of an authority when she may regard your advice as nagging. As a last resort you may have to take away the car keys. If you cannot do this, you can make it impossible to start a car by removing the distributor cap or the wire to the distributor. This is small and easy to replace when you want to drive. A car mechanic can show you how to do this.

Drivers are required by law to inform the licensing authorities if they suffer from any disability which affects their fitness to drive unless it is not likely to last for more than three months. Some insurance companies require older drivers to undergo medical examinations to assess their fitness to drive. If a driver is convicted of a motoring offence and their ability to drive is questioned, a magistrate may require them to pass a driving test before allowing them to drive.

Orange Badge Scheme

An 'Orange Badge Scheme' grants concessionary parking to people with disabilities. The regulations state that only those with permanent, substantial difficulty which causes inability to walk or very considerable difficulty in walking should be given badges. The badge is exhibited on the car's windscreen and can be obtained from the local authority Social Services or Borough Surveyors Departments. There is usually a fee and proof of eligibility will be sought, either evidence that the person holds a mobility allowance or a doctor's note.

When a person can no longer live alone

When a person has lived alone but can no longer continue to do so, the move to live with someone else can be difficult for everyone. Some people welcome the sense of security that living with others provides. Others vigorously resist giving up their independence.

Often patients go through a series of stages from complete independence to living with someone. When a gradual transition from independence is possible, it may be easier for the person to adjust and it may postpone the time when she must live with someone. For example, at first the help of the neighbours, a home help or provision of Meals-on-Wheels may be adequate; later, a family member or a paid voluntary helper may spend part of the day with the confused person. A person who is still fairly independent may only need someone to come in to give the medication or help with a meal but not constant supervision.

Eventually, however, the time may come when the care-giving family decides that the person cannot live alone. You will need to be alert to the possibility that the person's ability to function alone can change suddenly: some minor stress or even a mild case of the flu can make her worse. Or, you may not notice the gradual, insidious decline until something happens. Here are some questions that will help you decide if that time has come.

Is the person eating her meals and taking her medicines? A forgetful person may not eat, or may eat only sweets even when you have provided a hot meal. The person may take too much medicine or forget her medicine. This can make her mental impairment worse and can jeopardise her physical health. If the person is safe in other ways, she may be able to live alone if someone else helps daily with food and medicine, but it has been our experience that people who forget to eat properly are experiencing sufficient cognitive impairment that they probably cannot safely live alone.

Is the person able to manage her own personal care and grooming? Some forgetful people wear dirty clothes, forget (or refuse) to have a bath or brush their teeth, or in other ways neglect themselves.

Is the person wandering away from home? She may get lost or be robbed or assaulted. Is the person wandering around outside at night? Such behaviour is not uncommon and is dangerous.

Is the person forgetting to turn off the cooker or burning the food? People who appear to be managing well often forget to turn off the cooker. Is the person using candles or matches? It can be hard to believe that a person is really a danger to herself when she looks so well, but fire is a real and serious hazard. Cases of severe or even fatal accidental burns are not uncommon. If you suspect that the person is forgetting to turn off the cooker, you must intervene.

Is the person keeping the house tidy, reasonably clean, and free of hazards? Forgetful people may spill puddles of water in the kitchen or bathroom and forget to clean them up. A person can slip and fall on a wet floor. Sometimes people forget to wash the dishes or forget to flush the toilet or in other ways create unsanitary conditions. If the house is badly cluttered, they can trip and fall. A confused person may pile up newspapers and rags which become a fire hazard.

Is the person keeping warm? A forgetful person may keep her house too cold or dress inappropriately. Her body temperature can drop dangerously if she does not keep herself warm. In hot weather the confused person may dress too warmly or may be afraid to open the house for adequate ventilation. This can lead to heat stroke.

Is the person acting in response to 'paranoid' ideas or unrealistic suspiciousness? Such behaviour can get her in trouble in the community. Sometimes people call the police because of their fears and make their neighbours angry. Also confused elderly people may become the target of malicious teenagers. These problems can occur in suburban neighbourhoods as well as in the inner city.

Is the person showing good judgment? Some confused people show poor judgment about whom they let in the house and can be robbed by the people they invite in, or they may give away money or do other inappropriate things.

Moving to a new home

If some of these things are happening, you know that the person can no longer live alone and you must make other arrangements for her. You might consider full-time help or you may arrange for the person to move into a residential home, a nursing home, or a psychiatric hospital. (These facilities will be described in detail in Chapter 16.)

Mr Sawyer reports, 'Mother simply cannot live alone anymore. We hired a housekeeper and Mother fired her—and when I called the employment agency they said they could not send anyone else. So we talked with Mother, told her we wanted her to come live with us. But she absolutely refused. She says nothing is wrong with her, that I am trying to steal her money. She won't admit she isn't eating. She says she changed her clothes and we know she hasn't. I don't know what to do.'

If a confused person refuses to give up her independence and move into a safer setting, understanding something of what she may be thinking and feeling may help make the move easier. A move from living alone to living with someone else may mean giving up one's independence and admitting one's impairment. Moving means more losses. It means giving up a familiar place and often many familiar possessions. That place and those possessions are the tangible symbols of one's past and reminders when one's memories fail.

The confused person is dependent upon a familiar setting to provide her with cues that enable her to function independently. Learning one's way around in a new place is difficult or impossible. She feels dependent upon familiar surroundings to survive. The person with a dementing illness may forget the plans that have been discussed or may be unable to understand them. You may reassure your mother that she is coming to live in your house—which is very familiar to her—but all her damaged mind may perceive is that a lot of things are going to be lost.

As you make plans for this person to live with someone, there are several things to consider:

1 Take into careful consideration the changes that this move will mean in your life, and plan, before the move, for financial resources and emotional outlets and supports for yourself.

If the impaired person is to move in with you, what effect will this have on her income? You will also want to review such things as whether you can claim the person as your dependant on your income tax.

If the person is coming to live with you, how does the rest of the family feel about this? If there are children or teenagers in the family, will their activities upset the confused person or will the 'odd' behaviour of the confused person upset them? How does your spouse feel about this? Is your marriage already under stress? A demented person in the home creates burdens and stresses under the best of circumstances. If the demented person and her spouse are both moving in, you must also consider how the spouse will interact in the household. All of the people affected need to be involved in the decision and need the opportunity to express their concerns.

Assuming the care of a forgetful person may mean changes in other things: leisure time (you may not be able to go out because there is no one to sit with Mother), peace (you may not be able to read the newspaper or talk to your wife because Mother is pacing the floor), money (you may have to face higher heating bills, or bills for adapting the home), rest (the confused person may wake at night), visitors (people may stop visiting if the person's behaviour is embarrassing). These are the things that make life tolerable and that help to reduce your stress. It is important to plan ways for you and your family to relax and get away from the problems of caring for a sick person. Remember also that other problems are not going to go away. You may still worry about your children, come home exhausted from your job, have the car break down, etc.

Is the person you are bringing into your home someone you can live with? If you never could get along with your mother and if her illness has made her behaviour worse instead of better, having her move in with you may be disastrous. If you have had a long-standing poor relationship with the person who is now sick, that poor relationship is a reality that can make things more difficult for you.

2 Involve the person as much as possible in plans for the move, even if she refuses to move. The patient is still a person, and her participation in plans and decisions that involve her is important unless she is too severely impaired to comprehend what is happening. Confused people who have been hoodwinked into a move may become even more angry and suspicious and their adjustment to the new setting may be extremely difficult. Certainly the extent and nature of the impaired person's participation depend on the extent of her illness and her attitude toward the move.

Keep in mind that there is a major difference between making the decision, which you may have to do, and participating in the planning, which the confused person can be encouraged to do. Perhaps Mr Sawyer's story will continue like this:

'After we talked it over with Mother she still absolutely refused to consider a move. So I went ahead with the arrangements. I told Mother gently that she had to move because she was getting forgetful.

'I knew too many decisions at once would upset her, so we would just ask her a few things at a time. 'Mother, would you like to take all your pictures with you?' 'Mother, let's take your own bed and your lovely bedspread for your new bedroom.'

'Of course, we made a lot of decisions without her—about the cooker and the washing machine, and the junk in the attic. And of course she kept saying she wasn't going and that I was robbing her. Still, I think some of it sank in, that she was 'helping' us get ready to move. Sometimes she would pick up a vase and say, 'I want Carol to have this.' We tried to comply with her wishes. Then after the move, we could honestly tell her that the vase was not stolen: she had given it to Carol.'

When a person is too impaired to understand what is happening around her it may be better to make the move without the added stress of trying to involve her in it.

3 Be prepared for a period of adjustment. Changes are frequently upsetting to people with dementing illnesses. No matter how carefully and lovingly you plan the move, this is a major change, and the person may be upset for a while. It is easy to understand that it takes time to get over the losses a move involves. A forgetful person also needs extra time to learn her way around in a new place.

Reassure yourself that after an adjustment period the person usually will settle into her new surroundings. Signs on doors may help her find her way around an unfamiliar home. An additional sedative may help her sleep at night. Try to postpone other activities or changes until after everyone has adjusted to the move.

Occasionally an impaired person never really adjusts to moving. Don't blame yourself. You did the best you could and acted for her well-being. You may have to accept her inability to adjust as being the result of her illness.

5 Problems arising in daily care

Hazards to watch for

A person with a dementing illness is less able to take responsibility for his own safety. He is no longer able to assess the consequences of his actions the way the rest of us do, and, because he forgets so quickly, accidents can easily happen. He may attempt to do familiar tasks without realising that he can no longer manage them. For example, the disease may affect those portions of the brain which remember how to do simple things, such as buttoning buttons or slicing meat. This inability to do manual tasks is often unrecognised and causes accidents. Since the person also cannot learn, you will have to take special precautions to guard against accidents. Because a person seems to be managing well, you may not realise that he has lost the judgment he needs to avoid accidents. Families may need to take responsibility for the safety of even a mildly impaired person.

Accidents are most likely to occur when you are cross or tired, when everyone is hurrying, when there is an argument, or when someone in the household is ill. At these times you are less alert to the possibility of an accident and the impaired person may misunderstand or overreact to even the slightest mishap with a catastrophic reaction.

Do what you can to reduce confusion or tension when it arises. This is difficult when you are struggling with the care of a person with a dementing illness. If you are rushing with him to keep an appointment or finish a job, *stop*, even if it means being late or not getting something done. Catch your breath, rest a minute, and let the confused person calm down.

Be aware that mishaps can be warning signs of impending accidents: you banged your shin on the edge of the bed, or dropped and broke a cup, and the impaired person is getting upset. This is the time to create a change of pace before a serious accident occurs.

Alert others in the household to the relationship between increased tension and increased accidents. At such times everyone can keep a closer eye on the impaired person.

Be sure you know the limits of the impaired person's abilities. Do not take his word that he can heat up his supper or get into the bath alone. An occupational therapist can give you an excellent picture of what the person can do safely. If this assessment has not been done, observe the person closely as he does various tasks.

Have an emergency plan ready in case something does happen. Whom will you call if someone is hurt? How will you get the upset person out in case of a fire? Remember that he may misinterpret what is happening and resist your efforts to help him.

Change the environment to make it safer. This is one of the most important ways to avoid accidents. Hospitals and other institutions have safety experts who regularly inspect for hazards. You can and should do the same thing. Go thoughtfully through your home, garden, neighbourhood, and car, looking for things a person with a dementing illness could possibly misuse or misinterpret that might cause an accident.

In the house

A neat house is safer than a cluttered one. There are fewer things to trip over or knock over, and hazards are more easily seen. Knickknacks or clutter may distract or confuse an impaired person.

Remove things that cause problems. If a person tries to use the iron and leaves it on, causing a fire hazard, put it away where he cannot find it. Whenever possible take the easiest path to safety without conflict. Does the impaired person have access to power tools, lawn mower, knives, hairdryer, cooker, sewing machine, or car keys when he can no longer safely use them? You must put these in a locked cupboard.

Are all medications kept out of reach of a person who may forget that he has already taken them? Buy a medicine cabinet or any small cupboard or box with a lock and lock your medicines safely away from the forgetful person and visiting grandchildren.

Are things stored on the stairs? Clutter is always dangerous, particularly when a person is confused, clumsy, or misinterprets what he sees. Are electric flexes and wires stretched across the floor where a person might trip over them?

Lower the temperature on your water heater so that water is not hot enough to scald the person who accidentally turns it on. People with dementing illnesses can lose the ability to realise that hot water is too hot and they can burn themselves badly. Paint hot water taps bright red as a reminder. If hot water pipes are exposed, cover them with insulation.

If the confused person readjusts the boiler or water heater, you may need to lock the door of the room where it is situated.

If you have stairs, install gates at the top. The confused person can easily become disorientated and fall down the steps, especially at night. Check the handrails; be sure they are sturdy. Handrails should be anchored into the brick wall or wooden support beams and not into plaster. They will not hold a person's weight if they are not securely fastened. Install handrails if there are none. As the person becomes unsteady on his feet, he will need them. Put away rugs that slip. If stairs are carpeted, check to see that the carpet is securely tacked down.

Remove furniture with sharp corners or sharp edges. Put away or block off large areas of breakable glass; a person can fall against a glass china cabinet and be badly cut. Put away rocking chairs that tip over easily. Put away coffee tables and fragile antiques.

Use stable chairs that are easy to get out of (see p. 31). Check to see if fingers or toes could get caught in parts of reclining chairs. Furniture upholstery should be easy to clean; you may have to wipe up spills. Fabric for upholstery, curtains and cushions should be flame resistant.

Impaired people may not see well and it can become harder for them to distinguish colours that are similar to each other. Sometimes it helps to put bright reflector tape on handrails, doorways, and the corners of mantelpieces if a person has been bumping into them (also see Chapter 6: 'Vision Problems').

A confused person may fall out of a window. Lock windows securely. There are inexpensive devices to enable you to lock a window in an open position so that a person cannot get out but fresh air can get in. Open the window a little at the top and a little at the bottom and secure it.

Block off hot radiators by putting a sturdy chair in front of them. You will want to put a guard around all fires and stoves.

Can the person lock himself in a room so that you cannot get in? If so, remove the lock, take the levers out, and replace the knob, or tape the latch open with tape.

Never keep insecticides, petrol, paint, solvents, cleaning agents, etc., in other than their original, clearly labelled containers. Store them safely out of reach of the confused person. Child-proof (and patient-proof) cabinet locks are available at hardware stores, at large chemists such as Baby Boots, and Mothercare shops. Mildly confused people may try to use such materials inappropriately.

Impaired people forget what can be eaten and what cannot; they may drink solvents by mistake. These people may also eat other inappropriate items. Put small things such as pins and buttons out of reach. Give away poisonous houseplants. Some people will eat chips of loose paint from walls or furniture. This could be dangerous if the paint is old and contains lead. Watch closely for any behaviour that involves putting things in the mouth.

Most accidents happen in the kitchen and the bathroom. Confused people often try to turn on the cooker but forget they have done so, or try to cook but put empty pans on a hot burner. *This is a serious fire hazard.* You must watch for this and intervene immediately. People left alone at home or those who get up at night are especially at risk.

You may be able to take the knobs off the cooker so that the disabled person cannot operate it. If you have an electric cooker, you can have a switch installed behind it so that when the switch is off the burners will not operate. You can remove the fuse when you are not using the cooker.

If you have a gas cooker, ask the gas board to assist you in making the cooker safe. Depending on the cooker and your house, there are several things you can do. You may have to be quite persistent and talk to several people before you reach a gas board official who is helpful and understanding.

Confused people often spill water on the kitchen or bathroom floor and forget to wipe it up. It is easy to slip and fall on a wet spot, so watch for this and keep the floor dry. Perhaps you will want to give up polishing the floor, also. Polishing is work for you and makes the floor slippery.

Handrails and grab rails should be installed in the bathroom (see p. 61). They can best be supplied by local authority Social Services and installed by the local authority technician, or purchased at various hardware stores and chemists (the Disabled Living Foundation Information Service can give addresses of vendors). Put a non-slip mat on the floor of the bath or shower. It is sometimes helpful to replace the bathmat with bathroom carpeting. This is easily cleaned, doesn't slip, and soaks up puddles.

Outdoors

Both adults and children can easily put a hand through the sheet glass in a front or outside door. These doors should be covered with a protective grillwork. Sliding glass patio doors should be well marked with stick-on indicators.

Check to see if a confused person might fall off a verandah or balcony. If there are steps, paint them in bright, contrasting colours, attach outdoor non-slip tape to the edges, and install a banister.

Check for uneven ground, cracked pavement, holes in the lawn, fallen branches, thorny bushes, or molehills that the person can trip over.

Take down the clothesline so the person will not run into it.

Make sure the charcoals have cooled on an outside barbecue. If you have a gas barbecue, be sure the confused person cannot operate it.

Lock up garden tools.

Check garden furniture to be sure it is stable, will not tip or collapse, and has no splinters or chipped paint.

Fence in or dispose of poisonous flowers.

Outdoor swimming pools are very dangerous. If you have one be sure it is securely fenced and locked so that the person cannot get to it. Even if he has always been a good swimmer, a confused person may lose his judgment or his ability to handle himself in the water.

In the car

Problems with driving are discussed in Chapter 4. Never leave a confused person alone in a car. He may wander away, fiddle with the ignition, release the handbrake, be harassed by strangers, or run the battery down with the lights. Automatic windows are dangerous for confused people and for children, who may close the window on their head or arm.

Occasionally a confused person will open the car door and attempt to get out while the car is moving. Locking the door may help. If this continues to be a problem, you may need a third person to drive while you keep the impaired person calm. In some cases you can unscrew and remove the knobs on the door locks so that the person cannot unlock the door while you are driving, or childproof locks can be fitted.

Smoking

If the person smokes, the time will come when he lays lighted cigarettes down and forgets them. *This is a serious hazard.* If it occurs, you must intervene. Try to discourage smoking. Many families have taken cigarettes completely away from a patient. Things may be difficult for a few days or weeks, but much easier in the long run.

Other families allow the impaired person to smoke only under their supervision. All smoking materials and matches must be kept out of reach of the forgetful person. (The person who has cigarettes but no matches may use the cooker to light his cigarette and may leave the cooker on.)

Nutrition and mealtimes

Good nutrition is important to both you and the chronically ill person. If you are not eating well, you will be more tense and more easily upset. It is not known to what extent a proper diet affects the progress of dementing diseases, but we do know that forgetful people often fail to eat properly and can suffer nutritional deficiencies. Sometimes this can make symptoms worse. It is important that you and your dependant have a balanced diet and for detailed advice you should consult your doctor or health visitor. You may be referred to a nutritionist or dietician. Generally, however, you should try and have as much variety as possible in your diet and not eat too much of anything. There are no foods which you *must* have and it is best to have several small meals rather than one or two large ones over a day. If your doctor has recommended a special diet for managing other diseases like diabetes or heart disease, it is important that you know from him what foods you should eat in order to maintain a balanced diet. He can refer you to a dietician who can help you plan a special diet. Dieticians run outpatient clinics in most large hospitals and may also conduct clinics in some health centres.

There is no known link between nutrition and Alzheimer's disease and there are no special diets that have been proved to help memory problems.

Meal preparation

When you must prepare meals on top of all your other responsibilities you may find yourself taking short cuts such as fixing just a cup of coffee and toast for yourself and the confused person. If preparing meals is a job you had to take on for the first time when your spouse became ill, you may not know how to serve good nutritious meals quickly and easily and you may not want to learn to cook. There are several alternatives. We suggest you plan a variety of ways to get good meals with a minimum of effort. Lunch clubs and Meals-on-Wheels services exist in most areas. Both services provide one hot, nutritious meal a day. You can find out what meal services are available through a social worker or by calling the local Social Services Department. Meals-on-Wheels services bring a meal to your home. Lunch clubs provide lunch and sometimes recreation facilities in the company of other retired people at a community centre. Transport is often provided.

Some restaurants will prepare carry out meals if requested. This helps when a person can no longer eat in public.

There are numerous inexpensive cookbooks on the market that explain the basic steps in easy meal preparation. Some are in large print. An experienced housewife can show you how to prepare quick, easy meals. The health visitor may make some suggestions on budgeting, shopping, meal planning, and nutrition, and she can help you understand and arrange menus for special diets.

Use tinned and frozen snack meals only as an emergency back-up. They are not an adequate regular diet. They are low in vitamins, high in salt, and lack the roughage older people need to prevent constipation.

Problem eating behaviours

Forgetful people who are still eating some meals alone may forget to eat, even if you leave food where it can be clearly seen. They may hide food, throw food away, or eat it after it has spoiled. These are signals that the person can no longer manage alone and that you must make new arrangements. You may cope for a time by telephoning at midday to remind him to eat lunch now, but this is only a short-term solution. Confused people who live alone are frequently malnourished. Even when they appear overweight, they may not be getting the proper foods.

Many of the problems that arise at mealtime involve catastrophic reactions. Make mealtime as regular a routine as possible, with as little confusion as you can arrange. This will help prevent catastrophic reactions. Fussy or messy eaters do better when things are calm.

Check that dentures are tight fitting if the person uses them to eat. If they are loose, it may be safer to leave them out until they can be adjusted.

Check the temperature of foods—confused people often lack the judgement to avoid burning themselves.

People with dementing illnesses may develop rigid likes and dislikes and refuse to eat certain foods. Such people may be more willing to eat familiar foods, prepared in familiar ways. If the person never liked a particular food, he will not like it now. New foods may confuse him. If the person insists on eating only one or two things and if all efforts at persuasion or disguising foods fail, you will need to ask the doctor about vitamins and diet supplements.

If the person has a complicating illness, such as diabetes, which requires a special diet, it may be necessary to put foods he should not eat where he cannot get them, and allow him only those foods he should have. Remember, he may lack the judgement to decide responsibly between his craving and his well-being. Since a proper diet is important to his health, you may have to be responsible for preventing him from getting foods he should not have, even if he vigorously objects. A locksmith can put a lock on the refrigerator door if necessary. But before you invest in locks, ask yourself whether the foods you wish to lock away are really necessary.

People with dementing illnesses may be unable to recognise that some things are not good to eat. You may need to lock up foods like salt, vinegar, oil, or Worcestershire sauce, which can make the person sick if he eats them in quantity.

Nibbling

Sometimes a person seems to forget that he ate, and will ask for food again right after a meal. Sometimes people seem to want to eat all the time. Try setting out a tray of small, nutritious 'nibbles' such as small biscuits or cheese cubes. Sometimes people will take one at a time and be satisfied. If weight gain is a problem, put out carrots or celery.

Messiness

If the person has problems with coordination he may lose the ability to do tasks he has always done. When this happens, he may become a messy eater, and may use his fingers instead of cutlery or spill food. It is usually easier to adjust to this than to fight circumstances.

Use a plastic tablecloth or plastic placemats. Try a clear plastic cloth over a pretty tablecloth. Get the person an attractive smock to wear, rather than a bib, if spills are a problem. Turn the bottom up into a big pocket to catch crumbs.

Put only the fork or spoon that the person will need at his place. Knives, forks and spoons with large, built-up handles are easier for people with poor coordination. You can purchase these or build up your own handle with foam rubber. A fork or spoon with some weight will help the person remember that he is holding it. Forgetful people may not remember that they are holding plastic forks or they may bite off pieces of them.

In general, it is easier for a person to manage a bowl than a plate. Use sturdy plastic rather than glass or china dishes. Use dishes that are a different colour from the placemat. Glass is hard to see. To keep a plate from sliding, place a non-slip mat under the plate or attach a suction pad to the bottom of the plate. Plates with suction pads are available from chemists and are also sold for children. If neither is available, a damp washcloth under the plate will help keep it from sliding. To keep food from being pushed off a dish, a plate surround can be temporarily attached to any plate or you can use a Manoy or 'hemi' dish. Both are available from large chemist shops.

Some people lose the ability to judge how much liquid will fill a glass and overfill glasses. They will need your help. If a person dribbles or spills when drinking from a cup, use a feeding cup, which has a spout. Similar spillproof cups are also sold for children. Don't fill glasses or cups full. This will help prevent spilling. All these appliances can also be supplied by a domiciliary occupational therapist who can be contacted through your Social Services Department.

As eating becomes more difficult, limit the number of foods you put in front of the confused person at one time. For example, serve only his vegetables, then only his meat. Having to make choices often leads to playing with the food. Don't put salt, ketchup, etc., where he can reach it and mix it inappropriately into his food. Season his food for him. Be sure that food is cut into pieces that are small and tender enough to be eaten safely. People with dementing illnesses may forget to chew or fail to cut meats up properly, because the hands and brain no longer work together.

If you spoonfeed a person, put only a small amount of food on the spoon at a time, and wait until the person swallows before giving him the next spoonful. You may have to remind him verbally to swallow.

Fluids

Be sure that the person gets enough fluid each day. Even mildly impaired people may forget to drink, and inadequate fluids can lead to other physical problems (see p. 70).

Don't give the person a cup of tea or coffee that is too hot to drink. He will eventually lose the ability to judge this and will burn himself.

Puréed diet

If the person is on a puréed diet, use a liquidiser or food processor. You can purée normally prepared foods in them. This saves time and money. Home-cooked foods will be more appealing to the person than babyfoods.

Drooling or respiratory problems

If the person drools or has respiratory problems, milk or citrus juice may produce more mucus and make the problem worse. Check with your doctor to determine the cause of the problem. Then offer tea or fruit squash instead of orange juice or milk.

Weight loss

Sometimes a person with a severe dementia stops eating. This can be a difficult and frustrating situation. If a person stops eating or begins to lose weight, notify the doctor. This can be a signal of a complicating disease. It is important to search carefully for any contributory physical illness. Is the person depressed? Does he have any acute illness (see p. 68)? Has he had a stroke? Be sure to check for painful teeth or gums or poorly fitting dentures.

Sometimes a familiar person can coax a patient to eat. Offer his favourite foods. If they must be puréed, be sure that they are still tasty. Put only one thing on his plate at a time. Use a feeding beaker which has a plastic cover or spout. Often an impaired person eats slowly. Be sure he is not rushed. Ensure that his physical surroundings are pleasant, calm, and not distracting. We have had one patient respond by having her back gently stroked while she was being fed. One patient responded to a low dose of neuroleptic given one hour before meals.

You may give a person who is not eating well a liquid diet supplement like Complan or BuildUp. You can purchase these from most chemists. They contain the vitamins, minerals, and proteins the person needs. They come in different flavours; the person may like some better than others. Offer this as the beverage with a meal or as a milk drink between meals. Consult your doctor at all stages and especially if all efforts fail and the person continues to refuse to eat.

Choking

Sometimes people with coordination problems begin to have trouble swallowing. If the person has difficulty changing his facial expression, he may also have trouble chewing or swallowing. When this occurs, it is important to guard against choking. Do not give the person foods that he may forget to chew thoroughly, such as small hard sweets, nuts, or carrots. Soft, thick foods are less likely to cause choking. Easily handled foods include chopped meat, soft-boiled eggs, canned fruit, and yogurt. Foods can be liquidised in a blender. Seasoning will make them more appealing.

If the person has trouble swallowing, be sure that he is sitting up straight with his head slightly forward—his head should never tilt back while he is eating. He should be sitting in the same position in which a well person would sit at a table. He should remain sitting for fifteen minutes after he eats.

Do not feed a person who is agitated or sleepy.

Foods like milk and cereal may cause choking. The two textures —liquid and solid—make it hard for him to know whether to chew or swallow.

Some fluids are easier to swallow than others. If a person tends to choke on fluids like water, try a thicker liquid. A community nurse can help you cope with this problem.

First aid for choking

A nurse or the St John's Ambulance Brigade can teach you a very simple technique that can save the life of a choking person. It takes only a few minutes to learn this simple skill. Everyone should know how to do it.

If the person can talk, cough, or breathe, *do not interfere*. If the person cannot talk, cough, or breathe (and he may point to his throat or turn bluish), *you must help him*. If he is in a chair or standing, stand behind him, then reach around him and lock or overlap your two hands in the middle of his abdomen (belly) below the ribs. Pull hard and quickly back and up (toward you). If he is lying down, turn him so he is face up, put your two hands in the middle of his belly, and push. This will force air up through the throat and cause the food to fly out like a cork out of a bottle. (You can practise where to put your hands, but you should not push hard on a breathing person.)

Exercise

Remaining physically fit is an important part of good health. We do not know the precise role that exercise plays in good health, but we do know that it is important for both you and the confused person to get enough exercise. Perhaps exercise will refresh you after the daily burdens of caring for a chronically ill person. We do not know the relationship between tension and exercise, but many people who lead intense, demanding lives are convinced that physical exercise enables them to handle pressure more effectively.

Dementia is not caused by inadequate circulation. Therefore, improving circulation with exercise does not prevent or reverse memory disorders, but it does have other useful effects.

Some practitioners have observed that people with dementing illnesses who exercise regularly seem to be calmer and do less agitated pacing. Some have observed that motor skills seem to be retained longer if they are used regularly. Exercise is a good way to keep an impaired person involved in activities, since it may be easier for him to use his body than to think and remember. Perhaps of most importance to you is the fact that sufficient exercise seems to help confused people sleep at night, and it helps to keep their bowel movements regular.

You may have to exercise with the impaired person. The kind of exercise you do depends on what you and the impaired person enjoy. There is no point to adding an odious exercise programme to your life. Consider what the person did before he became ill and find ways to modify that activity so that it can continue. Sometimes exercises can also be a time for you and the impaired person to share closeness and affection without having to talk.

How much exercise can an older person safely do? If you or the impaired person has high blood pressure or a heart condition, check with the doctor before you do anything. If both of you can easily walk around the house, climb steps, and shop for groceries, you can cope with moderate exercises. Always start a new activity gradually and build up slowly. If an exercise causes either of you stiffness, pain, or swelling, do less of it or change to a gentler activity. Check the person's feet for blisters or bruises if you begin walking.

Simple exercises

Walking is excellent exercise. Try to take the person outside for a short walk in all but the worst weather. The movement and the fresh air may help him sleep better. If the weather is too rainy or cold, drive to the shops. Make a game of 'window shopping'. Be sure both of you have comfortable, low-heeled shoes, and soft, absorbent cotton socks. You may gradually build up the distance you walk, but avoid steep hills. It may be easier for a forgetful person to walk the same route each day. Point out scenery, people, smells, etc., as you walk.

Dancing is good exercise. If the person enjoyed dancing before he became ill, encourage some sort of movements to music.

If the person played golf or tennis, he may be able to enjoy hitting the ball around long after he has become unable to play a real game.

Confused people often enjoy doing movement to music as part of a group, for example, in a day care setting. If you are doing exercises in a group or at home, encourage him to imitate what you are doing. If he has trouble with specific movements, try gently helping him move.

If the person is able to keep his balance, standing exercises are better than those done sitting in a chair. However, if balance is a problem, do the same exercises from a chair.

Even people who are confined to bed can exercise. However, exercises for seriously chronically ill patients must be planned by a doctor or physiotherapist so they do not aggravate other conditions and are not dangerous to a person who has poor coordination or poor balance. You should check with your GP.

Lessons in recreational graded movement with music by specially trained leaders are given by EXTEND (Exercise Training for the Elderly and Disabled) who can be contacted at 5 Conway Road, Sheringham, Norfolk NR26 8DD (tel. 0263 8224 79). Exercise should be done at the same time each day, in a quiet, orderly way, so it does not create confusion that would add to the person's agitation. Follow the same sequence of exercises, starting from the head and working your way down toward the feet. Make the exercises fun and encourage the person to remember them. If the person has a catastrophic reaction, stop and try again later.

The impaired person may have other physical problems that interfere with his ability to exercise. You should notify your doctor of any new physical problems and of marked changes in existing ones.

When a person has been unwell or inactive, he may become weak and tire more easily. He may get stiff joints. Regular, gentle exercise can help keep his joints and his muscles in healthy condition. When stiffness or weakness is caused by other diseases such as arthritis or by injury, a doctor, physiotherapist or occupational therapist can plan an exercise programme that may help prevent further stiffness or weakness. There is usually a physiotherapist attached to a Day Hospital from whom you can seek advice. However, if your relative is not attending such a unit, your GP can arrange for the domiciliary physiotherapist to call and see you in your home.

Recreation

Recreation, having fun, and enjoying life are important for everyone. A dementing illness does not mean an end to enjoying life. It may mean that you will need to make a special effort to find things that give pleasure to the impaired person. Previously enjoyed activities may remain important and enjoyable even for seriously impaired people. However, the things the person used to enjoy, such as hobbies, guests, concerts or going out to dinner, can become too complicated to be fun for someone who is easily confused. These must be replaced by simpler joys, although it can be hard for family members to understand that simple things can now give just as much pleasure.

Music is a delightful resource for many confused people. Sometimes a severely impaired person seems to retain a capacity to enjoy old, familiar songs. He may be able to use a simple cassette player or radio with large knobs. Very impaired people are sometimes still able to play the piano or sing if they learned this skill earlier.

Some memory-impaired people enjoy television. Others get upset when they cannot understand the story any more. The quick shifts from one scene to another precipitate catastrophic reactions in some people.

Most confused people enjoy seeing old friends, although sometimes visitors upset them. If this happens, try having only one or two people visit at a time, instead of a group. It is often the confusion of several people at once that is upsetting. Ask visitors to stay for shorter periods, and explain to them the reason for the person's forgetfulness and other abnormal behaviour.

Some families enjoy going out to dinner, and many people with dementing illnesses retain their social graces well. Others embarrass the family by their messy eating. It is helpful to order for the confused person and select simple foods that can be eaten neatly. Remove unnecessary glasses and cutlery. Some families have found that it helps to explain to the waitress discreetly that the person is confused and cannot order for himself.

Consider the hobbies and interests the person had before he became ill, and look for ways he can still enjoy these. Often, for example, people who liked to read continue to enjoy leafing through magazines after they can no longer make sense of the text. Sometimes a person puts away a hobby or interest and refuses to pick it up again. This often happens with something a person had done well and can no longer do as effectively. It can seem degrading to encourage a person to do a simplified version of a once fine skill unless he particularly enjoys it. It may be better to find new kinds of recreation.

Everyone enjoys experiencing things through his senses. You probably enjoy watching a brilliant sunset, smelling a flower, or tasting your favourite food. People with dementia are often more isolated and may not be able to seek out experiences to stimulate their senses. Try pointing out a pretty picture, a bird singing, a familiar smell or taste. Remember the sense of touch. The person may enjoy stroking a furry animal, touching a smooth piece of wood, or putting his hand under running water. Like you, the person will enjoy certain sensations more than others.

Many families have found that confused people enjoy a ride in the car.

If the person has always enjoyed animals, he may respond with delight to pets. Some cats and dogs seem to have an instinctive way with mentally confused people.

As the dementing illness continues and the person develops trouble with coordination and language, it is easy to forget his need to experience pleasant things and to enjoy himself.

Never overlook the importance of holding hands, touching, hugging, and loving. Often when there is no other way we can find to communicate with a person, he will respond to touching. Touch is an important part of human communication. You may enjoy just sitting and holding hands. It's a good way to share some time when talking has become difficult or impossible.

Satisfying activity

Much of what a well person does during the day has a purpose that gives meaning and importance to life. We work to make money, to serve others, to feel important. We may knit a sweater for a grandchild, or bake a cake for a friend. We wash our hair and clothes so we will look nice and be clean. Such purposeful activities are important to us—they make us feel useful and needed.

When the person with a dementing illness is unable to continue his usual activities, you need to help him find things to do that are meaningful and still within his abilities. Such tasks should be meaningful and satisfying to him—whether they seem so to you or not. A man may be able to dig the garden for you and for the neighbours. A woman may be able to peel the vegetables or set the table when she is no longer able to prepare a complete meal. Confused people can wind a ball of wool, dust, or stack magazines while you do the housework. Encourage the person to do as much as he can for himself, although you can simplify the tasks for him.

Personal hygiene

The amount of help a person with a dementing illness needs in personal care varies with the extent of his brain damage. The person with Alzheimer's disease will be able to care for himself in the early stages of the disease, but may gradually begin to neglect himself and will eventually need total help.

Problems often arise over getting a person to change his clothes or take a bath. 'I've already changed,' the person may tell you, or he may turn the tables and make it sound as if you are wrong to suggest such a thing.

A daughter says, 'I can't get her to change her clothes. She has had the same clothes on for a week. She sleeps in them. When I tell her to change, she says she has already done so or she yells at me, "Who do you think you are, telling me when to change my clothes?"'

A husband relates, 'She screams for help the whole time I am bathing her. She'll open the windows and yell, "Help, I'm being robbed."'

A person with a dementing illness may become depressed or apathetic and lose any desire to keep clean. He may be losing the ability to remember how much time has passed: it doesn't *seem* like a week since he changed his clothes. To have someone telling him he needs to change his clothes may embarrass him. (If someone came up to you and told you that you should change your clothes, you might well become indignant.)

Dressing and bathing are personal activities. We each have our own individual ways of doing things. Some of us take showers, some take baths, some of us bath in the morning, some bath at night. Some of us change clothes twice a day, some every other day, but each of us is quite set in our way of doing things. Sometimes when a family member begins to help the demented person, he inadvertently overlooks these established habits. The change in routine can be upsetting to the confused person. A generation ago, people often did not wash and change as often as we do today. Once a week may have been the way the person did things in his childhood.

We begin to wash and dress ourselves as small children. It is a basic indication of our independence. Moreover, bathing and dressing are private activities. Many people have never completely bathed and dressed in front of anyone else. Having other people's hands and eyes on our naked, ageing, not-so-beautiful body is an acutely uncomfortable experience. When we offer to help with something a person has always done for himself—something everybody does for himself and does in private—it is a strong statement that this person is not able to manage for himself any longer, that he has, in fact, become like a child who must be told when to dress and must have help.

Changing clothes and bathing involve making many decisions. A man must select among many socks, shirts, and ties for an outfit that goes together. When he begins to realise he can't do this, when looking at a drawer full of blue, green, and black socks becomes overwhelmingly confusing, it can be easier just not to change.

Such factors as these often precipitate catastrophic reactions involved in bathing and dressing. Still, you are faced with the problem of keeping this person clean. Begin by trying to understand the person's feelings and his need for privacy and independence. Know that his behaviour is a product of his brain impairment, and is not deliberately offensive. Look for ways to simplify the number of decisions involved in bathing and dressing without taking away his independence.

Bathing

When a person refuses to take a bath, part of the problem may be that the business of bathing has become too confusing and complicated. Try to follow as many of the person's old routines as possible while you encourage him to have a bath, and at the same time simplify the job for him. If a man has always shaved first, then washed, then eaten breakfast, he is most likely to cooperate with your request if you time it for before breakfast. Then lay out his clothes and towels and start the water.

Be calm and gentle when you help with a bath. Avoid getting into discussions about whether a bath is needed. Instead, tell the person *one step at a time* what to do in preparation for the bath.

Avoid: *'Dad, I want you to take a bath right after breakfast.' ('Right after breakfast' means he has to remember something.)*

Avoid: *'I don't need a bath.'*
'Oh yes you do. You haven't had a bath for a week.' (You would not like him saying that to you, especially if you couldn't remember when you last had a bath.)

Try: *'Dad, your bath water is ready.'*
'I don't need a bath.'
'Here is your towel. Now, unbutton your shirt.' (His mind may focus on the buttons instead of on the argument. You can gently help him if you see him having difficulty.) 'Now stand up. Undo your trousers, Dad.'
'I don't need a bath.'
'Now step into the bath.'

The bath should be a regular routine, done the same way at the same time. The person will come to expect this and may put up less resistance. When bathing continues to be difficult, it is not necessary for the person to have a bath every day. Always check the temperature of the bath or shower water, even if the person has been successfully doing this for himself. The ability to gauge safe temperatures can be lost quite suddenly. Avoid using bubble bath or bath oils that can make the bath slippery. These can also contribute to vaginal infections in women.

Showers are more dangerous than baths because the unsteady person may fall. If you must use a shower, install grab rails or use a bath seat. There are several inexpensive appliances that you can borrow or purchase, such as a free standing or wall-hinged shower seat, that make bathing much safer and easier (see p. 61). These appliances can also be supplied by a domiciliary occupational therapist who can be contacted through your local Social Services Department.

Never leave the person alone in the bath. Use only two or three inches of water. This helps the person feel more secure, and is safer in case he slips. Put a slip resistant bath mat on the bottom of the bath. People can often continue to wash themselves if you gently remind them one step at a time of each area to wash.

Sometimes it is embarrassing for a family member to see that the genital area is thoroughly washed, but rashes can develop, so see that this is done. Be sure that you or the confused person has washed in folds of flesh and under breasts.

Use a bathmat that will not slip for the person to step out onto and be sure there are no puddles on the floor. It may be helpful to replace bathmats with bathroom carpeting that does not slip, soaks up puddles, and is washable. If the person still dries himself, check to see that he doesn't forget some areas. If you dry the person, be sure he is completely dry. Use talcum powder or baby powder under women's breasts and in creases and folds of skin.

While the person is undressed, check for red areas of skin, rashes, or sores. If any red areas or sores appear, ask your doctor or community nurse to help you manage them. Pressure sores or decubitus ulcers develop quickly on people who sit or lie down much of the time. Use body lotion on dry skin. There are unscented lotions for men.

Dressing

If all of the person's socks will go with all of his trousers, he doesn't have to decide which is right to wear with what.

Hang ties, scarves, or accessories on the hanger with the shirt or dress they go with. Eliminate belts, scarves, sweaters, ties, and other accessories that are likely to be put on wrongly.

Lay out a clean outfit for the confused person. Laying out clothes in the order in which he puts them on may also help.

Put away clothes which are inappropriate for the time of year or rarely worn clothes so they do not add to the decisions the person must make. If the person refuses to change clothes, avoid getting into an argument. Make the suggestion again later.

As the disease progresses, it becomes difficult for a person to get clothes on the right way round and in the right sequence. Buttons, zips, shoe laces, and belt buckles become impossible to manage. If the person can no longer manage buttons, replace them with Velcro tape, which you can purchase in a fabric shop. People can often manage this after their fingers can no longer cope with buttons. One wife, sensitive to her husband's need to continue to dress himself independently, bought him clothes that were reversible. She bought attractive t-shirts, which don't look too bad if they are worn back to front and which don't have buttons, trousers with elastic waistbands, and seamless socks. (These socks don't have heels, so it takes less skill to put them on.) Slip-on shoes are easier than shoes with laces or ties.

Women can look pretty in reversible, slip-on blouses and reversible, wrap-around or elastic-waistband skirts or slacks. Loose-fitting clothing is easier to manage.

Select clothing that is washable and that doesn't need ironing; there is no reason to add to your work load.

Sometimes bright, 'busy' patterns confuse and distract the impaired person. Try simpler patterns and pastel colours. Select colours with considerable contrast; these are easier for the older person to distinguish.

Women's underwear is difficult for a confused person to manage, and a mystery to many husbands. Buy soft, loose-fitting pants. It won't matter if they are on back to front or inside out. Don't bother with the slip; it is not necessary. If you must put a bra on a woman, ask her to lean forward to settle her breasts in the cups. Tights are difficult to put on, and knee socks are bad for people with poor circulation. Short cotton socks may be best to wear at home.

Grooming

Have the person's hair cut in an attractive, short style that is easy to wash and care for. Avoid a style that requires setting. People who have always gone to the hairdressers or barber's shop may still enjoy doing so. If this is too upsetting an experience, it may be possible to arrange for a hairdresser or barber to come to your home.

It may be safer (and easier on your back) to wash hair in the kitchen sink rather than the bath unless you have a shower attachment to the bath. Invest in a hose attachment for the sink. Be sure you rinse hair well. It should squeak when rubbed through your fingers.

You will need to trim fingernails and toenails or check to see that he can still do this.

Encourage the person to get dressed and to look nice. Moping around in a dressing gown will not help his morale. If a woman has always worn makeup it may be good for her to help her continue to wear simple makeup. It is not difficult for a husband to put powder and lipstick on his wife. Use pastel colours and a light touch on an older woman. Don't bother with the eye makeup.

When the bath and dressing are finished, encourage the person to look in the mirror and see how nice he looks (even if you are exhausted and exasperated). Get the rest of the family to compliment him also. Praise and encouragement are important in helping him continue to feel good about himself even when a task he has always been able to do, such as dressing, has become too much for him.

Oral Hygiene

With all the other tasks of caring for a chronically ill person it is easy to forget what we can't see, but good oral hygiene is important for the person's comfort and for his health. A person who appears to be able to care for himself in other ways may, in fact, be forgetting to care for his teeth or dentures.

Dentures are particularly troublesome. If they don't fit correctly, they interfere with chewing. The natural response is to stop eating those things one can't chew. This can lead to inadequate nutrition or constipation. Dentures should be in place when a person is eating. If they don't fit properly or are uncomfortable, insist that the dentist alter them. If a person forgets to take his dentures out and clean them, or if he refuses to let you do it, he can develop painful sores on his gums which also interfere with a proper diet.

Since you want the person to be as independent as possible, you can assume the responsibility of remembering, but let the person do as much of the actual care as possible. One reason people stop caring for their teeth or dentures is that these are actually complicated tasks with many steps and they get confused about what to do next. You can help by breaking down the job into simple steps and reminding the person one step at a time. If you take over the care of the person's dentures, you must remove them daily, clean them, and check the gums for irritation. The dentist can show you how to do this. If the person has his own teeth, you may have to brush them for him and check the mouth for sores. Make oral care a part of a regular, expected routine and do it calmly; you will get less resistance. Select a time of day when the person is most cooperative. If the person does get upset, stop, and try again later.

Healthy teeth or properly fitting dentures are critically important. People with dementing illnesses tend not to chew well and to choke easily. Poor teeth make this worse. Even mild nutritional problems caused by sore teeth can increase the person's confusion or cause constipation. Sores in the mouth can lead to other problems and can increase the person's impairment.

Bathroom supplies

Local Social Services can provide a variety of bathroom aids which are also stocked by larger chemists and which make the bathroom safer and easier for the impaired person.

Raised toilet seats make it easier for an impaired person to get off and on the seat. The seat should fasten securely to the toilet so it does not slip when the person sits on it. Padded (soft) toilet seats are more comfortable for the person who must sit for some time. This is especially important for the person who develops pressure sores easily.

You can loan portable commodes from your local Social Services or buy from various suppliers (information on these is available from the Disabled Living Foundation Information Service). They can be placed near a person's bed or on the ground floor, so that the person does not have to climb stairs. Urinals and bedpans are available to meet a variety of needs. Discuss your specific problem if possible with the domiciliary occupational therapist so that she can help you select the appliance that is best for you.

Grab rails are important. There are rails that help a person lift himself off and on the toilet and rails that he can grasp as he gets in and out of the bath. You can buy rails that mount into your wall or that are free standing or clamp onto the bath. These latter are helpful if you are renting your home and cannot attach things to the walls. You can also loan grab rails from Social Services and the Social Services technician will install those supplied, or if you are buying the grab rails, a local carpenter or builder can install them.

Towel rails and the handle on the soap dish in many homes are glued to the wall or fastened only into the wallboard. They may come loose if a person grabs them for balance or to lift himself up. Ask someone knowledgeable about carpentry to be sure they are anchored into a structural feature of the wall or are designed for the purpose. A seat for the shower or bath can be purchased or supplied by Social Services. This often makes a person feel more secure and raises him up so that you can reach him without so much bending and stretching. Shower hose attachments are helpful for rinsing the person thoroughly and they make washing hair much easier.

Grab rails, bath seats and shower hoses can be supplied by your local Social Services or can be purchased from some department stores and various manufacturers (consult the Disabled Living Foundation Information Service Department). They come in a variety of different designs to fit different bathrooms and to meet different needs. Much of the equipment mentioned can be obtained from your local Social Services after an initial assessment by an occupational therapist. The grab rails and bath seats are available from Social Services at no cost but there can be some delay before they are supplied.

Incontinence (wetting or soiling)

People with dementing illnesses may begin to wet themselves or have their bowel movements in their clothing. This is called, respectively, urinary incontinence and bowel or faecal incontinence. The two are really separate problems, and one often occurs without the other. There are many causes of incontinence, so it is important to begin by assessing the problem.

Urinating and moving one's bowels are natural human functions. However, ever since childhood we have been taught that these are private activities. Many of us have also been taught that they are nasty, dirty, or socially unacceptable. In addition, we associate caring for our own body functions in private with independence and personal dignity. When another person has to help us, it is distressing for both the helper and the disabled person. Often, too, people find urine or bowel movements disgusting and may feel sick when cleaning up. It is important for both family members and professional care givers to be aware of their own strong feelings in these areas.

Urinary incontinence

Urinary incontinence has many causes, some of which respond well to treatment. Ask yourself the following questions:

If the person is a woman, does she leak, especially when she laughs, coughs, lifts something, or makes some other sudden exertion? Do accidents happen only at certain times of a day, such as at night? (It is helpful to keep a diary for several days of the times accidents occur, the times the person successfully uses the toilet, and the times the person eats or drinks.) How often does the person urinate? Is the urination painful? Did the incontinence begin suddenly? Has the person's confusion suddenly become worse? Does the incontinence occur occasionally or intermittently? Is the person living in a new place? Is the person urinating in improper places, such as in cupboards or in flower pots? (This is different from the person who wets himself and his clothing wherever he happens to be.) Do accidents happen when the person cannot get to the bathroom on time? Are they happening on the way to the bathroom?

Whenever incontinence begins, it is important to consult the doctor. You can help him diagnose the problems by having the answers to these questions. If the person has a fever, report this to the doctor at once.

Incontinence may be brought on by either chronic or acute bladder infections, uncontrolled diabetes, a faecal impaction, an enlarged prostate, dehydration, medications, or many other medical problems (see Chapter 6: 'Medical Problems'). Do not let a doctor dismiss incontinence without carefully exploring all possible treatable causes.

A leakage can be caused by weakening muscles and other conditions that are potentially treatable.

If the problem is that the person who moves slowly or uses a walking aid or who is clumsy cannot get to the bathroom in time, you can bring the toilet closer to the person. For example, if a person must go upstairs to the toilet, buying or borrowing a commode for the ground floor may solve the problem. You can improvise a portable urinal that will help when you travel. You can also simplify clothing so the awkward person can manipulate it faster. Try Velcro tape instead of zips or buttons. Can the person easily get up out of his chair? If he is sunk into a deep chair, he may not be able to get up in time.

Sometimes people cannot find the bathroom. This often happens in a new setting. A clear sign or a brightly painted door may help. People who urinate in wastebaskets, cupboards and flowerpots may be unable to locate the bathroom or unable to remember the appropriate place. Some families find that putting a lid on the waste basket, locking cupboard doors, and toileting the person regularly help. Remember that older people may have been taught as children to urinate outdoors or in a chamber pot by the bed. If so, it may be easier to supply them with a pot than to clean up the waste basket.

Purchase washable chair cushion covers. Slide them on over a large rubbish bag to waterproof cushions. If you have a favourite chair or rug that you are afraid will be damaged, take the easy way out and put it where the person will not use it.

Sometimes people need help and are either unable to ask for it or embarrassed to ask for it. People may have used children's words such as *wee wees*, *pooh pooh*, or *widdle piddle*, or even obscure euphemisms such as *go for a walk*. The person with language problems may say 'I want tea'. If the care-giver (particularly someone unfamiliar with the patient) does not understand what the person is asking for, accidents can result. Learn what the person means and be sure that sitters or other care-givers know also.

If the person is incontinent at night, limit the amount of fluid he drinks after supper unless there is some medical reason why he needs extra fluid. (The rest of the day, be sure he is getting plenty of fluids.) Get him up once at night. It may be helpful to get a bedside commode he can use easily, especially if he has trouble moving around. Night lights in the bathroom and bedroom greatly help, too.

Falls often occur on the way to the bathroom at night. Make sure there are adequate lights and no slip mats, that the person can get out of bed, and that he has slippers that are not slippery or floppy.

A diary will provide you with the information you need to prevent many accidents. If you know when the person usually urinates (immediately upon awakening, about 10 a.m., an hour after he has his coffee), you can take him to the toilet just before an accident would occur. This is, in fact, training yourself to the confused person's natural routine. Many families find that they can tell when the patient needs to go to the bathroom. He may get restless or pick at his clothes. Routinely take him to the toilet every two to three hours. A regular schedule will avoid most 'accidents', reduce skin irritations, and make life easier for you.

Certain nonverbal signals that tell us it is time or not time to urinate may influence some impaired people. Taking down one's underpants or opening one's fly, or sitting down on a toilet seat is a clue to 'go'. Dry clothes, and being in bed or in public are signals to 'not go'. (Some people are unable to urinate when there are 'no go' clues, such as in the presence of another person or into a bedpan.) Taking down pants to undress a woman may cause her to urinate. You may be able to use such nonverbal clues to help a person go at the right time.

One man urinated every morning as soon as he put his feet on the floor. If this is what is happening, you may be able to be prepared and catch the urine in a urinal or bottle. There are urinals for women as well as men available from Social Services. Use a plastic bowl for a standing woman. People may also be inhibited and unable to go when you are in the bathroom with them or if you ask them to use a commode in a room that is not a bathroom. It is often this involuntary 'no go' response that leads families to say, 'He wouldn't go when I took him and then he wet his pants. I think he is only being difficult.'

Sometimes if a person has trouble urinating, it may help to give him a glass of water with a straw and ask him to blow bubbles. This seems to help the urine start.

Sometimes a person asks to go to the bathroom every few minutes. If this is a problem, it may be necessary for a urologist to see the person to determine whether there is a medical reason why the person feels he needs to urinate frequently. A urinary tract infection or other local causes can give a person this feeling. If you have ruled out medical reasons and are sure the person is completely emptying his bladder when he urinates, take him to the toilet every two to three hours and try to distract him in the interim period.

Faecal incontinence

Faecal incontinence, like urinary incontinence, should be discussed with the doctor. Temporary incontinence may be the result of an infection, diarrhoea, or constipation (see Chapter 6: 'Medical Problems').

Ensure that the bathroom is comfortable and that the person can sit without discomfort or instability long enough to move his bowels. His feet should rest on the floor and he should have something to hold onto. A bar, made from a broom handle and crossing in front of the person between two professionally installed supports, will give him something to hold and will encourage a restless person to stay put. Try giving him something to do or letting him listen to music.

Learn when the person usually moves his bowels and take him to the toilet at that time. Using a stool softener may help (see p. 72).

Avoid reprimanding the person who has accidents.

Cleaning up

A person who remains in soiled or wet clothing can quickly develop skin irritations and sores. It is important to watch for these. Keeping the skin clean and dry is really the best protection against skin problems. The skin must be washed after each accident. Powder will keep the skin dry.

Using a catheter as a continuing way to manage incontinence should be avoided if possible.

The personal care of an incontinent person can seem degrading for him and unpleasant or disgusting to you. Therefore, some families have made a deliberate effort to use the clean-up time as a time to express affection. This can help to make a necessary task less unpleasant.

There is clothing available for incontinent people. The doctor or nurse will help you decide what is right for you. Disposable adult nappies, pads and plastic outer pants are sold in chemists and can be ordered through the mail. Some are more comfortable and stay on better if regular underpants are worn over them. Before you buy any pads, pants or aids check what is available from the community nursing service.

There are both disposable and washable garments. Some washable garments are not lined with soft materials, so the protective layer comes in contact with the skin and is uncomfortable.

Many families find disposable pads are better because they hold larger volumes of urine. Pads with 'gel' hold more urine with less bulk than fibre-filled materials.

Several products consist of an outer, washable pant that holds a disposable pad (Kanga type pants). The ideal is a soft, cool material in which the absorbent pad tends to draw urine away from the crotch so that the person's skin feels dry. It is helpful if the garment is designed so the pad can be changed without lowering the garment and so the garment can be lowered for toileting. The leg of the pant should fit snugly to prevent leakage, but should not bind. This type of pad is suitable for both men and women.

Garments that don't fit or that are too saturated may leak. Don't expect the garment to hold more than one urination. Pads may say how much fluid they will hold. One full bladder may empty eight to ten ounces (one cup) of urine.

There may be an incontinence laundry service in your area which would save you the burden of washing bed linen and draw sheets.

Disposable pads are made to protect bedding, and you can also buy rubberised flannel baby sheets. These are much less unpleasant than the older rubber sheet you may remember from your childhood.

Use a draw sheet in bed. This is a regular sheet folded in half lengthwise and tucked in across the bed. It holds a plastic pad in place between it. Should the patient have an accident, you have only the draw sheet and the pad to change. Absorbent bed pads used in combination with a draw sheet and rubber pad will help keep the bed dry. Look for pads with a polymer (gelling) effect and an embossed back to keep them from slipping. Follow the manufacturer's washing and drying instructions.

Problems in walking and balance; falling

As the person's illness progresses, he may become stiff or awkward, and have difficulty getting out of a chair or out of bed. He may develop a stooped or leaning posture or a shuffling walk. He will need close supervision when he is at risk of falling.

A family member writes, 'His steps are very slow now. As he walks, he often raises his feet high, for he has little sense of space. He clutches door frames or chairs. Sometimes he just grasps at the air. His gaze is unfocused, like that of a blind man. He stops in front of mirrors, and he talks and laughs with the images there.'

Another wife says, 'He sometimes falls down. He trips over his own feet or just crumples up. But when I try to lift him—and he is a big man—he yells and struggles against me.'

Any of these symptoms *may* be caused by medications. Discuss with the doctor the onset of any change in walking, posture, stiffness, repetitive motions, or falling. He needs to be sure that there is not a treatable cause for them, such as medications, a delirium, or a small stroke. These same symptoms will occur when the dementing process has damaged the areas of the brain which control muscle movements. But do not assume this as the cause until the doctor has eliminated other causes.

Watch for the time the person can no longer safely negotiate stairs, or when he trips or has other difficulties walking. If a person is unsteady on his feet, get him to take your arm, rather than you grasping his, if he will. Hold your arm close to your body. This maximizes your ability to keep your balance. Or you may steady him by walking behind him and holding his belt.

Put away slip mats which may slide when the person steps on them. Install hand rails, especially in the bathroom. Pad the steps with rug samples. Staple or tack down rug edges. Round off shelf corners or pad them with foam rubber scraps. Be sure that chairs or other furniture that the person tends to lean on are sturdy; put unstable or antique furniture away. Get things out of the way in areas where the person usually walks. Stair rails and banisters in many homes are inadequately anchored, and will come loose if a person leans on them heavily. Get someone who is knowledgeable about carpentry to check this for you.

Some people can learn to use walking sticks or zimmer frames. Others will not be able to learn this new skill. A harness can help a person sit up in a chair if he cannot do so unassisted (see p. 86). Walking frames and advice should be sought from a physiotherapist or occupational therapist.

It is important that when you help the person, you don't hurt yourself or throw yourself off balance. A physiotherapist, occupational therapist or nurse can show you ways to assist a person without strain. Avoid leaning forward or bending over when you lift. If you must bend to lift something, bend at the knees, not at the waist. Take your time; accidents happen when you rush yourself or the confused person. If you lift a person, lift from under his arms in the armpit. Avoid pulling him up out of bed by the arms. Avoid trying to put an awkward or heavy person in the back seat of a two-door car.

When a person falls,

1. remain calm,
2. check to see if he is visibly injured or in pain,
3. avoid precipitating a catastrophic reaction, and
4. watch the person for signs of pain, swelling, bruises, agitation, or increased distress, and call the doctor if these symptoms appear or if you think there is any chance that he has hit his head or hurt himself. Instead of trying to get her husband up, one wife trained herself to sit down on the floor with him. (Obviously this took an effort to calm her own distress.) She would pat him and chat with him gently until he calmed down. When he was relaxed she was able to encourage him to get himself up one step at a time rather than having to lift him.

Wheelchairs

If the time comes when the person needs a wheelchair your doctor or occupational therapist can give guidance in selecting and using it, or you can contact the Disabled Living Foundation Information Service or visit the Aids Centre (by appointment only) for advice and 'hands on' experience of wheelchairs. Aids Centres exist in many major cities throughout the UK and a list can be obtained from the Disabled Living Foundation.

6 Medical problems

People with dementing illnesses can also suffer from other diseases ranging from relatively minor problems like the flu to serious illnesses. They may not be able to tell you they are in pain (even if they are able to speak well) or they may neglect their bodies. Cuts, bruises, or even broken bones can go unnoticed. People who sit or lie for long periods of time may develop pressure sores. Their physical health may gradually decline. *Correction of even minor physical problems can greatly help people who suffer dementing illnesses.*

You may have experienced a feeling of mental 'dullness' when you are sick. This phenomenon can be worse in the demented person, whose system seems to be especially vulnerable to additional troubles. A delirium can be brought about by other conditions (flu, a minor cold, pneumonia, heart trouble, reactions to medications, and many other things) and it may look like a sudden worsening of the dementia. However, the delirium (and the symptoms) usually goes away when the condition is treated. You should check routinely for signs of illness or injury and call them to the attention of your doctor.

All indications of pain or illness must be taken seriously. It is important to find a doctor who is gentle, who understands the patient's condition, and who will take care of general medical problems. Do not let a doctor dismiss a patient because she is 'senile' or 'old'. Insist that her infection be treated and her pains diagnosed and relieved. Because of the impaired person's vulnerability to delirium, it is wise to check with the doctor about even minor conditions such as a cold.

Signals of illness include:

fever (temperature over 100° F.). When taking a temperature, be careful that the person does not bite the thermometer. You can use a paper thermometer that is placed on the forehead or you can get an approximate temperature by holding the thermometer in the person's armpit for three to five minutes.

flushing or paleness,

a *rapid pulse* over 100 (not obviously associated with exercise). Normal for most people is between 60 and 100 beats per minute. Ask your doctor or a nurse to show you how to find a pulse in the wrist. Count for 20 seconds and multiply by 3. It is helpful to know what a normal pulse is for this individual.

vomiting or *diarrhoea*,

changes in the *skin* (it may lose its elasticity, or look dry or pale),

dry, pale gums or *sores* in the mouth,

thirst or *refusal of fluids* or *foods*,

a *change in personality*, increased irritability, or increased lassitude or drowsiness,

headache,
an *abrupt worsening of behaviour*, refusal to do certain things she was previously willing to do. (*Behaviour changes often signal illness.*)
moaning or *shouting*,
sudden onset of convulsions, hallucinations, or falls,
swelling of any part of the body (check especially hands and feet),
coughing, *sneezing*, signs of respiratory congestion, or difficulty breathing.

Ask yourself the following questions: Has the person had even a minor fall? Has she moved her bowels in the last seventy-two hours? Has she had a recent change in medication? Do mild pain killers such as aspirin relieve her? Does she have other health problems, such as heart disease, arthritis, or a cold?

If a person begins to lose weight, this may indicate the presence of a serious disease. It is important that your doctor determines the cause of any weight loss. A person who has lost 10 per cent of her weight needs to be seen by a doctor as soon as possible.

People who cannot express themselves well may not be able to answer yes or no when you ask them specific questions such as, 'Does your head hurt?'

Pain

Families ask if people suffer pain as part of a dementing illness. As far as is known, Alzheimer's disease does not cause pain and multi-infarct dementia causes pain only very rarely. People with dementing illnesses do suffer pain from other causes, such as stomach and abdominal cramps; constipation; hidden sprains or broken bones; sitting too long in one position; flu; arthritis; pressure sores, bruises, or cuts; sores or rashes resulting from poor hygiene; sore teeth or gums; and clothes or shoes that rub or are too tight. Indications of pain include a sudden worsening of behaviour, moaning or shouting, refusal to do certain things, and increased restlessness. All signals of pain must be taken seriously. If the person cannot tell you where or whether she is in pain, a doctor may have to search for a cause of the pain.

Falls and injuries

People with dementing illnesses may become clumsy. They can fall out of bed, bump into things, trip, or cut themselves. It is easy to overlook serious injuries for several reasons: (1) older people are more vulnerable to broken bones from seemingly minor injuries, (2) they may continue to use a fractured limb, (3) demented people may not tell you they are in pain, or (4) even minor head injuries can cause bleeding within the skull, which must be treated promptly to avoid further brain damage.

Check the person routinely for cuts, bruises, and blisters that may be caused by accidents, falls, pacing, or uncomfortable clothing. Changes in behaviour may be your only clue to an injury.

Pressure sores

Pressure sores (decubitus ulcers) develop when a person sits or lies down for prolonged periods, from tight clothing, swelling, or inadequate nutrition. Older people's skin may be quite sensitive to them. Pressure sores begin as red areas and can develop into open sores. They are more common over bony areas: heels, hips, shoulders, shoulder blades, spine, elbows, knees, buttocks, and ankles. You must watch for these, even in people who are able to walk, if the person spends a lot of time sitting or lying down. The doctor can show you how to treat existing sores or the district nurse may be required to dress the sores. You will want to take steps to prevent further problems.

Encourage the person to change position: ask her to change the TV channel, go for a walk, set the table. Ask her to come into the kitchen to see if the cake is baking correctly or to come to the window to see something.

Pressure prevention cushions can be obtained from statutory authorities. There are a wide variety of cushions available and guidance on the one most suitable can be obtained from an occupational therapist or the Disabled Living Foundation Information Service. It is also possible to obtain from your local community nurse or via private purchase heel and elbow pads made of sheepskin or soft synthetic materials that protect those bony areas.

Dehydration

Even people who can walk and appear to be able to care for themselves may become dehydrated. Because we assume that they are caring for themselves we may not watch for the signs of dehydration. Look for this problem especially in people who have vomiting, diarrhoea, or diabetes, or are taking diuretics (water pills) or heart medication. Symptoms include: thirst or refusal to drink; fever; flushing; rapid pulse; a dry, pale lining of the mouth or a dried, inelastic skin; dizziness or lightheadedness; and confusion or hallucinations.

The amount of fluid a person needs varies with the individual and with the season. People need more fluids during the summer months. If you are uncertain whether the person is getting enough fluid, ask your doctor how much the patient should be drinking.

Pneumonia

Pneumonia is an infection of the lungs caused by a bacteria or virus. It is a frequent complication of dementia, but may be difficult to diagnose because symptoms such as fever or cough may be absent. Delirium may be the earliest symptom, so pneumonia should be suspected when a person with dementia worsens suddenly.

Constipation

When a person is forgetful, she may not be able to remember when she last moved her bowels and she may not realise the cause of the discomfort that comes from constipation. Some people move their bowels less frequently than other people; however, they should have a bowel movement every two or three days.

Constipation can cause discomfort or pain, which can cause a worsening of the person's confusion. Constipation can lead to a faecal impaction, in which the bowel becomes partially or completely blocked and the body is unable to rid itself of wastes. You should consult a doctor or nurse if you suspect this. (A person can have diarrhoea accompanying a partial impaction.)

Many factors contribute to the development of constipation. One important factor is that most British people eat a diet high in refined, easy-to-prepare foods and low in fibre-containing foods that encourage bowel activity. Often when a person has a dementing illness or her dentures fit poorly or her teeth hurt, she makes further changes in her diet that aggravate the problem of constipation. The muscles of the bowel that move wastes along are believed to be less active as we age, and when we are less physically active, our bowel is even less active. Some drugs and some diet supplements (given to people who are not eating) tend to increase constipation.

If a person has a dementing illness, you cannot assume that she is able to keep track of when she last moved her bowels even if she seems to be only mildly impaired or if she tells you she is taking care of herself. If a confused person is living alone, she may have stopped eating things that take preparation skills and may be eating too much cake, biscuits and other low-fibre, highly refined foods. Since you do not live with her, it may be impossible to find out how regularly her bowels move. If you suspect that she may be getting constipated, you will need to keep track for her. Do this as quietly and unobtrusively as possible, so that you do not inadvertently make her feel that you are 'taking over'.

Most people are private about their bodily functions and a confused person can react angrily to your seeming invasion of her privacy. Also, keeping track of someone else's bowel movements is distasteful to many of us, and we tend to avoid doing it. These two feelings can conspire to cause a potentially serious problem to be overlooked.

When a demented person cannot talk and appears to be in pain or has a headache, do not overlook constipation as a possible cause. In the midst of providing care for a seriously impaired person, it is easy to forget to keep track of bowel movements. If you think the person may be constipated, you may want to talk this over with the doctor. He can quickly determine whether the person's bowels are working properly, and, if they are not, he can help manage the problem.

Regular or frequent use of laxatives is not recommended. Instead, increase the amount of fibre and water in the diet, and help the person get more exercise (perhaps a daily walk). The person should drink at least eight cupfuls of some form of beverage every day. Increase the amounts of vegetables (try putting them out as nibbles), fruits (including prunes, apples as more nibbles, or on cereal), whole grain cereals (bran, wholemeal bread, whole grain breakfast cereal), and salads she eats.

Ask your doctor whether you should add more fibre by giving ispaghula husk preparations (sold under various brand names, such as Regulan, Fybogel or Isogel). Do not use any such product without medical supervision.

Medications

Medications are a two-edged sword. They may play a vital part in helping the patient to sleep, in controlling her agitation, or in the treatment of other conditions. At the same time, people suffering from a dementing illness (and older people in general) are vulnerable to overmedication and to reactions from combinations of drugs. A sudden increase in agitation, a slow stooped walk, falling, drowsiness, incontinence, leaning, stiffness, or strange mouth or hand movements may be a side effect of medication and should be called to the doctor's attention. Doctors cannot always eliminate all the side effects of the medication and at the same time get the needed results. You and your doctor must work together to achieve the best possible balance.

Much of the responsibility for medications will fall on you. Here are some ways you can help.

Be sure that all of the doctors involved in the person's care know about all the medications she is taking. Sometimes combinations of drugs can make her confusion worse.

Some drugs must be taken before meals, some after. Some have a cumulative effect (that is, they gradually build up their effectiveness) in the body, some don't. Older people and people with dementing illness are especially sensitive to incorrect dosages, so it is imperative that you see that the patient gets her medications in the amounts and at the times the doctor specifies.

Some patients do not understand why you want them to take a medication and may have a catastrophic reaction. Avoid arguing about it. Instead, tell the person one step at a time what is happening: 'This is your pill. Dr Brown gave it to you . . . Put it in your mouth . . . Drink some water . . . Good.' If the person becomes upset, try again later to give her her medicine. Some people will take pills more easily if you routinely put each dose in a cup or envelope instead of handing the person the whole bottle.

Patients may fail or refuse to swallow pills. They may carry the pill around in their mouth and spit it out later. You may find the pills much later on the floor. Getting the person to drink something with the medication helps. If this continues to be a problem, ask the doctor if the medication is available in another form. Pills or a liquid may be easier to get down than capsules. Sometimes the pills can be crushed and mixed into food or given with a spoonful of jam. If you are not sure whether a person actually took her pill, find out from the doctor what you should do. If pills are going on the floor, be sure that grandchildren or pets don't find and swallow them.

Never assume that a forgetful person is able to manage her own medications. If you must leave a person alone, put out one dose for her and take the bottle away with you. Even people with mild memory impairments (and sometimes normal people) forget whether they have taken their pills.

When you are tired or upset, you may forget the person's pills. Some local chemists sell plastic containers with compartments labelled 'Monday', 'Tuesday', 'Wednesday', etc. You can tell at a glance whether today's pills have been taken. (This device is helpful for *you*: do not trust the patient to be able to use it.) If your local chemist has never heard of such pill dispensers, contact the Disabled Living Foundation Information Service for addresses of suppliers. It is also possible that the hospital the person is attending may have information of pill dispensers and supply you with one. You can ask the chemist for easy-to-open pill bottles if the child-proof ones are difficult for you to open. However, the child-proof caps may keep the confused person from taking pills she should not have.

Store medications where the confused person cannot reach them.

Dental problems

It is important that the person receive regular dental check-ups. Sores in her mouth may be hard for you to find and she may not be able to tell you about them. She may refuse to let you look in her mouth. Even mildly forgetful people may neglect their dentures and develop oral infections. The person's teeth must be pain-free or her dentures must fit well. Poor teeth or ill-fitting dentures can lead to poor nutrition, which can significantly add to her problems.

Vision problems

Sometimes it appears that the person cannot see well or is going blind. She may bump into things, pick her feet up very high over low curbs, be unable to pick up her food on her fork, or become confused or lost in dim light. One of several things may be happening. She may have a problem with her eyes such as long sightedness or cataracts. Arrange for her to be seen by an ophthalmologist. A correctable vision problem should be corrected if possible so that her impaired brain can get the best possible information from her eyes. If she is both not seeing well and not thinking well, she will be even less able to make sense out of her environment and will function more poorly. Do not let a doctor dismiss her vision problems because she is 'senile'. Even if he cannot help, he should explain to you what the problem is.

Brain-impaired people may be less able to distinguish between similar colour intensities. Thus, light blue, light green, and light yellow may all look similar. A white handrail on a white wall may be hard to see. It may be hard for some people to tell where a light green wall joins a blue green carpet. This may cause the person to stumble into walls.

Some people have difficulty with depth perception. Prints and patterns may be confusing. A black and white bathroom floor can look as if it is full of holes. It may be difficult to know whether one is close enough to a chair to sit down. It may be hard to tell how high a step or curb is. It can be difficult to see where to step on stairs. Glare from a window tends to obliterate the detail of objects near it. The older eye may adjust more slowly to sudden changes from bright light to darkness or vice versa.

When the brain is not working well the person will be less able to compensate for these vision problems, but you can help her. She needs to see as well as possible so that she can function at her best level. Paint a handrail dark if the wall is light. Paint skirting boards dark if the walls are light. The dark line will help the person see the change from floor to wall. Cover the bathroom with washable carpeting that is secured so that it does not slip. Delineate the edges and bottom of the bath with colourful strips of waterproof tape. Paint stair risers and treads in contrasting colours. The contrast will help. Outline doors, mantelpieces, and other things the person bumps into with bright tape in a contrasting colour and colour intensity (light on dark or dark on light).

Increase the light in rooms in the daytime and evening and leave nightlights on at night. Install lights in dark cupboards. Cover chairs in bright, contrasting colours without patterns. Put a towel or bedspread over the chair if you don't want to recover it. Leave chairs in their familiar places.

People with dementing illnesses can also lose the ability to *know* what they see. In this instance the eyes work all right but the brain is no longer correctly using what the eyes tell it. For example, the person may bump into furniture, not because she has a vision problem but because her brain is not working properly. What seem like vision problems may be part of the dementia. This condition is called agnosia and is discussed in Chapter 8. When problems are caused by agnosia, the ophthalmologist will not be able to help. In fact, it may be difficult for him to test the vision of a person with thinking or language impairments. Obviously, when this is the problem, it will do no good to tell the person to watch where she is going. She will need increasing care to protect her from injuries she cannot avoid, and you may need to check her frequently for cuts and bruises.

If the person is laying her glasses down and forgetting them, it often helps to have her wear them on a chain. Keep her old glasses, or buy her a spare pair in case she loses her glasses. Carry her prescription and your own with you if you travel away from home. With a prescription, you can replace lost or broken glasses with less trouble and expense.

If the person wears contact lenses, you may need to replace them with glasses before the person reaches a point where she is unable to manage contact lenses. If she continues to wear lenses, you must watch for irritations to the eye and be sure she cares for her lenses properly.

Hearing problems

Failing to hear properly deprives the confused brain of information needed to make sense of the environment, and hearing loss can cause or worsen suspiciousness or withdrawal (see Chapter 8). It is important to correct any hearing loss if possible. Ask your GP to refer the patient to an ENT clinic. An audiologist can determine the cause of the hearing loss and help you select an appropriate hearing aid. As with vision problems, it can be difficult for you to separate problems in thinking from problems in hearing. Since the ill person cannot learn easily, she may not be able to adjust to her hearing aid. (Hearing aids pick up background noises, which can sound loud and be upsetting to the wearer.)

If the person uses a hearing aid, you must be responsible for it and must check regularly to see that the batteries are working.

In addition to correcting the loss with a hearing aid, here are some things you can do:

1 Reduce background noises, such as noise from appliances, the television, or several people talking at once. It is difficult for the impaired person to distinguish between these and what she wants to hear.

2 Lower the pitch of your voice. High-frequency sounds are harder to hear.

3 Give the person clues to where sounds are coming from. It can be hard to locate and identify sounds, and this may confuse the person. Remind her, 'That is the sound of the dustman's cart.'

4 Use several kinds of clues at one time: point, speak, and gently guide the person, for example.

Visiting the doctor

Visits to the doctor or dentist can turn into an ordeal for you and the patient. Here are some ways to make them easier.

The forgetful person may not be able to understand where she is going or why. This, combined with the bustle of getting ready to go, may precipitate a catastrophic reaction. Look for ways to simplify things for her.

Some people do better if they know in advance that they are going to the doctor. Others do better if you avoid an argument by not bringing up the visit until you are almost there. Instead of saying, 'We have to get up early today. Hurry with your breakfast because today you will be going to see Dr Brown, and he has to change your medicine,' just get the person up with no comment, serve her breakfast, and help her into her coat. When you are almost there, say, 'We are seeing Dr Brown today.'

Rather than get into an argument, ignore or play down objections. If the person says, 'I am not going to the doctor,' instead of saying, 'You have to go to the doctor,' try changing the subject and saying something like 'We will stop and have a cup of tea while we are in town.'

Plan your trip in advance. Know where you are going, where you will park, how long it will take, and whether there are stairs or lifts. Allow enough time without rushing, but not so much time that you will be early and have a longer wait. Ask for an appointment at the person's best time of day. Take someone with you to help while you drive.

Talk to the receptionist. She may be able to tell you whether you have a long wait. If the waiting room is crowded and noisy, she may be able to arrange for you to wait in a quieter place. Take along some snacks or some activity the person enjoys doing. If the receptionist knows that you have a long wait, you may be able to take a short walk if you check in frequently with her. Never leave a forgetful person alone in the waiting room. The strange place may upset her or she may wander away.

The doctor may prescribe a sedative for the patient if other methods fail. Usually, however, your being calm and matter of fact and giving the person simple information and reassurance are all that is needed.

Seizures, fits or convulsions

The majority of people with dementing illnesses do not develop seizures. Because they are so uncommon, you are not likely to have to face this problem. However, seizures can be frightening for you if you are not prepared to deal with them. Various diseases can cause seizures. Therefore, if the person does have a seizure it may not be related to the dementia.

There are several types of seizure. In a generalised tonic-clonic seizure (the kind we usually associate with an epileptic fit), the person becomes rigid, falls, and loses consciousness. Her breathing can become irregular or even stop briefly. Then her muscles will begin to jerk and she may clench her teeth tightly. After some seconds the jerking will stop and the person will slowly regain consciousness. She may be confused, sleepy, or have a headache. She may have difficulty talking.

Other types of seizure are less dramatic. For example, just a hand or arm may move in a repetitive manner.

A single epileptic fit is not life-threatening. Most important, remain calm. Do not try to restrain the person. Try to protect her from falling or banging her head on something hard. If she is on the floor, move things out of the way. If she is seated you may be able to ease her to the floor or quickly push a sofa cushion under her to soften her fall if she should fall out of the chair.

Do not try to move her or stop the seizure. Stay with her and let it run its course. Do not try to hold the tongue and do not try to put a spoon in the patient's mouth. Never force her mouth open after her teeth are clenched. You may damage her teeth and gums. Loosen clothing if you can. For example, unfasten a belt, a necktie, or buttons at the neckline.

When the jerking has ceased, ensure that the person is breathing correctly. If she has more saliva than usual, turn her head gently to the side and wipe out her mouth. Let her sleep or rest if she wishes. She may be confused or irritable or even aggressive after the seizure. She may know something is wrong, but she will not remember having the seizure. Be calm, gentle, and reassuring. Avoid restraining her, restricting her, or insisting on what she should do.

Take a few minutes after the seizure to relax and collect yourself.

If the person has a partial fit nothing need be done. If the person wanders about, follow her and try to prevent her from hurting herself. When this type of seizure ends she may be temporarily confused, irritable, or have trouble talking. You may be able to identify the warning signals that a seizure is starting, such as specific repetitive movements. If so, you can make sure the person is in a safe place (away from traffic, away from stairs or cookers, etc.)

Your doctor can be helpful in advising on the management and treatment of epileptic fits. He should be called the first time the person has any type of seizure, so that he can check her and determine the cause of the seizure. Stay with the person until the seizure is over and you have had a chance to collect yourself. Then call the doctor. He can prescribe medication to minimise the likelihood of further epileptic fits.

If the patient is being treated for seizures, the doctor should be called if the person has many seizures over a short period of time, if the symptoms do not go away after several hours, or if you suspect that the person has hit her head or injured herself in some other way.

Epileptic fits are frightening and unpleasant to watch, but they are usually not life-threatening nor are they indications of danger to others or of insanity. They can become less frightening for you as you learn how to respond to them. Contact your GP, health visitor, district nurse or experienced family member with whom you can discuss your distress and who can knowledgeably reassure you.

Jerking movements (myoclonus)

Patients with Alzheimer's disease occasionally develop rapid jerking movements of their arms, legs, or body. These are called myoclonic jerks.

They are not epileptic fits: in an epileptic fit there are repeated movements of the same muscles, while myoclonic jerks are single thrusts of an arm or of the head.

Myoclonic jerks are not a cause for alarm. They do not progress to epilepsy. The only danger they may cause would be inadvertently hitting something and possible accidental injury. At present there is no effective treatment for the myoclonus associated with Alzheimer's disease. Drugs can be tried but these usually have significant side effects and offer little improvement.

The death of the impaired person

Whenever you have the responsibility for an ill or elderly person, you face the possibility of that person's death. You may have questions you are reluctant to bring up with the doctor. Often thinking about such things in advance will help relieve your mind and can make things easier if you have to face a crisis.

Cause of death

In the final stages of a progressive dementing illness, so much of the nervous system is failing that this profoundly affects the rest of the body. The person may be confined to bed, incontinent, and aphasic. The *immediate* cause of death is often a complicating condition such as pneumonia, malnutrition (these people sometimes stop eating), dehydration, or infection. Death certificates often list only this immediate cause of death and do not list the dementing illness as a cause of death. This has made it difficult for epidemiologists to determine accurately how prevalent dementing illnesses are.

Dying at home

Families sometimes worry that the ill or elderly person will die at home, perhaps in her sleep, and that they will find her. Because of this a care-giver may be afraid to sleep soundly or may get up to check on the sick person several times a night.

One daughter said, 'I don't know what I would do. What if one of the children found her?'

Perhaps you have heard of someone who found a husband or wife dead, and you wonder how you would cope with this. Most families find it reassuring to know what to do. Select a funeral director in advance. Should a death occur, you have only to call him or your doctor.

In some areas there are special resources available to people who have terminal illnesses and who, with their families, wish to die at home or in a hospice. Your hospital will know about hospices and other terminal care facilities in your area. Hospices will not usually accept severely demented patients, caring mainly for those dying of cancer, particularly where pain control is a problem. However, each case is judged individually and a demented patient who is dying of cancer with severe pain would of course be eligible for admission. The staff in the hospice or terminal care unit may be able to give you information about how to plan for a death and some advice and counselling.

Prolonging suffering?

There is another aspect to consider when a person has a slow, chronic, terminal illness: the question of whether it would be better to allow life to end rather than prolong suffering. This is a serious question, one doctors, judges, and ministers struggle with as well as the seriously ill and their families. Each of us must make that decision for himself based on his unique background, beliefs, and experiences.

Talking about death is often difficult. Yet getting these thoughts out in the open by talking with other family members, friends, a minister, or a doctor can often relieve us of the oppressive thought that we are alone. Such thoughts of death often reflect our underlying feelings of depression, anger, or hopelessness, and talking about our concerns can be a bridge to these emotions.

The post-mortem

Your doctor may ask you for permission to perform a post-mortem or you may decide to request one. We feel that it is important for post-mortems to be performed for several reasons. First, a post-mortem is the only way to confirm a diagnosis of Alzheimer's disease and many other causes of dementia. It can be reassuring to you to know the exact illness. In the future such knowledge may be important when specific treatment is available. Also, individual doctors frequently learn from the post-mortem information that they can use to help others. Finally, post-mortem studies advance our knowledge of the dementing illnesses. Post-mortems do not disfigure the body.

7 Problems of behaviour

Concealed memory loss

People with a deteriorating dementing disease can become skilful at hiding their declining abilities and forgetfulness. This is understandable; no one wants to admit that he is getting 'senile'.

This tendency to hide limitations can be distressing for families. The person living with someone suffering from a dementing illness may know that the person is impaired yet get no support or understanding from others who cannot see the problem. Friends may say that 'he looks and sounds perfectly all right. I don't see anything wrong, and I don't see why he cannot remember to phone me.' Family members may not be able to differentiate between real memory loss and plain contrariness.

When a person has been living alone, family, neighbours, and friends may be unaware for a long time that anything is wrong. When the person denies that he has any memory problems, he may manage for years until a crisis occurs. Families are often shocked and distressed by the extent of the problem when they finally learn of it.

You may wonder what the person is still able to do for himself and what needs to be done for him. If he is employed, has responsibility for his own money, or is driving, he may not realise or may be unwilling to admit that he can no longer manage these tasks as well as he once could. Some people recognise that their memory is failing. Different people cope with this in different ways. While some people don't want to admit that anything is wrong, others find relief and comfort in talking about what is happening to them. Listen to their thoughts, feelings, and fears if this is so. This can be comforting and can give you a chance to correct misconceptions.

Others may successfully conceal their impairment by keeping lists. They may use conversational devices, such as saying 'Of course I know that' to cover their forgetfulness. Some people get angry and blame others when they forget things. Some people stop participating in activities that they have always enjoyed.

A frequent characteristic of the dementing illnesses is that personality and social skills appear nearly intact while memory and the ability to learn are being lost. This condition enables a person to conceal his illness for a long time. One can talk with such a person about routine matters and fail to recognise that his memory or thinking is impaired. Psychological testing or an occupational therapy assessment can be helpful in such situations because the assessment will give you a realistic measure of how much you can expect from the impaired individual and what things the person can still do. Because dementing illnesses can be so deceiving, even to someone close to the person, the assessment these professionals can give is most important to you in helping you and your family plan realistically.

These professionals may also talk over their findings with the impaired person and show him ways he can remain as independent as possible.

Wandering

Wandering is a common and frequently serious problem that deserves thoughtful consideration. Wandering behaviour can make it difficult to manage a person at home. It can make it impossible for day centres, residential homes or certain nursing homes to care for a person. The impaired person is endangered when he wanders into busy streets or into strange neighbourhoods. When a confused person becomes disoriented and lost, he may feel frightened. Because so many people do not understand dementia, strangers who try to help may think the individual is drunk or insane. When wandering occurs at night it can deprive the family of needed rest. However, often it can be stopped or at least reduced.

Since it appears that there are different kinds of wandering and different reasons why brain-impaired people wander, identifying the cause of the behaviour may help you plan a strategy to manage it.

Wandering may result from getting lost. Sometimes a person sets out on an errand, such as going to the shops, takes a wrong turning, becomes disoriented, and gets completely lost trying to find his way back. Or he may go shopping with you, lose sight of you, and get lost trying to find you.

Wandering often increases when a person moves to a new home, starts to go to a day centre or day hospital, or for some other reason is in a new environment.

Some people wander around intermittently for no apparent reason.

Some wandering behaviour appears aimless and can go on for hours. It appears to be different from the wandering associated with being lost or with being in a new place. Some people develop an agitated, determined pacing. When this continues it gets on everyone's nerves. It can be dangerous when the person is determined to get away. This seemingly incomprehensible pacing may be associated with the damage to the brain. Occasionally, continuous pacing and wandering can cause the person's feet to swell.

Some people wander at night. This can be dangerous for the impaired person and exhausting for you. Night wandering can have different causes, from simple disorientation to agitated pacing.

Many of us can sympathise with the confused person's experience of becoming disoriented. We may have lost our car in a car park or become disorientated in a strange place. For a few minutes we feel unnerved until we get hold of ourselves and work out a logical way to find out where we are. The person with a memory impairment is more likely to panic, is less able to 'get hold of himself' and may feel that he must keep his disorientation a secret.

When wandering is made worse by a move to a new home or by some other change in the environment, it may be because it is difficult for a confused, memory-impaired person to learn his way around in a new setting. He may not be able to understand that he has moved and is determined to go 'home'. The stress of such a change may impair his remaining abilities, which makes it harder for him to learn his way around.

Aimless wandering may be the person's way of saying, 'I *feel* lost. I am searching for the things I feel I have lost.' Sometimes wandering behaviour is the person's way of trying to communicate feeling.

Mr Griffiths was a vigorous man of sixty who kept leaving the day centre. The police would pick him up several miles away walking along the main road. Mr Griffiths always explained that he was going to Cardiff. Cardiff represented home, friends, security, and family to Mr Griffiths.

Wandering may be the person's way of expressing restlessness, boredom, or the need for exercise. It may help to fill the need of an active person to be 'doing something'.

A constant or agitated pacing or a determination to get away may be difficult to manage. Sometimes this is a catastrophic reaction. Something may be upsetting the person. He may not be able to make sense out of his surroundings or may be misinterpreting what he sees or hears. Sometimes this agitated wandering appears to be a direct result of the brain damage. It is hard to know exactly what is happening to the brain, but we do know that brain function can be seriously and extensively disrupted. Remind yourself that this is not a behaviour that the person can control.

Night wandering can also have various causes, from simple disorientation to a seemingly incomprehensible part of the brain injury (see p. 86).

Management of wandering

The management of wandering behaviour depends on the cause of the wandering. If the person is getting lost and if you are sure he can still read and follow instructions, a card in his pocket may help him. Write *simple* instructions on a card he can carry in his pocket and refer to if he is lost. You might put at the top of the card the written reminder, 'Stay calm and don't walk away.' You might write on the card 'phone home' and put the telephone number, or write 'ask a shop assistant to show you to the men's wear department and stay there. I will come for you.' You may need different cards for different outings. This will make it possible for a mildly confused person to help himself.

It is essential that you get the person a bracelet with his name and your phone number on it, and the statement 'memory impaired'. A bracelet that is securely fastened (so the patient cannot take it off) and too small to slip off is most practical. This information will help anyone who finds the person if he gets lost. You can have an inexpensive bracelet engraved in a store that engraves rings, tankards, key rings, etc. Have a 'memory impaired' bracelet made *now* if there is any possibility that the person will wander or get lost. A lost, confused person will be afraid and upset, and this can cause him to resist help. He may be ignored or assumed to be crazy by the people around him. Under stress he may function more poorly than he usually does.

There are also Medic Alert bracelets and necklaces and SOS talismans that can be worn and which give information regarding the person and a telephone number to contact. These can be obtained from the Medic Alert Foundation, 11/13 Clifton Terrace, London N4 3JP (tel. 01 263 8597) or Talman Ltd, Grays Corner, Ley Street, Ilford, Essex (tel. 01 554 5579). You could also try a personal information wallet—information recorded in a plastic wallet with a 'disabled' motif and obtained from the Herts Association for the Disabled (County Office), 2 Townsend Avenue, St Albans, Herts AL1 3SG (tel. 0727 58810)—or a black medical ID box which contains personal information and a photograph, supplied by Medical ID Services Ltd, 67 High Street, Leatherhead, Surrey KT22 8AH (tel. 0372 374510).

Some forgetful people will carry a card in their pocket or wallet which gives their name, address, and phone number. Others will lose it or throw it away. However, they are worth trying.

To reduce increased wandering when the person moves to a new environment, you may want to plan in advance of the move to make it as easy as possible for the impaired person. When a person is still able to understand and participate in what is going on around him, it may help to introduce him gradually to his new situation. If he is moving to a new home, involve him in planning the move (see p. 40) and visit the new home as often as possible before he moves. When a person's impairment makes it impossible for him to understand what is happening, it may be easier not to introduce him gradually but simply to make the move as quietly and with as little fuss as possible. Each person is unique. Try to balance his need to participate in decision making with his ability to understand.

If the person is going to attend a day centre or day hospital you might go with him the first time, or arrange for him to spend only a few hours rather than a full day there the first few times. This will help him realise that you want him to be in the centre.

When a confused person finds himself in a new place, he may feel that he is lost, that you cannot find him, or that he is not supposed to be where he is. Reassure the disoriented person often about where he is and why he is there. 'You have come to live with me, Father. Here is your room with your things in it,' or 'You are at the day centre. You will go home at 3.00.'

Families tell us 'It doesn't work!' when we give this advice. It doesn't work in the sense that the person may continue to insist that he doesn't live here and to keep trying to wander away. This is because he is memory impaired and does not remember what you told him. He still needs to be gently and frequently reassured about his whereabouts. It takes time and patience to get him to accept the move and gradually come to feel secure. He also needs this frequent reassurance that you know where he is. A gentle reassurance and your understanding of his confusion help reduce his fear and the number of catastrophic reactions he has. Our experience with people who are admitted to hospital for their dementia is that, even with difficult people, frequent gentle reassurance about where they are sometimes helps them settle down (and become easier to manage). However, this may take several (five to seven) days.

A move often upsets a person with a dementing illness, causing him to wander more or making his behaviour worse for a period of time. It is helpful to know that this is usually a temporary crisis.

Because changes may make the person's behaviour or wandering worse, it is important to consider changes carefully. You may decide that a holiday or an extended visit is not worth the upset to the confused person.

When the wandering seems to be aimless, some professionals suspect that exercise helps to reduce this restlessness. Try taking the person for a long, vigorous walk each day. You may have to continue an activity plan for several weeks before you see whether it is making a difference.

When wandering seems to be the person's way of saying, 'I *feel* lost' or 'I am searching for the things I feel I have lost,' you can help by surrounding the person with familiar things, for example, pictures of his family. Make him feel welcome by talking to him or by taking time to have a cup of tea with him.

An agitated pacing or determined efforts to wander away are sometimes caused by frequent or almost constant catastrophic reactions. Ask yourself what may be happening that is precipitating catastrophic reactions. Does this behaviour happen at about the same time each day? Does it happen each time the person is asked to do a certain thing (like take a bath)? Review the way people around the confused person are responding to his wandering. Does their response increase his restlessness and wandering? If you must restrain a person or go after him, try to distract him rather than directly confronting him. Talking calmly can reassure him and prevent a catastrophic reaction that will change aimless wandering into a determination to get away. Wandering can often be reduced by creating an environment that calms the person.

When Mrs Davies came into the hospital, she had been making constant, determined efforts to leave the nursing home. In the hospital, which was also a strange place, the nurses had much less difficulty with her.

In both places Mrs Davies felt lost. She knew this was not where she lived and she wanted to go home. Also, she was lonely; she wanted to go back to her job, where her confused mind remembered friends and a sense of belonging. So she wandered toward the door. The overworked nursing staff at the nursing home would yell loudly to her 'Come back here!' After a few days, one of the other residents in the home began to 'help'. 'Mrs Davies has escaped again!' she would shout. The noise confused Mrs Davies, who doubled her efforts to get out. This brought a nurse on the run; Mrs Davies would panic and run away as fast as she could, straight onto a busy street. When an attendant caught her arm and held her, Mrs Davies bit him. This happened several times, exhausting the staff and precipitating almost constant catastrophic reactions. The family was told that Mrs Davies was unmanageable.

In the hospital Mrs Davies headed for the door almost at once. A nurse approached her quietly and suggested they have a cup of tea together (distraction rather than confrontation). Mrs Davies never stopped wandering to the door, but her vigorous effort to escape and aggressive behaviour did stop.

Medication may reduce the patient's restlessness. However, some drugs can induce restlessness as a side effect. Medications must be closely supervised by a doctor. Occasionally, the judicious use of major tranquillisers, under close medical supervision, can lessen wandering significantly.

If incessant wandering causes the person's feet to swell, try sitting down with him and helping him to put his feet up. He may sit still as long as you sit with him. Other measures (see p. 86) may be necessary if you cannot get him off his feet. Ask your GP to examine the patient should he develop swollen or injured feet. The discomfort can make the person's behaviour worse.

Changing the environment to protect the person is an important part of coping with wandering. One family found that the confused person would not go outside if he did not have his shoes on. Taking his shoes away and giving him slippers kept him inside.

It is often helpful to install locks that are difficult to undo or that are unfamiliar to the confused person, so that he cannot go outside unsupervised. Sometimes inexpensive devices such as a spring-operated latch are sufficient because the impaired person cannot learn the new task of opening them. A confused person is less likely to look for a lock at the bottom of the door. Make sure you can undo the locks quickly in case of a fire.

Check other means of exit as well as doors. Confused people may climb out of second storey windows. Secure locks protect you as well as ensure the person's safety. The police can advise you about inexpensive ways to secure your windows and doors.

If the person does go outside, be alert to hazards in the neighbourhood such as busy streets or dogs. The person may no longer possess the *judgment* to protect himself from these things. You may want to walk through the neighbourhood in which the person lives and look around thoughtfully for things that are dangerous for a person who no longer has the ability to assess his surroundings appropriately. At the same time you may want to alert people in the neighbourhood to the problem, reassuring them that the person is not crazy or dangerous but just disoriented.

The person himself can be his own worst enemy. When he looks healthy and acts in a reasonable manner, people tend to forget that he may have lost the judgment that would keep him from stepping in front of a car.

Other people are also an environmental hazard to the confused person who wanders. In addition to those who don't understand are the cruel and vicious who seek out the elderly and the frail in order to harass, torment, or rob them. Unfortunately, there seem to be enough such people, even in the 'nicest' neighbourhoods, for you to recognise this hazard and protect the confused person from them.

There are physical devices to restrain a person in a chair or bed. The decision to use a restraint should be made jointly between you and the health care professional who knows the person best, and these *should be used only after all other possibilities have been tried.* (We are addressing here the use of restraints at home. The use of restraints in a hospital or nursing home involves other issues and will be discussed in Chapter 16.) There are different types of harnesses and restraints available. Those restraining straps used by wheelchair users can be adapted for use with demented people (contact the Disabled Living Foundation Information Service).

A geriatric-type chair is a chair which can be reclined and have a tray fitted to it. It can also be mobile. In the reclined position with the tray in place, it can be difficult for a person to get out of. On prolonged use, however, this type of chair can sometimes further impair balance and posture. These chairs can be loaned by Social Services or purchased from various suppliers (contact the Disabled Living Foundation Information Service).

Nurses occasionally find that a restraint, especially at night, provides the person with a firm reassurance that he must stay where he is. However, restraints further agitate some people. Either a chair or a harness may help to keep a person still and safe long enough for you to take a bath or prepare supper.

Very agitated people can hurt themselves fighting against the bed while in restraints or may tip over a chair in which they are restrained. People cannot be left unsupervised for long periods in either harnesses or geriatric-type chairs. *Never* leave a person alone in the house while he is restrained, because of the possibility of a fire.

People with dementing illnesses can be difficult to manage and wandering can be a serious problem. The responses vary with each person. One confused lady was only looking for the bathroom when she wandered away. A sign solved the problem. Another man got a screwdriver and took the door off its hinges when he found that he could not undo the lock.

You may reach a point when the wandering behaviour is more than you can manage or when a person cannot be kept safely in a home setting. If this time comes, you will have done all you can, and will need to plan realistically for institutional care for the person. Many places will not accept a patient who is agitated, aggressive, or a wanderer. See Chapter 16 for a discussion of placement issues.

Sleep disturbances; night wandering

Many people with dementing illnesses are restless at night. They may wake to go to the bathroom and become confused and disoriented in the dark. They may wander around the house, get dressed, try to cook, or even go outside. They may 'see things' or 'hear things' that are not there. Few things are more distressing than having your much needed sleep disrupted night after night. Fortunately, there are ways to reduce this behaviour.

Older people seem to need less sleep than younger people. People with dementing illnesses may not be getting enough exercise to make them tired at night, or they may be dozing during the day. Often it seems that the internal 'clock' within the brain is damaged by the dementing illness. Some night-time behaviour problems may be in response to dreams that the impaired person cannot separate from reality.

If the person is napping during the day he will be less tired at night. Try to keep him occupied, active, and awake in the daytime. If he is taking tranquillising drugs to control his behaviour, these may be making him drowsy during the day. Discuss with the doctor the possibility of giving most of the tranquilliser in the evening instead of spreading the dose throughout the day. This may provide the behaviour control without making the person sleepy during the day. If he must sleep during the day, try to get some rest yourself at the same time.

Often people with dementing illnesses are not very active and don't get much exercise. It may be helpful to plan a regular activity—a long walk, for example—in the late afternoon. This may make the person tired enough to sleep better at night. A car ride makes some people sleepy.

See that the person has been to the toilet before going to sleep.

Older people may not see as well in the dark and this may add to their confusion. As our eyes age, it becomes more difficult to distinguish dim shapes in poor light. The confused person may misinterpret what he sees, so he thinks he sees people or thinks he is in some other place. This can cause catastrophic reactions. Leave a night-light on in the bedroom and bathroom. Night-lights in other rooms may also help the person orient himself at night. Reflector tape around the bathroom door may help. Try putting a commode right beside the bed.

Many of us have had the experience of waking from a sound sleep and momentarily not knowing where we are. This may be magnified for the confused person. Your quiet reassurance may be all that is needed.

Be sure the sleeping arrangements are comfortable: the room is neither too warm nor too cool, and the bedding is comfortable. Continental quilts are less likely to tangle than blankets and sheets. Cotsides help some people remember they are in bed. Other people get upset and try to climb over them, which is dangerous. Cotsides and bedrails may help people remember they are in bed. Cotsides and bedrails can be loaned or provided by local Social Services or the Community Nursing Services. Cotsides and bedrails can be fitted to most beds. Information on purchasing of cotsides and bedrails can be obtained from the Disabled Living Foundation Information Service.

If the confused person gets up in the night, speak softly and quietly to him. When you are awakened suddenly in the night, you may respond irritably and speak crossly. This may precipitate a catastrophic reaction in the impaired person, which will get everybody up in the middle of the night. Often all that is needed is gently to remind the person that it is still night-time and that he should go back to bed. A person will often go back to sleep after he has had a cup of warm milk. Encourage him to go back to bed and sit with him quietly while he drinks his milk. A radio playing softly will quiet some people. Quietly remind the disoriented person that it is dark and the curtains are drawn, therefore it is time to stay in bed.

Sometimes a person who will not sleep in bed will sleep in a lounge chair or on a sofa. If the person gets up in the night and gets dressed, he may sit back down again and fall asleep in his clothes if you don't interfere. It may be better to accept this than to be up part of the night arguing about it.

If the person does wander at night, you must examine your house for safety hazards. Arrange the bedroom so the person can move around safely. Lock the window. Can he turn on the cooker or start a fire while you are sleeping? Can he unlock and walk out through the outside doors? Can he, while trying to go to the bathroom, fall down the stairs? A gate across the stairs may be essential in houses where a disoriented person sleeps.

Finally, if these measures fail, sedative-hypnotics are helpful. However, you cannot simply give the person a sleeping pill and solve the problem. Sedatives affect the chemistry of the brain, which is complex and sensitive. Your doctor faces a series of difficult, interacting problems when he begins to prescribe sedatives.

Older people, including the well elderly, are more subject to side effects from drugs than are younger people. Side effects of sedatives are numerous and some are serious. Brain-injured people are more sensitive to drugs than well people. Older people are more likely to be taking other drugs that can interact with a sedative or to have other illnesses that can be aggravated by a sedative.

Sedating the person may make him sleep in the day-time instead of at night or it may have a hangover effect that worsens his cognitive functioning during the day. It can make him more confused, more vulnerable to falls, or incontinent. Paradoxically, it may even worsen sleep. Each person is different; what works for one may not work for another.

The effect of the sedative may change—for many reasons—after it has been used for a while. Your doctor may have to try first one drug and then another, carefully adjusting the dosage and the time at which it is given. Drugs may not make the person sleep all night. Therefore, it is important that you do all you can to help the person sleep with other methods. This does not mean that we discourage the use of sedatives; they are a very useful tool, but only one of several tools used to manage a difficult problem.

Worsening in the evening

People with dementing illnesses often seem to have more behaviour problems in the evening. We do not know what causes this. It may be that the person cannot see clearly in dim light and misinterprets what he sees, causing catastrophic reactions. Leaving lights on often helps. Telling the person where he is and what is happening may help.

A whole day of trying to cope with confusing perceptions of the environment may be tiring, so a person's tolerance for stress is lower at the end of the day. You are also more tired and may subtly communicate your fatigue to the confused person, causing catastrophic reactions.

Plan the person's day so that fewer things are expected of him in the evening. A bath (which is often difficult), for example, might be timed for morning or midafternoon if this works better.

Sometimes there are more things going on at once in the house in the evening. This may overstimulate the already confused and tired person. For example, do you turn on the TV? Are more people in the house in the evening? Are you busy preparing supper? Are children coming in? Being tired may make it harder for him to understand what is going on and may cause him to have catastrophic reactions.

If possible, try to reduce the number of things going on around the person at his worst times of day or try to confine the family activity to an area away from the impaired person. It is also important to try to plan your day so that you are reasonably rested and not too pressed for time at the time of day that you observe are worst for the confused person. For example, if he gets most upset while you are getting supper, try to plan meals that are quick and easy, that are left over from lunch, or that you can prepare in advance. Eat the larger meal at midday, if possible.

Sometimes the trouble is that the person wants your constant attention and becomes more demanding when you are busy with other things. Perhaps you can occupy the person with a simple task close to you while you work, or get someone else in the family to spend some time with him.

You may want to talk to the doctor about changing the timing of giving medications if other methods don't help change this pattern.

Periods of restlessness or sleeplessness may be an unavoidable part of the brain injury. Reassure yourself that the person is not doing this deliberately, even though it may seem like he acts up at the times of day that are hardest for you.

Losing things and hiding things

Most people with dementing illnesses put things down and forget where they put them. Others hide things and forget where they hid them. Either way, the result is the same; just when you need them most the person's dentures or your car keys have vanished and cannot be found.

First, remember that you probably cannot ask the impaired person where he put them. He will not remember, and you may precipitate a catastrophic reaction by asking him.

There are several things you can do to reduce this problem. A neat house makes it easier to locate misplaced items. It is almost impossible to find something hidden in a cluttered cupboard or drawer. Limit the number of hiding places by locking some cupboards or rooms.

Take away valuable items such as rings or silver so they cannot be hidden and lost. Do not keep a significant amount of cash around the house. Make small, easily lost items larger and/or more visible—for example, put a large attachment on your key ring. Have a spare set of necessary items such as keys, spectacles, and hearing aid batteries if at all possible.

Get into the habit of checking the contents of waste-paper baskets before you empty them. Check under mattresses, under sofa cushions, in wastepaper baskets, in shoes, and in desk drawers for lost items. Ask yourself where the confused person used to put things for security. Where did he hide Christmas gifts or money? These are good places to look for lost dentures.

Inappropriate sexual behaviour

Sometimes confused people take off their clothes or wander out into the living room or down the street undressed. For example,

One teenage boy came home to find his father sitting in the back garden reading the newspaper. He was naked except for his hat.

Occasionally confused people will expose themselves in public. Sometimes very confused people will fondle their genitals. Or they will fidget in such a way that their fidgeting reminds others of sexual behaviour, which is upsetting.

One man repeatedly undid his belt buckle and unzipped his trousers.

A woman kept fidgeting with the buttons of her blouse.

Sometimes brain damage will cause a person to demand sexual activities frequently or inappropriately. But much more common than actual inappropriate sexual behaviour is the myth that 'senile' people will develop inappropriate sexual behaviour.

One wife who asked for her husband to be referred to the hospital for care confessed that she had no problems managing him but that she had been told that, as he got worse, he would go into his 'second childhood' and start exposing himself to little girls.

There is *no* basis to this myth. Inappropriate sexual behaviour in people with dementing illnesses is uncommon. In a recent study of our patients we found no instances of such behaviour.

Accidental self-exposure and aimless masturbation do sometimes happen. Confused people may wander out in public undressed or partially dressed simply because they have forgotten where they are, how to dress, or the importance of being dressed. They may undo their clothes or lift up a skirt because they need to urinate and have forgotten where the bathroom is. They may undress because they want to go to bed or because a garment is uncomfortable.

Don't overreact to this. Just lead the person calmly back to his room or to the bathroom. If you find the person undressed, calmly bring him a dressing gown and matter-of-factly help him put it on. The man who sat in the garden undressed had taken off his clothes because it was hot. He was unable to recognise that he was outside, was in sight of other people, and was not in the privacy of his home. Most confused people will never exhibit even this kind of behaviour because their lifelong habits of modesty may remain.

Undressing or fidgeting with clothing can often be stopped by changing the kind of clothing the person wears. For example, use trousers that pull on instead of trousers with a fly in them. Use blouses that slip on or zip up the back instead of buttoning in front.

In our culture we have strong negative feelings about masturbation and such actions are upsetting to most families. Remember, this behaviour, when it occurs, is a part of the brain damage. The person is only doing what feels good. He has forgotten his social manners. This does not mean that the person will develop other offensive sexual behaviour. If this occurs, try not to appear upset, because it may precipitate a catastrophic reaction. Gently lead the person to a private place. Try distracting him by giving him something else to do. If a person's fidgeting is suggestive or embarrassing, also try giving him something else to do or something else to fidget with.

We know of no case in which a person with a dementing illness has exposed himself to a child and we do not wish to contribute to the myths about 'dirty old men' by focusing on such behaviour. However, should such an incident occur, react matter-of-factly and without creating any more fuss than is absolutely necessary. Your reaction may have much more impact on the child than the actual incident had. Remove the person quietly and explain to the child, 'He forgets where he is.'

We have observed that some people with dementing illnesses have a diminished sex drive, and some have more interest in sex than they did previously. If a person develops increased sexuality, remember that, however distressing this is, it is a factor of the brain injury. It is not a factor of personality or a reflection on you or your marriage (see p. 150).

Don't hesitate to discuss upsetting sexual behaviour with the doctor, a counsellor, or even other families. They can help you understand and cope with it. The person you choose should be knowledgeable about dementia and comfortable discussing sexual matters. He may make specific suggestions to reduce the behaviour. Also see Chapter 12: 'Sexuality' and 'Getting Help'.

Changing annoying behaviour

Sometimes it is the little things that the impaired person does which really upset you. You may have some success reducing or eliminating this annoying behaviour with this method.

First, select *one* specific behaviour that happens often and that you would really like to change. You will have most success with certain kinds of behaviour, such as repeating the same question over and over. Behaviour that arises out of catastrophic reactions is not easily changed by this method but is best managed by eliminating the precipitating cause. Next, get the cooperation of everyone in the household in your plan. This method works only if everyone participates. Finally, respond with warmth and affection to all the pleasant things the person does and *absolutely ignore* the selected annoying behaviour. Do not try to argue with the person, scold him, or respond *in any way at all* to the annoying behaviour. A negative response, such as scolding, can have the opposite effect from what you want, so that the person continues the behaviour. This is not because he is obstinate (he can't remember long enough to do it deliberately) but because you have reminded him of his habit by calling his attention to it.

This system works best if you focus on one specific problem area at a time. It works only if everyone cooperates by *always* ignoring the behaviour. It will not work if you occasionally respond to the behaviour. This is why everyone in the house must participate. A vital part of the process is giving the person obvious attention when he behaves pleasantly. It may take several weeks of patient effort before you see a change.

This method worked for one husband who was particularly upset when his wife asked every night, 'Who are you? What are you doing in my bed?' He stopped trying to explain to her and began simply ignoring the question. He would turn his head away slightly or turn his back on her and pretend she had not said anything. Eventually she stopped asking the question.

A similar method for changing annoying physical activities is to follow the same patterns except to respond to the behaviour by distracting the person each time the behaviour occurs. Again, do not scold the person for the behaviour. For example,

> *One woman was restless much of the time. She paced, fidgeted, and wandered. Her husband stopped telling her to sit down and instead began handing her a deck of cards, saying, 'Here, Helen, play some solitaire.' He took advantage of her lifelong enjoyment of this card game, even though she no longer played it correctly.*

Repeating the question

Sometimes it is the little things that seem to be the last straw in living with a person with a dementing illness. Many families find that confused people ask the same question over and over and that this is extremely irritating. In part, this may be a symptom of the fear and insecurity of a person who can no longer make sense out of his surroundings. The person may not remember things for even brief periods, so he may have no recollection of having asked you before or of your answer. Try the technique described for changing annoying behaviour.

Sometimes, instead of answering the question again, it is helpful to reassure the person that everything is fine and that you will take care of things. Sometimes the person is really worried about something else, which he is unable to express. If you can correctly guess what this is and reassure him, he may relax. For example,

Mr Rockwell's mother kept asking, 'When is my mother coming for me?' When Mr Rockwell told her that her mother had been dead for many years, she would either get upset or ask the question again in a few minutes. Mr Rockwell realised that the question really expressed her feelings that she was lost, and began responding by saying, 'I will take care of you.' This obviously calmed his mother.

Repetitious actions

An occasional and distressing behaviour that may occur in people with a brain disease is the tendency to repeat the same action over and over again.

Mrs Weber's mother-in-law folded the laundry over and over again. Mrs Weber was glad the older woman was occupied, but this same activity upset her husband. He would shout, 'Mother, you have already folded that towel five times.'

Mrs Andrews had trouble with baths. She would wash just one side of her face. 'Wash the other side,' her daughter would say, but she kept on washing the same spot.

Mr Barnes paces around and around the kitchen in the same pattern, like a bear in a cage.

It seems as if the damaged mind has a tendency to 'get stuck' on one activity and has difficulty changing gear to a new activity. When this happens, gently suggest that the person do a specific new task, but try not to pressure him or sound upset, because you can easily precipitate a catastrophic reaction.

In the case of Mrs Weber's mother-in-law, ignoring the problem worked well. As Mr Weber came to accept his mother's illness, the behaviour ceased to bother him.

Mrs Andrews's daughter found out that gently patting her mother's cheek where she wanted her to wash next would get her out of the repetitious pattern. In this example, a stroke had lessened her mother's awareness of one side of her body. Touch is a very good way to get a message to the brain when words fail. Touch the arm you want a person to put into a sleeve; touch the place you want the person to wash next; touch a hand with a spoon to get a person to pick it up.

Mr Barnes's wife found ways to distract his pacing by giving him something to do. 'Here, Joe, hold this,' she would say, and hand him a spoon. 'Now hold this', and she would take the spoon and give him an oven glove. 'Helping' would enable him to stop pacing. It kept him busy and perhaps also made him feel needed.

Clinging or persistently following you around

Families tell us that forgetful people sometimes follow them from room to room, becoming fretful if the care-giver disappears into the bathroom, or that they constantly interrupt whenever the care-giver tries to rest or get a job done. This can be distressing. Few things can irritate more than being followed around all the time.

This behaviour can be understood when we consider how strange the world must seem to a person who constantly forgets. The trusted care-giver becomes the only security in a world of confusion. When one cannot depend on oneself to remember the necessary things in life, a form of security is to stick close to someone who does know.

The memory-impaired person cannot remember that if you go into the bathroom, you will soon be out again. To his mind, with his confused sense of time, it may seem as if you have vanished. Child-proof doorknobs on the bathroom door may help give you a few minutes of privacy. Sometimes setting a timer and saying 'I will be back when the timer goes off' will help. One husband got himself a set of headphones so he could listen to music while his wife continued to talk. (Then he got her a set because he discovered that she enjoyed the music.)

It is most important that you try not to let annoying behaviour such as these wear you down. You must find other people who will help you with the person so you can get away and do the things that relax you—go visiting or shopping, take a nap, or enjoy an uninterrupted bath.

Find simple tasks that the person can do, even if they are things that you could do better or things that are repetitious. Winding a ball of wool, dusting, or stacking magazines may make a person feel useful and will keep him occupied while you do your work.

Mrs Hunter's mother-in-law, who has a dementing illness, followed Mrs Hunter around the house never letting her out of her sight and always criticising. Mrs Hunter hit upon the idea of encouraging her mother-in-law to fold up the washing. Since Mrs Hunter has a large family, she has a lot of washing. The older woman folds, unfolds, and refolds (not very neatly) and feels that she is a useful part of the household.

Is it being unkind to give a person made-up tasks to keep her occupied? Mrs Hunter doesn't think so. The confused woman needs to feel that she is contributing to the family and she needs to be active.

Complaints and insults

Sometimes people with dementing illnesses repeatedly complain, despite your kindest efforts. The confused person may say things like 'You are cruel to me', 'I want to go home', 'You stole my things', or 'I don't like you'. When you are doing all that you can to help, you may feel hurt or angry when the confused person says such things. When he looks and sounds well or when such criticism comes from someone you have looked up to, your first response may be to take the criticism personally. You can quickly get into a painful and pointless argument, which may cause him to have a catastrophic reaction and perhaps even scream, cry, and throw things at you, leaving you exhausted and upset.

If this happens, step back and think through what is happening. Even though the person looks well, he actually has an injury to his brain. The experiences of having to be cared for, feeling lost, and losing possessions and independence may seem to the confused person like a cruel experience. 'You are cruel to me' may really mean 'life is cruel to me'. Because the person cannot accurately sort out the reality around him, he may misinterpret your efforts to help as stealing from him. He may not be able to accept, understand, or remember the facts of his increasing impairment, his financial situation, the past relationship he had with you, and all of the other things you are aware of. For example, he knows only that his things are gone and you are there. Therefore, he feels that you must have stolen his things.

A family member contributed the following interpretations of the things her husband often said. Of course, we cannot know what a brain-impaired person feels or means, but his wife has found loving ways to interpret and accept the painful things her husband says.

He says: 'I want to go home.'
He means: 'I want to go back to the condition of life, the quality of life, when everything seemed to have a purpose and I was useful, when I could see the products of my hands, and when I was without the fear of small things.'

He says: 'I don't want to die.'
He means: 'I am ill although I feel no pain. Nobody realises just how ill I am. I feel this way all of the time, so I must be going to die. I am afraid of dying.'

He says: 'I have no money.'
He means: 'I used to carry a wallet with some money in it. It is not in the back pocket of my trousers now. I am angry because I cannot find it. There is something at the shops that I want to buy. I'll have to keep looking.'

He says: *'Where is everyone?'*
He means: *'I see people around me but I don't know who they are. These unfamiliar faces do not belong to my family. Where is my mother? Why has she left me?'*

In coping with remarks such as these, avoid contradicting the person or arguing with him; those responses may lead to a catastrophic reaction. Try not to say 'I didn't steal your things', 'You *are* home', 'I gave you some money'. Try not to reason with the person. Saying 'Your mother died thirty years ago' will only confuse and upset him more.

Some families find it helpful to ignore many of these complaints or to use distractions. Some families respond sympathetically to the feeling they think is being expressed: 'Yes, dear, I know you feel lost', 'Life does seem cruel', 'I know you want to go home'.

Of course, you may get angry sometimes, especially when you have heard the same unfair complaint over and over again. To do so is human. Probably the confused person will quickly forget the incident.

Sometimes the impaired person loses the ability to be tactful. He may say, 'I don't like John' and you may know he never did like this person. This can be upsetting. It helps for those involved to understand that the person is unable to be tactful, that while he may be being honest he is not being purposefully unkind.

Perhaps you can cope with these remarks, but what about other people? Sometimes people with dementing illnesses make inappropriate or insulting remarks to other people. These can range from naive directness, such as telling the minister's wife she has a ladder in her tights, to insults, such as shouting at the neighbour who brings lunch in 'Get out of my house, you're trying to poison us.'

Confused people may pick up things in a shop and not pay for them, or may accuse the sales assistant of stealing their money. They may tell casual friends or strangers stories such as 'My daughter keeps me locked in my room.' When you take a confused person to visit someone he may put on his coat and say, 'Let's go home. I can't stand this place.'

Each brain-impaired person is different. Some will retain their social skills. In others a tendency toward bluntness may emerge as open rudeness. Some are fearful and suspicious, leading them to make accusations. Catastrophic reactions account for some of this behaviour. The confused person often misjudges who the person is that he is speaking to or he misjudges the situation.

A secretary was talking with a confused man while the doctor talked to his wife. He was obviously trying to make polite conversation, but he had lost the subtlety he once had. 'How old are you?' he asked, 'You look pretty old.' When she answered another question that no, she was not married, he said, 'I suppose no one would have you.'

People chuckle at this sort of behaviour in a small child because everyone understands that a child has not yet learned good manners. It will be helpful to you if most of the people around you understand that the person has a dementing illness that affects his memory of good manners. Dementing illnesses are common enough that as public awareness develops more people will recognise that this behaviour is the result of specific diseases and that, while such behaviour is sad, it is not deliberate.

To those people who see you and the confused person often, such as neighbours, friends, church members, and perhaps familiar shop assistants, you may want to give a brief explanation of the person's illness. When you make this explanation, you should reassure people that this illness does not make the person dangerous, and that the person is not crazy.

Should a confused person create a scene in a public place, perhaps due to a catastrophic reaction, remove him gently. It may be best to say nothing. While this can be embarrassing, you do not necessarily owe strangers any explanation.

Distraction is a good way to get a confused person out of what might become an embarrassing situation. For example, if he is asking personal questions, change the subject. When a person is telling others that you are keeping him prisoner or not feeding him, try distracting him. Avoid denying directly, as this can turn into an argument with the confused person. If these are people you know, you may want to explain to them later. If they are strangers, ask yourself whether or not it really matters what strangers think.

If a person is taking things from shops, he may be doing so because he has forgotten to pay for them or because he does not realise that he is in a shop. Several families have found that giving the person things to hold or asking him to push the shopping trolley, so that his hands are occupied, will stop the problem. Before you leave the shop, check to see if he has anything in his pockets. You may want to dress him in something that has no pockets the next time you go shopping.

Sometimes there is a gossip or insensitive person in a community who may build upon the inappropriate remarks of a person with a dementing illness. It is important that you should not be upset by such gossip. Usually other people have an accurate estimate of the truth of such gossip.

Forgetting telephone calls

Forgetful people who can still talk clearly often continue to answer the telephone or to make calls. However, they may not remember to write down telephone messages. This can upset friends, confuse people, and cause you considerable inconvenience and embarrassment.

It is therefore advisable to tell your friends, tradesmen, and health advisers that you are looking after someone who is confused and cannot be relied upon to take messages. They should be asked to call again to speak to you if they find that you are out when they call.

Demands

Mr Cooper refused to stop living alone, even though it was clear to his family that he could not manage. Instead, he called his daughter at least once a day with real emergencies that sent her dashing over to help out. His daughter felt angry and manipulated. She was neglecting her own family, and she was exhausted. She felt that her father had always been a self-centred, demanding person, and that his current behaviour was deliberately selfish.

Mrs Dawes lived with her daughter. The two women had never got along well and now Mrs Dawes had Alzheimer's disease. She was wearing her daughter out with demands: 'Get me a cigarette', 'Make me some coffee'. The daughter could not tell her mother to do these things for herself because she started fires.

Sometimes people with dementing illnesses can be demanding and appear to be self-centred. This is especially hard to accept when the person does not appear to be significantly impaired. If you feel that this is happening, try to step back and objectively assess the situation. Is this behaviour deliberate or is it a symptom of the disease? The two can look very much alike, especially when the person had a way of making people feel manipulated before he developed a dementing brain disease. However, what is often happening with an impaired person is *not* something he can control. Manipulative behaviour really requires the ability to plan, which the person with a dementing illness is losing. What you experience are old styles of relating to others which are no longer really deliberate. An assessment can be helpful because it tells you objectively how much of such behaviour is something the person can remember to do or not to do.

Some demanding behaviour reflects the impaired person's feelings of loneliness, fright, or loss. For example, when a person has lost his ability to comprehend the passage of time and to remember things, being left alone for a short time can make him feel that he has been abandoned and he may accuse you of deserting him. Realising that this behaviour reflects such feelings can help you not to feel so angry and it can help you respond to the *real* problem (for example, that he feels abandoned) instead of responding to what seems to you like selfishness or manipulation.

Sometimes you can devise ways for the confused person to continue to feel a sense of control over his life and mastery over his circumstances which are not so demanding of you.

Mr Cooper's daughter was able to find a flat for her father in a sheltered housing scheme where meals were provided. This reduced the number of emergencies but enabled Mr Cooper to continue to feel independent.

A medical assessment confirmed for Mrs Dawes's daughter that her mother could not remember her previous requests for a cigarette for even five minutes. With the help of the doctor, she was able to deal with her mother's addiction to cigarettes and coffee.

Families often ask whether they should 'spoil' the person by meeting his demands or whether they should try to 'teach' him to behave differently. The best course may be neither of these. Since he cannot control his behaviour, you are not 'spoiling' him, but it may be impossible for you to meet endless demands. And since the impaired person has limited ability, if any, to learn, you cannot teach him and scolding may precipitate catastrophic reactions.

If the person demands that you do things you think he can do, check that he really can do these things. He may be overwhelmed by the tasks. Simplifying them may make him willing to do them. Sometimes being very specific and direct with the person helps. Saying, 'I am coming to see you on Wednesday' is more helpful than getting into an argument over why you don't visit more often. Say, 'I will get you a cigarette when the timer goes off. Do not ask me for one until the timer goes off.' Ignore further demands until then.

You may have to set limits on what you realistically can do. But before you set limits, you need to know the extent of the impaired person's disability and you need to know what other resources you can mobilise to replace what you cannot do. You may need to enlist the help of an outside person—a health visitor or social worker who understands the disease—to help you work out a plan that provides good care for the sick person without leaving you exhausted or trapped.

When demands make you feel angry and frustrated, try to find an outlet for your anger which does not involve the impaired person. Your anger can precipitate catastrophic reactions, which may make him even more recalcitrant.

When the sick person insults the sitter

When a family is able to arrange for someone to stay with the impaired person, he may fire her. He may get angry or suspicious, insult her, not let her in, or accuse her of stealing. This can make it seem impossible for you to get out of the house, or mean that the impaired person can no longer live in his own home. Often you can find ways to solve the problem.

As with many other problems, this situation may arise out of the impaired person's inability to make sense out of his surroundings or to remember explanations. All he may recognise is that a stranger is in the house. Sometimes the presence of a 'babysitter' means a further loss of his independence, which he may realise and react to.

Make sure that the sitter or housekeeper knows that it is you, not the confused person, who has the authority to hire and fire. If possible, find a sitter the person already knows or introduce the person to the sitter gradually. For the first few times ask the sitter to come while you remain at home. Eventually the person may become accustomed to the idea that the sitter belongs there. This will also give you an opportunity to teach the sitter how you manage certain situations and to assess how well the sitter relates to the confused person.

Ensure that the sitter understands the nature of a dementing illness and knows how behaviour such as catastrophic reactions are managed. (Finding a sitter is discussed in Chapter 10.) Try to find sitters who are adept at engaging the person's trust and who are clever about managing the person without triggering a catastrophic reaction. Just as there are some people who are naturally good with children and others who are not, there are some people who are intuitively adept with confused people. However, they are often hard to find.

Make sure that the sitter can reach you, another family member, or the doctor in the event of a problem.

Often the confused person will adjust to the presence of a sitter if both you and the sitter can weather the initial, stormy period.

8 Problems of mood

Depression

People with memory problems may also be sad, low, or depressed. When a person has memory problems and is depressed it is very important that a careful diagnosis be made and the depression treated. The memory problems may not be caused by Alzheimer's disease and may get better when the depression improves. The person may have both Alzheimer's disease and a depression that will respond to treatment.

When a person with an incurable disease is depressed, it can seem logical that she is depressed about the chronic illness. But not all people with Alzheimer's disease or other chronic illnesses are depressed. Some seem not to be aware of their problems. A certain amount of discouragement about one's condition is natural and understandable, but a deep despondency or a continuing depression is neither natural nor necessary. Fortunately, this kind of depression responds well to treatment, so the person can feel better whether or not she also has an irreversible dementing illness.

Researchers are trying to understand why we get depressed, but the total answer is not yet known. We obviously feel sad or low when something bad happens to us. But this does not completely explain the phenomenon of depression. For example, researchers are linking some depressions to changes in the brain. It is important that a doctor assesses the nature of each depression and determines whether it is a response to a situation or a deeper despondency, and then treats the depression appropriately. Indications of a deeper despondency include weight loss, a change in sleep patterns, feelings that one has done something bad and deserves to be punished, or a preoccupation with health problems.

It may be impossible for a depressed person to 'snap out of it' by herself. Telling her to do so may only increase her feelings of frustration and discouragement. For some people, trying to cheer them makes them feel that they are not understood.

You can encourage a depressed or discouraged person to continue to be around other people. If she has memory problems, be sure that the activities she tries are things she can still do successfully and are of some use, so that she can feel pleased with herself for doing them. Help her avoid tasks that are too complicated. Even small failures can make her feel more discouraged about herself. Ask her to set the table for you. If she doesn't have that much energy, have her set just one place. If that task is too complicated, have her set out just the plates.

If groups of people upset her, encourage her not to withdraw completely but instead to talk with one familiar person at a time. Ask one friend to visit. Urge the friend to talk to the depressed person, to meet her eyes and involve her.

If the person often complains about health problems, it is important to take these complaints seriously and have a doctor determine whether there is a physical basis for the complaints. (Remember that chronic complainers can become ill. It is easy to overlook real illnesses when a person often focuses on things with no physical basis.) When you and the doctor are sure that there is no physical illness present, he can treat the depression that is the underlying cause of the problem. Never let a doctor dismiss a person as 'just a hypochondriac'. People who focus on health problems are really unhappy and need appropriate care.

Suicide

When a person is depressed, demoralised, or discouraged, there is always a possibility that she will harm herself. While it may be difficult for a person with Alzheimer's disease to plan a suicide, you do need to be alert to the possibility that she will injure herself. If the person has access to a knife, power tools, solvents, medications, or car keys, she may use them to kill or maim herself.

Alcohol or drug abuse

Depressed people may use alcohol, tranquillisers, or other drugs to try to blot out the feelings of sadness. This can compound the problem. In a person with a dementing illness it can also further reduce her ability to function. You need to be especially alert to this possibility in a person who is living alone or who has used medications or alcohol in the past.

People who are heavy drinkers and who also develop a dementing illness can be difficult for their families to manage. The person may be more sensitive to small amounts of alcohol than a well person, so even one drink or one beer can significantly reduce her ability to function. These people often do not eat properly, causing nutritional problems that further impair them. They may also be nasty, stubborn, or hostile.

It helps to recognise that the brain impairment may make it impossible for the person to control her drinking or her other unpleasant behaviour, and that you may have to provide this control for her. This will include taking steps to end her supply of alcohol. Do so quietly but firmly. Try not to feel that her unpleasant behaviour is aimed at you personally. Avoid saying things that put the blame for the situation on anybody. Do what needs to be done, but try to find ways for the person to retain her self-esteem and dignity. There should be no alcohol in the house unless it is locked away. One family was able to arrange with the local off-licence to stop selling to the patient.

You may need help from a psychiatrist to manage the behaviour of a person with a memory problem who also abuses alcohol or drugs.

Apathy, listlessness

Sometimes people with brain diseases become apathetic and listless. They just sit and don't want to do anything. Such people may be easier to care for than people who are upset, but it is important not to overlook them.

As with depression, we are not sure why some people become apathetic and listless. However, it is important to keep them as active as possible. People need to move around and to use their minds and bodies as much as they can.

Withdrawing may be a person's way of coping when things get too complicated for her, and if you insist on her participation she may have a catastrophic reaction. Try to reinvolve her at a level at which she can feel comfortable, can succeed, and can feel useful. Ask her to do a simple task, take her for a walk and point out interesting things, play some music, or go for a car ride.

It often seems that getting the body moving helps cheer a person up. Once a person gets started doing something, she may begin to feel less apathetic. Perhaps she can peel only one potato today. Tomorrow she may feel like doing two. Perhaps she can dig the garden. Even if she digs for only a few minutes, it may have helped her to get moving. If she stops a task after a few minutes, instead of urging her to go on, focus your attention on what she has accomplished and compliment her on that.

Occasionally, when you try to get a person active, she may become upset or agitated. If this happens, you need to weigh the importance of her being active against her being upset.

Anger

Sometimes people with dementing illnesses become angry. They may lash out at you as you try to help them. They may slam things around, hit you, refuse to be cared for, throw food, yell, or make accusations. This can be upsetting for you and may cause problems in the household. It can seem as if all this hostility is aimed at you, despite your best efforts to take care of the person and you may be afraid that the person will hurt herself or someone else when she lashes out in anger. This is certainly a real concern. However, our experience has been that it actually occurs rarely and can usually be controlled.

Angry or violent behaviour is usually a catastrophic reaction and should be handled as you would any other catastrophic reaction. Respond calmly; do not respond with anger. Remove the person from the situation or remove the upsetting stimulus. Look for the event that precipitated the reaction so that you can prevent or minimise a recurrence.

Try not to interpret anger in the same way as you would if it came from a well person. Anger from a confused person is often exaggerated or misdirected. The person may not really be angry with you at all. The anger is probably the result of misunderstanding what is happening. For example,

Mr Jones adored his small grandson. One day the grandchild tripped and fell and began to cry. Mr Jones grabbed a knife, began to shout, and would allow no one near the child.

Mr Jones had misinterpreted the cause of the child's crying and overreacted. He thought someone was attacking the child. Fortunately, the child's mother understood what was happening. 'I will help you protect the baby,' she said to Mr Jones. She gave Mr Jones a job to do: 'Here, you hold the door for me.' Then she was able to pick up and quiet the child.

Forgetfulness is an advantage, since the person may quickly forget the episode. Often you can distract a person who is behaving this way by suggesting something you know she likes.

Mrs Williams's mother-in-law often got angry and nasty when Mrs Williams tried to prepare supper. Mr Williams began distracing his mother by spending that time each day talking with just her in another part of the house.

Once in a while a person experiencing a catastrophic reaction will hit someone who is trying to help her. Respond to this as you would to a catastrophic reaction. When at all possible, do not restrain her. If this occurs frequently you may need to ask the doctor to help you review what is upsetting the person and if necessary to consider prescribing medication.

Nervousness and restlessness

People with dementing illnesses may become worried, anxious, agitated, and upset. They may pace or fidget. Their constant restlessness can get on your nerves. The person may not be able to tell you why she is upset. Or she may give you an unreasonable explanation for her anxiety. For example,

Mrs Berger was obviously upset over something, but whenever her husband tried to find out what it was, she would say that her mother was coming to get her. Telling her that her mother had been dead for years only caused her to cry.

Some anxiety and nervousness may be caused by the changes within the brain. Other nervousness may come from real feelings of loss or tension. Even severely ill people remain sensitive to the moods of the people around them. If there is tension in the household, no matter how well you try to conceal it, the person may respond to it. For example, Mrs Powell argued with her son over something minor, and just when that was solved, her confused mother began to cry because she 'felt that something dreadful was going to happen.' Her feeling was a real response to the mood in the house, but because she was cognitively impaired, her interpretation of the cause of the feeling was incorrect.

The person may be sad and worried over losing some specific item, such as her watch. Reassuring her that you have the watch may not seem to help. Again, she has an accurate *feeling* (something is lost: her memory is lost, time is lost, many things are lost), but the *explanation* of the feeling is inaccurate. Respond with affection and reassurance to her feeling, which is real, and avoid trying to convince her that what she expresses is unreasonable.

Trying to get the person to explain what is troubling her or arguing with her ('there is no reason to get upset') may only make her more upset. For example,

> *Every afternoon at 2.00, Mrs Novak began to pace and wring her hands at the day centre. She told the staff that she was going to miss the train to London. Telling her she was not going to London only upset her more. The staff realised that she was probably worried about going home, and they reassured her that they would see that she got home safely. This always calmed her down. (They had responded appropriately to her feelings.)*

Not all anxiety and nervousness may go away so easily. Sometimes these feelings are inexplicable. Offering the person comfort and reassurance and trying to simplify her environment may be all that you can do to counteract the effects of her brain disease.

When people with dementing illnesses pace, fiddle with things, resist care, shove the furniture around, run away from home or from the day centre, or turn on the cooker and all the water taps, they may make others around them nervous. Their restless, irritable behaviour is hard for families to manage without help.

Agitation may be a part of depression, anger or anxiety. It may be restlessness or boredom, a symptom of pain, caused by medications, or an inexplicable part of the dementing illness. Respond calmly and gently; try to simplify what is going on around the person, and avoid 'overloading her mental circuits'. Your calmness and gentleness will communicate to her.

You may find it helpful to give the person who is mildly restless something to fiddle with. Some people will play with worry beads or with coins in their pockets. Giving the person something constructive to do with her energy, such as walking to the postbox to post a letter with you, may help. If the person is drinking caffeinated beverages (coffee, tea), switching to noncaffeinated drinks might help.

Sometimes this behaviour is the result of frequent or almost continuous catastrophic reactions. Try to find ways to reduce the confusion, extra stimulation, noise, and change around the confused person. (Read the sections on catastrophic reactions and on wandering.) Medications may help very agitated or restless people.

False ideas, suspiciousness, paranoia, and hallucinations

Forgetful people may become unreasonably suspicious. They may suspect or accuse others of stealing their money, their possessions, and even things nobody would take, like an old toothbrush. They may hoard or hide things. They may shout for help or call the police. An impaired person may begin accusing her spouse of infidelity.

People with dementing illness may develop unshakable ideas that things have been stolen from them or that people are going to harm them. Carried to an extreme, these ideas can make the person fearful and resistant to all attempts at care and help. Occasionally they develop distressing and strange ideas that they seem to remember and insist upon. They may insist that this is not where they live, that people who are dead are alive and are coming for them, or that someone who lives in the house is a stranger and perhaps dangerous. Occasionally a person will insist that his wife is not his wife—she is someone who looks like his wife, but is an impostor.

A person with a dementing illness may hear, see, feel, or smell things that are not there. Such hallucinations may terrify her (if she sees a strange man in the bedroom) or amuse her (if she sees a puppy on the bed).

This behaviour is upsetting for families because it is strange and frightening and because we associate it with insanity. It may never happen to your family member, but you should be aware of it in case you have to respond to such an experience. When these symptoms occur in the presence of a dementing illness, they are usually the result of the brain injury or a superimposed delirium (see p. 198) and are not symptoms of other mental illness.

Misinterpretation

Sometimes these problems are due to the person's misinterpretation of what she sees and hears. If she sees poorly in the dark, she may misinterpret the moving curtains as a strange man. If she hears poorly, she may suspect conversations to be people talking about her. If she loses her shoes, she may misinterpret the loss as a theft.

Is the person seeing accurately in the dark or is she not hearing as well as she should? The cognitively impaired person must be seeing and hearing as well as possible because she may not realise her sensory limitations. Ensure that her glasses and/or hearing aid are working well. If the room is dimly lit, see if improving the lighting helps. If the room is noisy or if sounds are muted, the person may need help identifying sounds (see Chapter 6: 'Hearing Problems').

If you think the person is misinterpreting things, you may be able to help by explaining what she sees or hears. Say, for example, 'That movement is the curtains' or 'That tapping noise is the bush outside your window.' This is different from directly disagreeing with her, which may cause her to have a catastrophic reaction. Avoid saying, 'There is no man in the bedroom' or 'Nobody is trying to break in. Now go to sleep.'

If the person does not hear well, it may help to include her in the conversation by addressing her directly rather than talking about her. Look directly at her. Some people read lips enough to supplement their hearing. You might say, 'Dad, John says the weather has been terrible lately,' or 'Dad, John says the new grandchild is sitting up now.' Never talk about someone in the third person, as if she weren't there, no matter how 'out of it' you think she is. This is dehumanising, and can understandably make a person angry. Ask other people not to do it.

Sometimes the impaired person's brain incorrectly interprets what her senses see or hear correctly. This is often what happens when a person becomes unrealistically suspicious. Sometimes you can help by giving the confused person accurate information or writing down reminders. You may have to repeat the same information frequently, since the person will tend to forget quickly what you say.

Failure to recognise people or things (agnosia)

People with dementing illnesses may lose the ability to recognise things or people, not because they have forgotten them or because their eyes are not working but because the brain is not able to put together information properly. This is called *agnosia*, from Latin words meaning 'to not know'. It can be a baffling symptom. For example,

> *Mrs Robinson said to her husband, 'Who are you? What are you doing in my house?'*

This is not a problem of memory. Mrs Robinson had not forgotten her husband; in fact, she remembered him quite well, but her brain could not work out who he was from what her eyes saw.

> *Mr Clark insisted that this was not his house, although he had lived there many years.*

He had not forgotten his home, but, because his brain was not working correctly, the place did not look familiar.

You can help by giving the person other information. It may help to say 'I know it doesn't look familiar, but this is your house.' Hearing your voice may help her remember who you are. Help her focus on one familiar detail. 'Here is your chair. Sit in it. It *feels* familiar.'

'You are not my husband'

Occasionally a person with a dementing illness will insist that her spouse is not her spouse or that her home is not her real home. She may insist that it looks just like her real house, but someone has taken the real one away and replaced it with a fake one. We do not understand exactly what is happening but we do know that this distressing symptom is a part of the brain damage.

Reassure the person, 'I am your wife,' but avoid arguing. Although this may seem heartbreaking, it is important for you to reassure yourself that it is not a rejection of you (the person *does* remember you). It is just an inexplicable confusion of the damaged brain.

'My mother is coming for me'

Someone with a dementing illness may forget that a person she once knew has died. She may say, 'My mother is coming for me,' or she may say that she has been visiting her grandmother. Perhaps her memory of the person is stronger than her memory of the death. Perhaps in her mind the past has become the present.

Instead of either contradicting her or playing along with her, try responding to her general feelings of loss, if you feel that this is what she is expressing.

Sometimes people feel that this idea is 'spooky' or that the impaired person is 'seeing the dead'. It is much more likely to be just another symptom like forgetfulness, wandering, or catastrophic reactions.

Perhaps you will decide that this issue is not worth the argument.

Suspiciousness

If a person is suspicious or 'paranoid', one must consider the possibility that her suspicions are founded on fact. Sometimes when a person is known to be unusually suspicious, real causes for her suspiciousness are overlooked. In fact, she might be being victimised, robbed, or harassed. However, some people with dementing illnesses do develop a suspiciousness that is inappropriate to the real situation.

Paranoia and suspiciousness are not really difficult to understand. We are all suspicious; it is necessary for our survival. The innate naivety of the child is carefully replaced by a healthy suspicion. We are taught to be suspicious of strangers who offer us sweets, door-to-door salesmen, and people with 'shifty' eyes. Some of us were also taught as children to be suspicious of people of other races or religions. Some people have always been suspicious, others always trusting. A dementing illness may exaggerate these personality traits.

Ms Henderson returns to her office to find her purse missing. Two other purses have disappeared this week. She suspects that the new filing clerk has stolen it.

As Mr Starr comes out of a restaurant at night, three teenagers approach him and ask for change for the telephone. His heart pounds. He suspects that they plan to rob him.

Mrs Bolton called her friend three times to meet her for lunch and each time the friend refused, giving the excuse that she had extra work. Mrs Bolton worries that her friend is avoiding her.

Situations like these occur frequently. One difference between the response of a well person and that of a brain-impaired person is that the latter's ability to reason may become overwhelmed by the emotions the suspiciousness raises or her inability to make sense out of her world.

Ms Henderson searched for her purse and eventually remembered that she had left it in the cafeteria, where she found it being held for her at the till.

The confused person lacks the ability to remember. Therefore, she will never find her purse and will continue to suspect the filing clerk, as Ms Henderson would have if she had not been able to remember where it was.

Knowing that he is in a well lit, populated area, Mr Starr suppresses his panic and gives a ten pence piece to the three teenagers. They thank him and run to the phone.

The confused person lacks the ability to assess his situation realistically and to control his panic. He often overreacts. Therefore, he might have called for help, the boys would have run, the police would have been called, etc.

Mrs Bolton discussed her concerns with a mutual friend and learned that her friend had been ill and had got behind in her work and was always eating lunch at her desk.

The confused person lacks the ability to test out her suspicions against the opinions of others and then to evaluate them.

The person with the dementing illness who becomes 'paranoid' has not gone crazy. She lives in a world in which each moment is beginning again with no memory of the moments that went before, in which things disappear, explanations are forgotten, and conversations make no sense. In such a world it is easy to see how healthy suspiciousness can get out of hand. For example, the person with a dementing illness forgets that you carefully explained that you have hired a housekeeper. Lacking the information she needs to assess accurately what is going on, she makes exactly the same assumption we would if we found a strange person in the house—that she is a thief.

The first step in coping with excessive suspiciousness is to understand that this is not behaviour the person can control. Second, it only makes things worse to confront the person or to argue about the truthfulness of the complaint. Avoid saying 'I've told you twenty times I put your things in the attic. Nobody stole them.' Perhaps you can make a list of where things are: 'Love seat given to cousin Mary. Cedar chest in Ann's attic.'

When she says, 'You stole my dentures,' don't say, 'Nobody has stolen your teeth, you've lost them again.' Instead, say, 'I'll help you find them.' Locating the lost article will often solve the problem. Articles that are mislaid seem stolen to the person who cannot remember where she put them and who cannot reason that nobody would want her dentures.

One son securely fastened a key to the note board (so his mother could not remove and hide it). Every time she accused him of stealing her furniture, he replied gently, 'All your things are locked in the attic. Here is your key to the attic where they all are.'

Sometimes you can distract a person from her focus on suspiciousness. Look for the lost articles; try going for a ride or getting her involved in a task. Sometimes you can look for the real cause of her complaints and respond with sympathy and reassurance to her feelings of loss and confusion.

When many of a person's possessions must be disposed of so she can move into your home or a residential or nursing home, she may insist that they have been stolen. When you have assumed control over a person's finances, she may accuse you of stealing from her. Repeated explanations or lists sometimes help. Often they do not, because the person cannot make sense out of the explanation or will forget it. Such accusations can be discouraging when you are doing the best you can for someone. These accusations are often, at least in part, an expression of the person's overwhelming feelings of loss, confusion, and distress. They are not really harmful to anyone, except that they are distressing for you. When you understand that they occur because of the brain damage, you will be less upset by them.

Few things make us more angry than being falsely accused. Consequently, the impaired person's accusations can alienate sitters, other family members, neighbours, and friends, causing you to lose needed sources of friendship and help. Make it clear to people that you do not suspect them of anything and explain to them that accusatory behaviour results from the confused person's inability to assess reality accurately. Your trust in them must be obvious and strong enough to override the accusations made by the impaired person. Sometimes it is helpful to share with others written material such as this book, which explain how the brain impairment affects behaviour. Part of the problem is that the confused person may look and sound reasonable. She may not look and sound as if this behaviour were beyond her control, and, because dementing illnesses are often poorly understood, people may not realise what is happening.

Hiding things

In a world that is confusing and in which things inexplicably disappear, it is understandable that a person would put things of importance in a safe place. The difference between being well and being impaired is that the impaired person forgets where that safe place is more often than the well person. Hiding things often accompanies suspiciousness, but because it causes so many problems, we have discussed it separately in Chapter 7.

Delusions and hallucinations

Delusions are untrue ideas unshakably held by one person. They may be suspicious in nature ('The mafia are after me,' or 'You have stolen my money') or self-blaming ('I am a bad person,' or 'I am rotting inside and spreading a terrible disease'). The nature of the delusion can help doctors diagnose the person's problem. Self-blaming ideas, for example, are often seen in people who are severely depressed. However, when delusions occur in a person who is known to have a brain impairment from strokes, Alzheimer's disease, or other conditions, the delusion is believed to arise out of the injury to brain tissue. It can be frustrating to have a person who seems to be able to remember a false idea and yet is unable to remember real information.

Sometimes delusions appear to come from misinterpreting reality. Sometimes they are tied to the person's past experiences. (A note of caution: not all odd things older people say are delusions.)

Hallucinations are sensory experiences that are real to the person having them but that others do not experience. Hearing voices or seeing things are most common, although occasionally people feel, smell, or taste things also.

Mrs Singer sometimes saw a dog asleep in her bed. She would call her daughter to 'Come and get the dog out of my bed.'

Mr Davis saw tiny little men on the floor. They distracted him, and often he sat watching them instead of taking part in activities at the day centre.

Mrs Ellis heard burglars outside her window trying to break in and discussing how they would hurt her. She called the police several times and earned herself the reputation of being a crackpot.

Mr Vaughan tasted poison in all his food. He refused to eat and lost so much weight that he had to be admitted to hospital.

Hallucinations are a symptom, like a fever or sore throat, which can arise from many causes. Certain drugs can induce hallucinations in otherwise well people. Several disease processes can produce hallucinations. Just as with a fever or sore throat, the first step is to identify the cause of the hallucination. In an elderly person hallucinations are not necessarily an indication of a dementing illness. They may result from several causes, many of which are treatable. Delirium is one example. If hallucinations or delusions appear in a person who has previously been functioning well, they are probably not associated with dementia. Do not let a doctor dismiss this symptom as 'senility'. The examples we have given are not all examples of people in whom the hallucination is a symptom of dementia.

When hallucinations do develop as an inexplicable part of the dementing illness, your doctor can help. Often these symptoms respond to medications that make the patient more comfortable and life easier for you.

When delusions or hallucinations occur, react calmly so that you do not further upset the confused person. Although this is not an emergency situation, you will want to seek advice from the doctor as soon as it is convenient. Reassure the person that you are taking care of things and that you will see that things are all right.

Avoid denying the person's experience or directly confronting her or arguing with her. This will only further upset her. Remember, the experience is real for her. At the same time you should not play along with a delusion or a hallucination. You don't have to agree or disagree; just listen or give a noncommittal answer. You can say 'I don't hear the voices you hear, but it must be frightening for you. This is not the same as agreeing with the person. Sometimes you can distract the person so that she forgets her hallucination. Say 'Let's go into the kitchen and have a cup of warm milk.' When she returns to her bedroom, she may no longer see a dog in her bed and you will have avoided an upsetting confrontation.

It is often comforting to touch the person physically, as long as she does not misinterpret your touch as an effort to restrain her. Say, 'I know you are so upset. Would it help if I held your hand (or gave you a hug)?'

9 Special arrangements if you become ill

Anyone can become ill or suffer an accident. If you are tired and under stress from caring for a chronically ill person, your risk of illness or accident increases. The spouse of a person with a dementing illness, himself no longer young, is at risk of developing other illnesses.

What happens to the confused, forgetful person if you, the care-giver, are injured or become ill? It is important that you have a plan ready. Perhaps you will never need to put your plan into effect, but because dementia disables a person in such a way that he cannot act in his best interests, you must make advance plans that protect you and the impaired person.

You will, of course, have a GP who is familiar with your health to whom you can turn if you become ill, and who is available quickly in a crisis. In addition, you need to plan in advance for several kinds of possible problems: the sudden, severe problems that would arise if you had a heart attack or stroke or fell and broke a bone; the less sudden problems that would arise if you had a long illness, or required a hospital admission for medical or surgical reasons; and the problems that would arise if you got the flu or were at home, ill, for a few days.

Mrs Brady suddenly began having chest pains and knew she should lie quietly. She told her confused husband to fetch their neighbour but he kept pulling at her arm and shouting. When she finally was able to telephone for help, he refused to let the ambulance men into the house.

Even when an impaired person appears to function well he may become upset and unable to do things he usually can do. Should you suddenly become ill and unable to summon help yourself, the upset and confused person may not be able to summon help for you. He may misinterpret what is happening and impede efforts to get help.

There are several possible ways you can plan to summon help. If you have a telephone you can dial emergency services on 999, so try to teach the person to call for help. Stick the number over the phone. Or give the number of a relative or friend who lives nearby and who will respond to a confused telephone call. British Telecom offers an automatic dialing service. With this device the telephone will automatically dial a pre-recorded number of your choice if you or the confused person is able to dial one digit. You can paint this digit red with fingernail polish so that it is easily identified.

There are also telephone alarm systems which you can carry with you and activate as necessary. The alarm links via the telephone to a central control.

If you live near someone who is willing to respond in a crisis, you may be able to use fairly inexpensive walkie-talkies, citizen band radio, or intercoms to summon help. You will need a CB licence which is available from your local post office.

In some areas there are neighbourhood care schemes whereby someone will telephone regularly, every day or so, to see if you are all right. This may mean a long delay in getting help, but it is better than nothing.

Ensure that the person who would respond in a crisis has a key to your house. The upset, confused person may refuse to let anyone in.

If you must go into the hospital or if you are unwell at home, you will want to plan carefully in advance for the care of the confused person. Changes are upsetting for them, and it is helpful to minimise changes as much as possible. The substitute care-giver should be someone the person knows and someone who knows your routines for managing him. Ensure that the names and telephone numbers of your doctor, the patient's doctor and social worker if he has one, your solicitor, and close family members are written down where the person helping out in an emergency can find them.

Some families have made up a 'cope notebook' in which they have jotted down the things another person would need to know. For example, 'Dr Brown (tel. 824 8787). John gets a pink pill one hour before lunch. He will take it best with orange juice. The cooker won't work unless you turn on the switch that is hidden behind the toaster. John starts to wander around suppertime. You will need to watch him then.'

In the event of your death

When someone close to you has a dementing illness, you have a special responsibility to provide for him if you should die. Probably your plans will never have to be put into action, but they must, for the sake of the sick person, be made.

When a family member is unable to take care of himself, it is important that you have a will that provides for his care. Find a solicitor whom you trust, and have him draw up a will and any other necessary legal papers. If you do not make a valid will your estate may be divided in a way you do not wish. In addition to the usual matters of disposing of property to one's heirs, the following questions must be addressed, and appropriate arrangements made (see Chapter 15).

What arrangements have been made for your funeral, and who will carry these out? You can select a funeral director in advance and agree with him, in writing, what kind of funeral you will have and how much it will cost. Far from being macabre, this is a considerate and responsible act that ensures that things will be done as you wish and that saves your family from having to do this in the midst of their grief. Funerals can be expensive, and advance plans make it possible for you to see that your money is spent as you wish.

What immediate arrangements have been made for care of the person with a dementing illness, and who will be responsible for seeing that they are carried out? Someone must be available immediately who will be kind and caring. Do the people who will be caring for the person with a dementing illness know his diagnosis and his doctor, and do they know as much as possible of what you know about how to make him comfortable?

What financial provisions have been made for the person with a dementing illness, and who will administer them? If he cannot manage his own affairs, someone must be available with the authority to care for him. You will want to select a person whom you trust to do this rather than leave such an important decision to a court or judge.

Sometimes a husband or wife cares for years for a spouse with a dementing illness and does not want to burden sons or daughters with the knowledge of this illness.

Said a daughter, 'I had no idea anything was wrong with Mum because Dad covered up for her so well. Then he had a heart attack and we found her like this. Now I have the shock of his death and her illness all at once. It would have been so much easier if he had told us about it long ago. And we didn't know anything about dementia. We had to find out all the things he had already learned, and at such a difficult time for us.'

All members of the family need to know what is wrong with the impaired person and what plans have been made. An experience like this is one example of the disservice of 'protecting' other members of the family.

You should have a succinct summary of your assets available for the person who will take over. This should include information on the location of wills, deeds, stocks and share certificates, cemetery plot deeds, and information about the care of the confused person.

10 Getting outside help

Throughout this book we have emphasised the importance of finding time for yourself away from the responsibilities of caring for the impaired person. You may also need other kinds of help; someone to see that a person who is alone during the day gets her meals; someone to give the person a bath; someone to watch the person while you shop, rest or take a break; someone to help with the housework; or someone with whom you can talk things over. Some of this help can come from family members, friends or neighbours.

Sometimes a neighbour will look in on the confused person; the pharmacist keeps track of prescriptions for you; the clergy may listen when you are discouraged; a friend will sit with the person in an emergency; and so forth. As you plan, you should consider these resources because they are important to you. However, at some point most families look for outside help in obtaining information, making decisions, and planning for the long-term care of their afflicted family member. Many families find the help they need and manage effectively without extensive outside assistance. However, the burdens of caring for a demented person can be enormous.

Sometimes people have mixed feelings about seeking assistance. At the same time that you know you need help, you may feel that another person will not do the job as well as you, or you may find that changes upset the confused person. You may worry about the cost of help.

The decision to help should be shared by all involved members of the family. It is not unusual for differences of opinion to arise. Fewer misunderstandings develop when everyone is kept informed about what resources are available, what they cost, and what services they offer. When you seek help, you will need to think about what kind of help is right for you and the confused person. For example, it may be more difficult to find help for a person who is aggressive or who wanders.

You may need to work with your doctor to modify this abnormal behaviour in order to get the assistance you need.

There are a variety of individuals, local agencies, and national organisations which can offer help. These may be statutory or voluntary, national or local. The process of finding these resources on your own can be long and tedious. The first contacts you make may not provide the needed information or assistance, or the ideal resources may not be available. You may be brushed off by busy staff. A social worker should be helpful to you. She knows how to get around these problems and locate the best available help for you. She also knows how to assess your needs and match them with the resources available in the community (see Chapter 2).

Locating resources yourself

If you do not have available the skills of a social worker, here are some suggestions on how to locate outside resources on your own.

When you begin to look for help, know what kind of help you need and what you want to know. Writing down your questions may help you organise them. It may be helpful to keep a notebook. List the potential places you can look for help, what they can do, and their cost, advantages and drawbacks. Add to them as you learn of others. For example,

Mrs Connors wrote:

Needs	*Ideas*	*Pros*	*Cons*
Someone to stay with Bill when I shop	Aunt Mary	She is willing, no cost	She is critical of me
	Day care	Good care, nice people, gets him out and active	He gets upset if I take him there
	Crossroads or sitting service	A regular service	He will take time getting used to the attendant
	An Age Concern volunteer	May provide help as needed	A volunteer may not always be available

It is also useful to take notes on any conversation, including the name of the person you speak with. (Don't hesitate to ask people to spell their names.) If you speak with someone else in the organisation for more detailed information, it can be helpful to have a record of your prior contacts. This will help you keep information straight. Don't be ashamed or afraid to call back if you didn't understand the first time. Sometimes the person to whom you first speak will be unable to answer your questions.

Always ask to speak to someone who can answer your questions. The officer-in-charge should be able to answer your questions or direct you to someone else who can. It may take you many telephone calls and personal contacts before you reach someone who can offer the kind of help you need. It is important to keep looking and keep asking questions until you find some person or organisation who can offer the help you need.

Even when an agency cannot provide the needed help, ask them to direct you to some other person or agency who may be able to help. Be patient but be persistent.

Sometimes you may not find what you need, even after a long and tiring search. Don't get discouraged about yourself if there is no help. The quality and quantity of available services vary from area to area.

Unfortunately, the needed resources for families of people with dementing illnesses may not be available; some agencies have a waiting list, or they will only take certain kinds of people, while other agencies may be too expensive. Inadequate resources and services are major problems that can be changed only through public recognition of the dementing diseases and the needs of families. It is not your fault if you cannot locate a service that is not available.

Perhaps you will want to accept what resources are available, even if they are not ideal, since you may find that obtaining even some help is better than trying to cope alone.

Kinds of services

Not all people who have dementing illnesses are elderly. However, there may be additional resources for patients of sixty or over. There may be free or reduced charged services for people over sixty or over sixty-five. Some areas have free bus passes for pensioners, for example.

Some programmes serve only those people who have rehabilitative potential, i.e. who can be 'cured'. People who have had strokes or who have a depressive illness may qualify, while people who have been diagnosed as having Alzheimer's disease or who are described as 'senile' do not. Communities and policy makers must be educated to the facts that these are diseases and not old age, that aiding families is both fiscally sound and humane, and that facilities providing only rehabilitation is shortsighted.

The rising cost of residential care is leading policy makers to look at various alternatives to institutionalisation, including day care and help at home.

Many of the services for elderly people will not directly help the person with a chronic dementing illness, but they may help you. For example,

Mr Harrigan was eligible for a free admission to the local swimming pool. His daughter stayed with Mrs Harrigan while he swam two evenings a week. This got Mr Harrigan out of the house without making further demands on his limited income.

Some recreational facilities are often reduced or waived for senior citizens.

Some businesses, hairdressers for example, offer discounts to senior citizens.

Some areas offer some free or reduced cost travel. This can be valuable if you do not drive. British Rail offers concessions.

There are various forms of income maintenance.

In most areas, Meals-on-Wheels services will bring a daily hot meal to people who cannot get out. These meals are often delivered by friendly, dedicated volunteers who will also check to see how a person living alone is doing, but they provide limited help for a person who is becoming confused and are no substitute for supervision.

There are many voluntary services. Some may provide help for you. Others may provide a way for you and the forgetful person to remain active and spend time with other people. For example,

> *Mr Gillis had always been active. Now that he had a mild dementia, he was unable to continue his job, and was bored and restless. His daughter arranged for him to work as a volunteer at a nearby nursing home, where he spaded gardens and weeded flowerbeds. He felt active and useful and the nursing home staff was able to remind him frequently what to do next.*

There are many other care programmes; we have referred to some of them in other parts of this book. You should find out just what is available in your area even if you don't feel you need the service now by making enquiries at your local Social Services Department, Citizens Advice Bureau, or Age Concern office.

Help from friends and neighbours

Often friends and neighbours offer to help you care for the confused person. How much help should you accept or ask for from friends and neighbours? Most people like to help, yet making too many demands on some may eventually cause them to shy away.

When you turn to friends and neighbours for help, there are several things you can do to help them feel comfortable helping you. Because dementing illnesses are unfamiliar to many people, those who help you need to understand why the sick person acts as she does. Offer information about the ill person's condition.

Some people are uncomfortable around those who are visibly upset. You may not want to express all of your distress to such people. Close friends may be more willing to share some of the emotional burden with you than people who do not know you well.

When you ask people to help you, give them enough advance notice, if possible, so that they can plan the time to help you. Remember to thank them, and avoid criticising what they have done if their efforts are less than perfect.

Look for things others can do to help which they will not consider inconvenient. For example, neighbours may not mind 'looking in' since they live close by, while more distant friends might resent being asked to make a long drive. Suggest things a helper can do which he will feel are useful or productive and which he can do without upsetting the confused person or precipitating a catastrophic reaction.

Also, do not forget those facilities and services which do not directly affect your dependant's mental functioning but which may nevertheless improve his well-being. For example hearing aids, dental fitness, incontinence aids, and so on may all help.

Services for elderly people

Adaptations to the home
Adult Education classes
Aids to daily living
Alarm systems
Carer's support groups
Chiropody
Clubs
Concessionary schemes, e.g. hairdressing, transport, entertainment
'Crossroads Care' schemes
Day care, day centres
Day hospitals
District nursing, nursing auxiliaries
Domiciliary aid services, intensive home help services
Fostering or family placement schemes
General practitioner and primary health care services
Health visitors
Holidays
Home helps
Home repairs and practical jobs, e.g. decorating, gardening, adaptations
Incontinence services
Laundry services
Leisure activities and programmes
Library services including those for the housebound
Lunch clubs
Meals-on-Wheels
Nailcutting services
Night Nurses
Occupational therapy
Physiotherapy
Short stay residential care including rotational
Sitting services
Social clubs and activities
Social work
Telephones
Visiting service, by volunteers

Having someone come into your home

Many families can continue to care for a person if they are able to arrange for someone to come into their home to help. Such a person may be another family member, friend, neighbour, church member, paid or volunteer visitor, care attendant, home help, hired housekeeper or nurse. Unfortunately, resources for help at home are limited, and help may not be available, or may be more than you can afford. When outside help is available, the helpers may be reluctant to serve the so-called senile. A social worker can help you utilise what is available.

It is important that helpers understand the nature of the person's disability and that they know how to avoid or respond to catastrophic reactions. Helpers need to know how to reach you or another responsible family member in case of an emergency. Ensure the helper knows from you what the person can or cannot do and what special care he needs. Remember that the impaired person might give the helper misleading information.

If the sick person has complicating health problems, such as a heart or respiratory condition, a tendency to choke or fall, or epilepsy, you must carefully consider the skills of the person with whom you leave him. If the person gets upset easily you may need to discuss with the doctor ways to reduce this behaviour. We have mentioned the problems that arise when the confused person rejects the visiting care giver on p. 99.

Church groups are often involved in neighbourhood care schemes and will sometimes organise a team of helpers. Sometimes they will bring in meals for a short period (for example, while you are unwell).

Some voluntary groups are able to find a person who will sit with the impaired person part of the day and who may even prepare meals.

Sometimes the helper is paid a small honorarium or hourly wage. This may make it easier for you to ask for help.

Good people who you might employ on an occasional or a casual basis are often found through word of mouth. Ask your friends if they know of someone. One woman who does this sort of work may recruit her friends. Sometimes a person can be found by advertising in the newspaper.

Obviously, as with anyone you are taking into your home, you should check a person's references and be sure that she understands the person's condition and is willing to care for a confused person. Have the person come into your home several times while you are there before you leave the person in her care. This helps the forgetful person get used to the presence of another person in the house.

Discuss payment and exact responsibilities before you hire anyone.

It is unreasonable to expect a woman to clean and watch an ill person for the same salary she would be paid for housecleaning. Realistically, a domestic helper probably cannot look after the confused person and clean the house. It is challenging to do both and often impossible for someone unfamiliar with your home and with the impaired person. You may have to settle for a sitter and not a clean house.

Occasionally families are able to exchange services. This could be arranged through a carers' support group. Plans can be simple or elaborate; basically, two or three families agree to take turns sitting. You may sit with two confused people in your home for one afternoon a week. Then the next week someone else will sit, while you get an afternoon out. This works best when the impaired people are not agitated and do not wander. Such people enjoy the contact with others.

Nursing and other employment agencies may arrange for private nurses and other staff, such as companions, to help you on a paid basis. A nurse, for example, may care for the patient, change a catheter, bath an ill person, give injections and so on. A speech therapist may help a stroke patient regain language skills, or a physiotherapist may exercise the patient. Companions, either live-in or non-residential, may provide a variety of services including personal care, meals, shopping.

A number of voluntary organisations may be able to help you with support from either paid or volunteer staff. These groups include local Age Concerns, Red Cross, Alzheimer's Disease Society, Women's Royal Voluntary Service, Crossroads Care Attendant schemes, Councils for Voluntary Service and volunteer bureaux. Services offered may comprise carer's support groups, day care and night sitting, practical jobs and other forms of care.

Care outside your home

Another way for you to obtain help with the care of a person with a dementing illness is to arrange for him to have care outside your home part of the time. There are several potential resources, one or more of which may be available in your community. Your local Social Services Department or Age Concern group may be your best source of information. As with domiciliary services, care providers outside the home are often reluctant to accept people with dementing illnesses and you may have to help them learn how to care for such people.

It is not unusual for a family to be discouraged by the first visit to a day centre.

Mr Wilson said, 'I went to see the day centre. The social worker told me this was an excellent centre. But I can't put Alice in there. Those people are old and sick. One of them was dragging a shopping bag around and mumbling. One was drooling. Some of them were in these chairs with a tray across them, hanging on the tray or sleeping.'

The sight of other disabled or elderly people can be distressing, and our perception of a person we love is coloured by our memory of how she used to be.

You may feel that such a facility does not offer the individualised care that you can give at home. However, we have observed that getting out of the house and being with other people is good for the forgetful person. She may feel comfortable in a setting that does not demand much of her and may make friends with other impaired people.

If you find yourself reacting this way to places you visit, you may find it helpful to talk to other families who are already using the service. They can tell you how they felt, what places they found that they like, and how they have been able to accept things that upset them at first. You may need to weigh the importance of respite for yourself and the benefits of the impaired person's being with others against this concern.

Kinds of settings

Lunch clubs provide not only a hot meal but serve as a social occasion. They do not provide medical care, give medicines or take wandering or disruptive people. They are often staffed by paid and voluntary members and can be helpful for the mildly or moderately confused individual.

Lunch clubs are run by the local authority and voluntary agencies such as Age Concern and the Women's Royal Voluntary Services. Sometimes the voluntary agencies run the service on behalf of the local authority. There is usually a charge but these vary from area to area.

Day care offers several hours a day of structured recreation and therapy for people with limited abilities. The centres provide mental stimulation within the capabilities of a confused person. People frequently seem to enjoy life more, sleep better, and are more manageable at home once they are regularly attending day care. We believe they are among the most important resources for families.

Day centres vary in staff, services offered, and clients accepted. They are run by both local authorities and voluntary organisations. Some day centres cater just for elderly mentally confused people. There is usually a charge for transport and meals but these may be assessed according to the client's means. Some centres are attached to or part of a residential home.

Psychogeriatric day hospitals offer medical services, recreational activities, and occupational therapy for impaired people who live at home. They are staffed by nurses, social workers, doctors and other professionals. Transport is often provided to the day hospital.

Because only a limited number of places are available in most districts, the vacancies in these units are only offered to patients who are moderately to severely demented. The impaired person will be assessed by a psychiatrist or psychogeriatrician to determine whether or not they are suitable to attend such day hospitals. The mildly confused person can probably manage to go to a day centre and there are also day care places available in some Part III residential homes (see p. 183).

Geriatric day hospitals admit patients with physical problems (e.g. the impaired person may have had a stroke) but the patients must have rehabilitative potential and so only mild to moderately demented patients would be considered. The time a person may stay in these day hospitals is usually limited to the period of assessment and treatment.

11 You and the impaired person as part of a family

Chapters 2 to 10 have discussed how to get help for the sick person and ways to care for him. However, you and your family are important also. A chronic dementing illness places a heavy burden on families: it may mean a lot of work or financial sacrifices; it may mean accepting the reality that someone you love will never be the same again; it continues on and on; it may mean that responsibilities and relationships within the family will change; it may mean disagreements within the family; it may mean that you feel overwhelmed, discouraged, isolated, angry, or depressed. You and the person with a dementing illness, as well as the other people close to him, all interact as part of a family system. This system can be severely stressed by a dementing illness. It is helpful to consider the changes that may occur in families that are faced with a chronic illness and to identify the feelings you may experience. Sometimes just knowing that what is happening to you has happened to others can make life easier. Often recognising what is happening suggests ways to improve things.

It is important to know that almost all families do care for their elderly and sick as long as possible. It is simply not true that most British people abandon their elderly in hospitals or 'dump' them into nursing homes. Studies have shown that although many older people do not live with their children, they are closely involved with or cared for by them. Families usually do all they can, often at great personal sacrifice, to care for ill elderly members before seeking help. Of course, there are families who do not care for ill family members. There are some who, because of illness or other problems, are unable to care for their elderly; there are a few who do not wish to; there are some elderly people who have no family to help them. But in the majority of cases, families are struggling to do the best they can for their ill elderly.

Most family members discover a closeness and cooperation as they work together to care for someone with a dementing illness. Sometimes, however, the pressures of caring for an ill person create conflicts in families or cause old disagreements to flare up. For example,

Mr Higgins said, 'We can't agree on what to do. I want to keep Mother at home. My sister wants her in a nursing home. We don't even agree on what is wrong.'

Mrs Tate said, 'My brother doesn't call and he refuses even to talk about it. I have to take care of Mother alone.'

In addition, the burden of caring for a person with a dementing illness can be exhausting and distressing for you.

Mrs Friday said, 'I get so depressed. I cry. Then I lie awake at night and worry. I feel so helpless.'

Watching someone close to you decline can be a painful experience. This Chapter discusses some of the problems that arise in families, and Chapter 12 will discuss some of the feelings you may have.

It is important to remember that not all of your experiences will be unhappy ones. Many people feel a sense of pride in learning to cope with difficult situations. Many family members rediscover one another as they work together to care for an ill person. As you help a forgetful person enjoy the world around him, you may experience a renewed delight in sharing little things—playing with a puppy or enjoying flowers. You may discover a new faith in yourself, in others, or in God. Most dementing illnesses progress slowly, so you and your family member can look forward to many good years.

Mrs Morgan said, 'Although it has been hard, it's been good for me in a lot of ways. It's given me confidence to know that I can manage things my husband always took care of, and in some ways my children and I have grown closer as he has become ill.'

Since this book is designed to help you with problems when they do occur, most of what we discuss are unhappy feelings and problems. We know that this is a one-sided view that reflects only part of what life is like for you.

The feelings and problems you and your family experience interact and affect one another. However, for simplicity, we have organised them into separate topics: changes in roles within the family, finding ways to cope with changes in roles and the family conflict that can arise, your own feelings, and finding ways to care for yourself.

Changes in Roles

Roles, responsibilities, and expectations within the family change when one person becomes ill. For example,

A wife said, 'The worst part is writing out cheques. We have been married thirty-five years and now I have to learn how to write out cheques and balance the bank account.'

A husband said, 'I feel like a fool washing ladies' underwear in the launderette.'

A son said, 'My father has always been the head of the household. How can I tell him he can't drive?'

A daughter said, 'Why can't my brother help out and take his turn looking after Mother?'

Roles are different from responsibilities, and it is helpful to recognise what roles mean to you and to others in the family. Responsibilities are the jobs each person has in the family. Roles include who you are, how you are seen, and what is expected of you. By 'role' we mean a person's place in his family (e.g. head of the household, mother, or 'the person everyone turns to'). Roles are established over many years and are not always easy to define. Tasks often symbolise our roles. In the examples above, family members describe both having to learn new tasks (doing the washing or balancing the bank account) and changes in roles (money manager, homemaker, head of the household).

Learning a new responsibility, such as balancing the bank account or washing clothes, can be difficult when you are also faced with the many day-to-day needs of the confused person, yourself, and your family. However, changes in roles are often more difficult to accept or adjust to. Understanding that each person's responsibilities change and that roles and expectations of others change also will help you to understand other personal feelings and problems that may arise in families. It is helpful to remember that you have coped with changes in roles at other times in your life and that this experience will help you adjust to new responsibilities.

There are many relationships in which role changes occur as the person becomes demented. Here are four examples.

The relationships between a husband and wife change when one of them becomes ill. These changes may be sad and painful. Others can be enriching experiences.

John and Mary Douglas had been married forty-one years when John became ill. John has always been the head of the household: he supported the family, paid the bills, made most of the big decisions. Mary saw herself as a person who always leaned on her husband. When he became ill, she realised that she did not know how much money they had, what insurance they had, or even how to balance their bank account. Bills were going unpaid, yet when she asked John about it, he yelled at her.

For their anniversary Mary cooked a small turkey and planned a quiet time together when they could forget what was happening. When she put the electric carving knife in front of John he threw it down and shouted at her that the knife did not work and she had ruined the turkey. Trying to keep the peace, Mary took the knife, and then realised that she had no idea how to carve a turkey. Mary cried and John stormed. Neither of them felt like eating supper that night.

Having to carve a turkey seemed like the last straw for Mary. She realised that John could no longer do this, nor could he manage their finances, but she suddenly felt overwhelmed and lost. Throughout their marriage Mary had looked to John to solve problems. Now she had to learn to do the things he had always done at the same time that she had to face his illness.

Learning new skills and responsibilities involves energy and effort and means work added to what you already have to do. You may not want to take on new tasks. Few husbands want to learn to do the washing and more than one has had a load of shrunken sweaters and pale pink pants before he finds out that he can't wash red sweaters with white underwear. A spouse who has never managed the chequebook may feel that he doesn't have the ability to manage money and may be afraid of making errors.

In addition to having to do the job itself, the realisation that you must take this job away from your spouse may symbolise all of the sad changes that have taken place. For Mary, carving the turkey symbolised John's loss of status as head of the family.

A spouse may gradually realise that he is alone with his problem—he has lost the partner with whom he shared things. Mary could no longer see herself as leaning on her husband. She suddenly found herself, at sixty, on her own and forced to be independent with no one to help her. No wonder she felt overwhelmed by the task. But at the same time, learning new skills gradually gave Mary a sense of accomplishment. She said, 'I was surprised at myself, really, that I could handle things. Even though I felt so upset, it was good for me to learn that I could manage so well.'

Sometimes problems that seem insurmountable appear that way because they involve both changes in roles and the need for you to learn new tasks. Having to learn new skills when you are upset and tired can be difficult. As well as recognising the distress that may be caused by changing roles, you may need some practical suggestions for getting started with new responsibilities.

If you must take over the housework, often you can do it gradually and learn as you go. But you can save yourself the frustration of burned suppers and ruined laundry by getting the advice of experts. The Citizens' Advice Bureau may be able to direct you to sources of information on shopping, meal preparation, laundry, budgeting, and home maintenance, or you can get advice from a social worker or a visiting nurse. You may even find useful brochures or recipes in the supermarket.

Mrs Stearns says, 'I know my husband can't manage his money any more, but it seems as though it is taking away the last of his manhood to take away the chequebook. I know I have to, but I just can't seem to do it.'

Having to take this symbol of independence away from someone you love can be difficult. It can be worse when you are not accustomed to managing money.

If you have never balanced a chequebook or paid the bills you may find it hard to learn this new responsibility. Actually, managing household finances is not difficult, even for people who dislike maths. Most banks have staff who will advise you, without charge. They also will show you how to balance a chequebook. There are books in the library on this subject. The fact that you must take over this role, rather than the task itself, sometimes is what makes it hard to do.

The bank or a solicitor can also help you draw up a list of yours or the confused person's assets and debts. Sometimes a person has been private about financial affairs, has told no one, and now cannot remember them. Chapter 15 lists some of the potential resources you should look for.

If you can't drive or do not like to drive and must take over the driving responsibilities, look for a driver education course designed for adults. Inquire through the police or the RSPA (Royal Society for the Prevention of Accidents), Cannon House, Queensway, Birmingham B4 6BS (tel. 021 233 2461) which runs courses on defensive driving and has leaflets describing this. Life will be much easier if you are comfortable behind the wheel.

2 *The relationship of a parent with a dementing illness and his adult children often has to change*. The changes that occur when an adult child must assume the responsibility and care of a parent are sometimes called 'role reversal'. Perhaps this is better described as a shift in roles and responsibilities, in which the adult son or daughter gradually assumes increasing responsibility for a parent while the roles of the parent change accordingly. These changes can be difficult. You, the adult son or daughter, may feel sadness and grief at the losses you see in someone you love and look up to. You may feel guilty about 'taking over'.

'I can't tell my mother she shouldn't live alone any more,' Mrs Russell says. 'I know I have to, but every time I try to talk to her she manages to make me feel like a small child who has been bad.'

To varying degrees many of us as adults still feel that our parents are parents and that we, the children, are less assured, capable, and 'grown up'. In some families the parents seem to maintain this kind of relationship with their adult children past the time when adult sons and daughters usually come to feel mature in their own right.

Not everyone has had a good relationship with his parents. If a parent has not been able to let his grown children feel grown up, a lot of unhappiness and conflict may develop. Then as the parent develops a dementing illness he can seem to be demanding and manipulative of you. You may find yourself feeling trapped. You may feel used, angry, and guilty at the same time.

What seems demanding to you may feel different to the impaired person. He may be feeling that with 'just a little help' he can hold on to his independence, perhaps continue to live alone. As he senses his decline, this may seem the only way he can respond to his losses.

Adult children often feel embarrassed by the tasks of physically caring for a parent—for example, giving their mother a bath or changing their father's underwear. Look for ways to help your parent retain his dignity at the same time as you give needed care.

3 *The sick person must adjust to his changing roles in the family*. This often means giving up some of his independence, responsibility, or leadership, which can be difficult for everyone (also see Chapter 4). He may become discouraged or depressed as he realises his abilities are waning.

The roles a person has held within the family in the past, and the kind of person he is, will influence the new roles he assumes as he becomes ill. You can help him to maintain his position as an important member of the family even when he can no longer do the tasks he once did. Consult him, talk to him, listen to him (even if what he says seems confused). Let him know by these actions that he is still respected.

4 *As the roles of the sick person change, the expectations of each member of the family for the others change.* Your relationships and expectations of members of the family are based on family roles that have been established for years. Changes often lead to conflicts, misunderstandings, and times when people's expectations of each other do not agree. At the same time, adjusting to changes and facing problems can bring families closer together, even when they have not been close for years.

Understanding family conflicts

Mrs Eaton says, 'My brother doesn't have anything to do with Mum now—and he was always her favourite. He won't even come to see her. All the burden is on my sister and me. Because my sister's marriage is shaky, I hate to leave Mum with her for long. So I end up taking care of Mum pretty much alone.'

Mr Cooke says, 'My son wants me to put her in a nursing home. He doesn't understand that, after thirty years of marriage, I can't just put her in a nursing home.' His son says, 'Dad isn't being realistic. He can't manage Mother in that big two-storey house. She's going to fall one of these days. And Dad has a heart condition that he refuses to discuss.'

Mr Vane says, 'My brother says if I kept her more active, she would get better. He says I should answer her back when she gets nasty, but that only makes things worse. He *doesn't live with her. He just stays in his own home and criticises.'*

Division of responsibility

The responsibility of caring for an impaired person often is not evenly shared by the family. Like Mrs Eaton, you may find that you are carrying most of the burden of taking care of the person who has a dementing illness. There are many reasons why it is difficult to divide responsibility evenly. Some members of the family may live far away, may be in poor health, may be financially unable to help, or may have problems with their children or marriage.

Sometimes families accept stereotypes about who should help without really considering what is best. One such stereotype is that daughters (and daughters-in-law) are 'supposed' to take care of the sick. But the daughter or daughter-in-law may already be heavily burdened and not be able to take on this task. Perhaps she has young children, or a full-time job. Perhaps she is a single parent.

Long-established roles, responsibilities, and mutual expectations within the family, even when we are unaware of them, can play an important part in determining who has what responsibility for the impaired person. For example,

'My mother brought me up; now I must take care of her.'

'She was a good wife, and she would have done the same for me.'

'I married him late in life. What responsibility is mine and what responsibility is his children's?'

'He was always hard on me, deserted my mother when I was ten, and he's willed all his money to some organisation. How much do I owe him?'

Sometimes expectations are not logical and may not be based on the most practical or fair way to arrange things.

Sometimes family members fail to help as much as they might because it is difficult for them to accept the reality of the impaired person's illness. Sometimes a person just can't bear to face this illness. It is painful, as you know, to watch a loved one decline. Sometimes family members who do not have the burden of daily care stay away because seeing the decline makes them feel sad. However, others in the family may view this as deserting the declining person.

Sometimes one family member assumes most of the burden of care. He may not tell other members of the family how bad things are. He may not want to burden them or he may not really want their help.

Mr Newman says, 'I hesitate to call on my sons. They are willing to help, but they have their own careers and families.'

Mrs King says, 'I don't like to call on my daughter. She always tells me what she thinks I am doing wrong.'

Often you and other members of the family have strong and differing ideas of how things should be done. Sometimes this happens because not all family members understand what is wrong with the person who has a dementing illness, or why he acts as he does, or what can be expected in the future.

Family members who do not share the day-to-day experience of living with a person suffering from a dementing illness may not know what it is really like, and may be critical or unsympathetic. It is hard for people on the outside to realise how wearing the daily burden of constant care can be. Often, too, people don't realise how you are feeling unless you tell them.

Sometimes there have been long-established disagreements, resentments, or conflicts in the family which are aggravated by the crisis of an illness.

Your marriage

When the ill person is your parent or in-law, it is important to consider the effect of his illness on your marriage. Maintaining a good marriage is often not easy, and caring for a person with a dementing illness can make it much more difficult. It may mean more financial burdens and less time to talk, to go out, and to make love. It may entail being involved with your in-laws, having more things to disagree over, often being tired, and not giving the children enough attention. It can mean having to include a difficult, disagreeable, seemingly demanding, and sick person in your lives.

A dementing illness can be painful to watch. It is understandable that a person may look at his impaired in-law and wonder if his spouse will become like that, and if he will have to go through this again.

A son or daughter can easily find himself or herself torn between the needs of an impaired parent, the expectations of brothers and sisters (or the other parent), and the needs and demands of a spouse and children. It's easy to take out frustrations or fatigue on those we love and trust most—our spouse and our children.

The spouse of an ill parent may also add problems. He or she may be upset, critical, or ill, or he may even desert his ill partner. Such problems can add to the tension in your marriage, and, if at all possible, should be discussed with everyone involved. It is sometimes easier if a son initiates a solution with his own family or a daughter with her own relatives.

A good relationship can survive for a while in the face of stress and trouble, but we believe it is important that the husband and wife find time and energy for each other—to talk, to get away, and to enjoy their relationship in the ways that they always have.

Coping with role changes and family conflict

When the family does not agree, or when most of the burden is on one person, it adds to the problems you face. The burden of caring for a chronically ill person is often too much for one individual. It is important that you have others to help—to give you 'time out' from constant care, to give you encouragement and support, to help with the work, and to share the financial responsibility.

If you are getting criticism or not enough help from your family, it is usually *not* a good idea to let your resentment smolder. It may be up to you to take the initiative to change things in your family. When families are in disagreement or when long-established conflicts get in the way, this may be difficult to do.

How do you handle the often complex, painful role changes that are set in motion by a chronic, dementing illness? First, recognise these as aspects of family relationships. Just knowing that roles in families are complex, often unrecognised or unacknowledged, and that changes can be painful will help you to feel less panicked and overwhelmed. Recognise that certain tasks may be symbolic of important roles in the family and that it is the shift of role, rather than the specific issue, which may be painful.

Find out all you can about the disease. What family members believe to be true about this illness affects how much help they provide for a person and whether there will be disagreements about caring for the impaired person.

Think about the differences between the responsibilities or tasks that an impaired person may have to give up and the roles that he may be able to retain. For example, although John's illness means he can no longer carve a turkey or make many decisions, his *role* as Mary's loved and respected husband can remain.

Know what the impaired person is still able to do and what is too difficult for him. Of course, one wants a person to remain as self-reliant as possible, but expectations that exceed his abilities can make him upset and miserable. (Sometimes such expectations of how well he can function come from others, sometimes they come from the impaired person himself.) If he cannot do a task independently, try to simplify the job so that he can still do part of it.

Recognise that role changes are not one-off things, but are continuing processes. As the illness progresses, you may again have to take on new responsibilities. Each time you will probably re-experience some of the feelings of sadness and of being overwhelmed by your job. This is a part of the grief process in a chronic disease.

Talk over your situation with other families. This is one of the advantages of family support groups. You may find it comforting to learn that other families have struggled with similar changes. Laugh at yourself a little. When you have just burned the supper or hacked up a turkey, try to see the humour in the situation. Often where families of people with dementing illnesses get together they share both tears and laughter over such experiences.

Look for ways to help each other. When a wife has most of the responsibility of daily care for an impaired person, she may badly need her husband's help with such untraditional jobs as the housework or sitting with the parent while she goes out. She will certainly need his love and encouragement and may need his help with the rest of the family.

You may reach a point where the extent and demands of your job are exhausting you. You must be able to recognise this and to make other arrangements when that time comes. Your responsibilities as decision maker may eventually include making the decision to give up your role as primary care giver.

A family conference

We feel that a family conference is one of the most effective ways to help families cope. Have a family meeting, with help from a social worker or the doctor if needed, to talk over the problems and to make plans. Together you can make definite decisions about how much help or money each person will contribute.

There are ground rules for a family conference which you might suggest at the beginning: everyone comes (including children who will be affected by the decision), each person has his say uninterrupted, and everyone listens to what the others have to say (even if they don't agree).

If family members disagree about what is wrong with the confused, forgetful person or about how to manage his care, it may be helpful to give other members of the family this book and other written material about the specific disease, or to ask the doctor to talk to them. It is surprising how often this reduces the tensions between family members.

Here are some questions to ask of each other when you get together. What are the problems? Who is doing what now? What needs to be done, and who can do it? How can you help each other? What will these changes mean for each of you? Some of the practical questions that need to be discussed might be: Who will be responsible for daily care? Does this mean giving up privacy? not having friends over? not being able to afford a holiday? Does this mean that parents will expect their children to act in a more grown up way because the parents will be busy with the sick person? Who will make the decision to put a parent in a nursing home or seek hospital care? Who will be responsible for the sick person's money?

If a well spouse of the impaired person is to move into a son or daughter's home with the impaired person, what will this person's roles in the family be? Will she have responsibility for the grandchildren? Will there be two women in the kitchen? An expanded family can be enriching but it also can create tensions. Anticipating and discussing areas of disagreement in advance can make things easier.

It is also important to talk about several other practical areas in which family relationships can get into trouble. It can seem insensitive even to think about matters of money or inheritance when a loved one is ill. But financial concerns are important, and questions about who will get the inheritance are real—if often hidden—factors in determining responsibility for a family member. They can be the underlying cause of much bitterness. Money matters need to be brought out in the open. Ask yourself the following questions.

Does everyone know what money and inheritance there is? It is surprising how often one son is thinking, 'Dad has those shares he bought twenty years ago, he owns his house, and he has his pension. He ought to be quite comfortable.' The other son, who is taking care of his father, knows 'the house needs a new roof and a new boiler, those old mining shares are worthless, and he gets barely enough to live on from his pension. I have to dip into my own pocket to pay some bills.'

Is there a will? Does someone know or suspect that he has been shortchanged in the will? Do some members of the family feel that others are greedy for inherited money, property, or personal possessions? This is not unusual and it can best be handled when it is openly faced. Hidden resentments often smolder and can emerge as conflicts over the daily care of the person.

How much does it cost to care for the sick person, and who is paying these bills? When a family cares for a person at home, there are many 'hidden' costs to consider: special foods, special door latches, a sitter, transport, another bed and bedroom furniture on the ground floor, grab rails for the bathroom, perhaps the cost of a wife's not working because she must care for the confused person.

Does everyone know what it costs to care for a person with a dementing illness in a nursing home, and does everyone know who is legally responsible for those costs? (We discuss nursing home costs in Chapter 16.) Sometimes when a daughter says, 'Mother must put Dad in a nursing home,' she does not realise that doing so may deprive her mother of most of their joint income and leave her mother nearly destitute.

Do some members of the family feel that money has been unequally distributed in the past? For example,

> *'Dad put my brother through college and gave him the down payment on his house. Yet now my brother won't take him, so* I *get the work—and the cost—of taking care of him.'*

Families sometimes say, 'It is inconceivable that my family will come together to talk about things like that. My brother won't even discuss it on the phone. And if we did get together it would just be a big fight.' If you feel that your family is like this, you may be discouraged. Although you need your family's aid, you may feel trapped because you feel that your family will not help. It is not unusual for families to need the assistance of an outside person—a counsellor, minister, or social worker—to work out their problems and to help them arrive at equitable arrangements (see p. 161).

One of the advantages of seeking the assistance of a counsellor is that he can listen objectively and help the family to keep the discussion on the problems you are facing and not drift aside into old arguments. Your doctor, a social worker, or a counsellor may be able to intervene on your behalf and convince everyone involved of the need for a family to discuss issues of concern to them all. Sometimes a family solicitor can help. If a family is having difficulty and you ask a third party to help you, the first topic of conversation may be to agree that the third party will not take sides with any one person.

You need your family. Now is an excellent time to put aside old conflicts for the sake of the impaired person. Perhaps if your family cannot resolve all your disagreements, you can, in a discussion, find one or two things upon which you do agree. This will encourage everyone and the next discussion may be easier.

Your children

Having children at home can create special problems. They, too, have a relationship with the sick person, and they have complex feelings—which they may not express—about his illness and the roles in the family. Parents often worry about the effect that being around a person with a dementing illness will have on children. It is hard to know what to tell a child about a parent's or grandparent's 'odd' behaviour. Sometimes parents worry that children will learn undesirable behaviour from people with dementing illnesses.

Children are usually aware of what is going on. They are excellent observers and, even when things are carefully concealed from them, often sense that something is wrong. Fortunately, children are marvellously resilient. Even small children can benefit from an honest explanation of what is happening to the person with a dementing illness—in language they can understand. This helps them not to be frightened. Reassure the child that this illness is not 'catching' like chickenpox and that neither the children nor his parents are likely to get it. Tell the child directly that nothing he did 'caused' this illness. Sometimes children secretly feel to blame for the things that happen in their family.

One father put a pile of dried beans on the table. He took little pieces of the pile away as he gave his young son the following explanation of his grandfather's illness: 'Grandpa has an illness that makes him act like he does. It isn't catching. None of us is going to get like Grandpa. It's like having a broken leg, only little pieces of Grandpa's brain are broken. He won't get any better. This little piece of Grandpa's brain is broken, so he can't remember what you just told him; this little piece is broken, so he forgets how to use his cutlery at the table; this little piece is broken, so he gets angry too readily. But this part, which is for loving, Grandpa still has left.'

It is usually best to involve children actively in what is happening in the family and even to find ways in which they can help. Small children frequently relate well to impaired, confused people, and can establish special and loving relationships with them. Try to create an atmosphere in which the child can ask you questions and express his feelings openly. Remember that children also feel sadness and grief, but they may be able to enjoy the childlike ways of an impaired person without feeling at all sad. The more comfortable you feel in your understanding of this illness, the more easily you will be able to explain it to your child.

Children may need help knowing what to tell playmates who tease them about a 'funny' parent or grandparent.

It is unlikely that children will mimic the undesirable behaviour of a person with a dementing illness for long if you don't make a big issue out of this if it happens and if the child is getting enough love and attention. Clearly explain (probably several times) to the child that his parent or grandparent has a disease and cannot help what he does but that the child can, and is expected to, control his behaviour.

Young people may be frightened by unexplained, strange behaviour. Sometimes they worry that something they did or might do will make the person worse. It is important to talk about these concerns and to reassure the young person.

One family with children ranging from ten to sixteen shared with us the following thoughts based on their own experience:

> *What's going on in a child's head is not what we think! Anyone who has been around children much can think of examples of this. Don't assume that you know what a youngster is thinking.*
>
> *Children, even small children, also feel pity, sadness, and sympathy.*
>
> *If we had it to do all over again, we would talk more with the children.*
>
> *The effects of this illness linger long after the confused person has gone to a hospital or nursing home. Get together with the children afterwards and continue to discuss things.*
>
> *Make an effort to involve all of the children equally in the person's care. Children can find it hard to be depended on or they can feel left out. Sharing in care gives them a sense of responsibility.*
>
> *The parent closest to the sick person needs to be aware of the children and the effect of her grief and distress on them. Sometimes a person can be so overwhelmed by her own troubles that she forgets the children. Her behaviour can be as hard on the children as the illness itself.*

Perhaps the biggest problem when there are children at home is that the parent's time and energies are divided between that person and the children—with never enough for both. In order to cope with this double load you will need every bit of help available—the assistance of the rest of the family, the resources of the community, and time—for you to replenish your own emotional and physical energies. You may find yourself torn between neglecting the children and neglecting a 'childish' or demanding person with a dementing illness.

As the person's condition worsens, so may your dilemma. The declining person may need more and more care, and may be so disruptive that children cannot feel comfortable at home. You may not have the physical or emotional energy to meet the needs of children or adolescents and the sick person. Children growing up in such a situation may suffer as a result of the person's illness.

You may make the painful decision to place the sick person in a hospital if a place is available or in a nursing home in order to create a better home environment for the children. If you face such a decision, you and your children need to discuss what is to be done, talking over what your alternatives will mean to each member of the family. 'We will have less money for luxuries but we wouldn't have Dad shouting all night.'

The support of your doctor, clergy, or a counsellor is helpful at such times. Families often find it easier to make decisions when they know they are not alone.

Teenagers

Adolescents may be embarrassed by 'odd' behaviour, reluctant to bring friends home, resentful of the demands made on you by the confused person, or hurt by the confused person's failure to remember them. Adolescents can also be extraordinarily compassionate, supportive, responsible, and altruistic. They often have an unspoiled sense of humanitarianism and kindness which is refreshing and helpful. Certainly they will have mixed feelings. Like you, they may experience the grief of seeing someone they love change drastically at the same time that they may feel resentful or embarrassed. Mixed feelings lead to mixed reactions that are often puzzling to other family members. Adolescent years can be hard for young people, whether there are problems at home or not. However, many adults, looking back, recognise that sharing in family problems helped them to become mature adults.

Ensure that your adolescent understands the nature of the disease and what is happening. Be honest with him about what is going on. Explanations, given gently, help a lot. Children seldom benefit from mistaken attempts to shelter them. Involve the adolescent in the family discussions, groups, and conferences with health professionals, so that he, too, understands what is happening.

Spend time away from the sick person, when you are not exhausted or cross, to maintain a good relationship with your adolescent and to listen to his interests. Remember that he has a life apart from this illness and this situation. Try to find space for his teenage friends away from the impaired person.

Remember that you may be less patient or more emotional because of all you are dealing with. Again, breaks for you may help you be more patient with your children.

When a grandparent moves into your home, it is important that both he and your children know who sets the rules and who disciplines the children. When the grandparent is forgetful, it is important that your children know *from you* what is expected of them to avoid conflicts like, 'Grandmother says I can't go out on dates.' 'Grandad says I have to turn off the TV.'

12 How caring for an impaired person affects you

Family members tell us that they experience many feelings as they care for a person with a chronic, dementing illness. They feel sad, discouraged, and alone. They feel angry, guilty, or hopeless. They feel tired or depressed. In the face of the reality of a chronic illness, emotional distress is appropriate and understandable. Sometimes families of people with dementing illnesses find themselves overwhelmed by their feelings.

Human feelings are complex and they vary with each person. In this chapter we have tried to avoid oversimplifying feelings or offering simplistic solutions. Our goal is to remind you that it is not unusual to experience many feelings.

Emotional reactions

People have different ways of handling their emotions. Some people experience each feeling intensely; others do not. Sometimes people think that certain feelings are unacceptable—that they should not have certain feelings or that, if they do, no one could possibly understand them. Sometimes they feel alone with their feelings.

Sometimes people have mixed feelings. One might both love and dislike the same person, or want to keep a family member at home and put her in a hospital or nursing home, all at the same time. Having mixed feelings might not seem logical but it is common. Often people do not realise that they have mixed feelings.

Sometimes people are afraid of strong emotions, perhaps because such feelings are uncomfortable, perhaps because they are afraid they might do something rash, or perhaps because they are concerned about how others will view them. These and other responses to our feelings are not unusual. In fact, most of us will have similar responses at one time or another.

We do not believe there is a 'right' way to handle emotions. We think that recognising how you feel and having some understanding of why you feel the way you do are important, because your feelings affect your judgment. Unrecognised or unacknowledged feelings can influence the decisions a person makes in ways that he does not understand or realise. You can acknowledge and recognise your feelings—to yourself and to others—but you have a choice of when, where, and whether to express your feelings or to act on them.

People sometimes worry that not expressing feelings causes 'stress-related' diseases. Suppose you know that you are often angry with the behaviour of a person with a dementing illness, but you decide not to shout at her because it only makes her behaviour worse. Will you develop ulcers, or migraines, or hypertension? Researchers disagree about the relationship between expressing feelings and diseases. However, at present, the causes of diseases such as ulcer, migraines, and hypertension are unknown. It has not been our observation that these conditions are more common among families who care for people with dementing illnesses. We do believe that as families appreciate that the irritating behaviour of a confused person is a symptom of her disease, they feel less frustrated and angry and they can care better for the confused person.

As you read this section, remember that each person and each family is different. You may not have these feelings. We have discussed them in order to help those family members who do feel angry or discouraged, tired or sad, etc. Rather than read all this material, you may want to refer to it when you feel a particular section will help you.

Anger

It is understandable that you feel frustrated and angry: angry that this has happened to you, angry that you have to be the care-giver, angry with others who don't seem to be helping out, angry with the sick person for her irritating behaviour, angry that you are trapped in this situation.

Some people with dementing illnesses develop behaviour patterns that are extremely irritating and that can seem impossible to live with. You will understandably get angry and may sometimes react by shouting or arguing.

Mrs Palling felt that she must not get angry with her husband. They had had a good marriage and she knew that he could not help himself now that he was ill. She says, 'We went to dinner at my son and daughter-in-law's house. I have never felt comfortable with my daughter-in-law, anyway, and I don't think she understands about Joe. As soon as we got inside the door Joe looked around and said, "Let's go home." I tried to explain to him that we were staying for dinner and all he would say is, "I've never liked it here. Let's go home."

'We sat down to dinner and everyone was tense. Joe wouldn't talk to anyone and he wouldn't take his hat off. As soon as dinner was over he wanted to go home. My daughter-in-law went into the kitchen and shut the door and started banging the dishes. My son made me go into the study with him and all the time Joe was shouting. "Let's get out of here before she poisons us."

'My son says I'm letting Dad ruin my life, that there is no reason for Dad to act that way, that that isn't sickness, it's that he's become spiteful in his old age. He says I have to do something.

'So we got in the car to go home and all the way home Joe shouted at me about my driving, which he always does. As soon as we got home he started asking me what time it was. I said, "Joe, please *be quiet. Go and watch television." And he said, "Why don't you ever talk to me?" Then I started yelling at him and I yelled and yelled.'*

Episodes like this can wear out even the most patient person. It seems as if they always start when we are most tired.

The things that are most irritating sometimes seem like little things —but little things mount up, day after day.

Mrs Jackson states, 'I had never got along with my mother that well, and since she's come to live with us, it's been terrible. In the middle of the night she gets up and starts packing.

'I get up and tell her, "It's the middle of the night, Mother," and I try to explain to her that she lives here now, but I'm thinking if I don't get my sleep I won't be any good at work tomorrow.

'She says she has to go home, and I say she lives here, and every night a fight starts at two o'clock in the morning.'

Sometimes a person with a dementing illness can do some things very well and appear unwilling to do other, seemingly identical tasks. When you feel that the sick person can do more or is just acting up to upset you it can be infuriating. For example,

Mrs Graham says, 'She can load the dishwasher and set the table at my sister's house but at my house she either refuses to do it or she makes a terrible mess. Now I know *it's because I work and she knows I come home tired.'*

Often the person who has most of the responsibility for the care of a sick person feels that other members of the family don't help out enough, are critical, or don't come to visit. A lot of anger can build up around these feelings.

You may be irritated with doctors and other professionals at times. Sometimes your anger toward them is legitimate; at other times you may know that they are doing the best they can, yet you are still angry with them.

People with a religious faith may question how God could allow this to happen to them. They may feel that it is a terrible sin to be angry with God or they may fear that they have lost their faith. Such feelings can deprive them of the strength and reassurance faith offers at just the time when they need it most. To struggle with such questions is part of the experience of faith.

Said a minister, 'I wonder how God could do this to me. I haven't been perfect, but I've done the best I could. And I love my wife. But then I think I have no right to question God. For me that is the hardest part. I think I must be a very weak person to question God.'

Never let a person make you feel guilty about your anger with God. There are many thoughtful and meaningful writings discussing such things as feeling anger with God or questioning how He could do such a thing as this. C. S. Lewis's book *A Grief Observed* eloquently describes his own struggle with these questions. Reading this and other books, and talking honestly with your minister, priest, or rabbi can be comforting.

Remember, it is only human to be angry when faced with the burdens and losses a dementing illness often brings.

Expressing your anger to the sick person often makes her behaviour worse. Her illness may make it impossible for her to respond to your anger in a rational way. You may find that it improves her behaviour when you find other ways to manage both your frustrations and the problems themselves.

The first step in dealing with anger is to know what you can reasonably expect from a person with a dementing illness, and what is happening to the brain to cause irritating behaviour. If you are not sure whether the person can stop acting the ways she does, find out from your doctor or other professional staff. For example,

An occupational therapist discovered that Mrs Graham's sister had an old dishwasher that her mother had operated before she became ill. Mrs Graham had a new dishwasher that her mother could not learn to use because her brain impairment made it impossible for her to learn even simple new skills.

It may be possible to change the person's irritating behaviour by changing the environment or the daily routine. However, just knowing that unpleasant behaviour is the result of the disease that the person cannot help can be reassuring.

It is often helpful to think about a difference between being angry with the person's *behaviour* and being angry with the *person herself*. She is ill and often cannot stop her behaviour. Certainly, the behaviour can be infuriating, but it is not aimed at you personally.

A dementing illness might make it impossible for a person to be deliberately offensive because she has lost the ability to take purposeful action. Mrs Palling's husband was not deliberately insulting his family. His behaviour was the result of his illness.

It often helps to know that other families and professional care-givers have the same problems.

Says Mrs Kemp, 'I didn't want to send my husband to the day hospital, but I did it. It helped me so much to find out that his constant questions made trained professionals angry too. It wasn't just me.'

Many families find that discussing their experiences with other families helps them to feel less frustrated and upset.

Sometimes it is helpful to find other outlets for your frustrations: talking to someone about it, cleaning out cupboards, or chopping wood—whatever ways you have used in the past to cope with your frustrations. A vigorous exercise programme, a long walk, or taking a few minutes to relax totally may be helpful for you.

Helplessness

It is not uncommon for family members to feel helpless, weak, or demoralised in the face of a chronic dementing illness. These feelings are often made worse when you cannot find doctors or other professionals who seem to understand dementing illnesses. We have found that families and the people with dementing illnesses have many resources within themselves with which they can overcome feelings of helplessness. Although you may not be able to cure the disease, you are far from helpless. There are many ways to improve life for both the forgetful person and the family. Here are some places to start:

Things often seem worse when you look at everything at once. Instead, focus on changing small things that you can change.
Take one day at a time.
Be informed about the disease. Read and talk about ways others manage.
Talk with other families who face similar problems.
Get involved in exchanging information, supporting research, and reaching others.
Discuss your feelings with the doctor, social worker, or clergyman.

Embarrassment

Sometimes the behaviour of a person with a dementing illness is embarrassing and strangers often do not understand what is happening.

Says Mrs McGregor, 'I say my husband has Alzheimer's disease. "Old timer's disease?" they say. "No, Alzheimer's disease!" I say, and I spell it. If my husband had a brain tumour they would understand. How I wish he didn't have a disease nobody has ever heard of!'

Says one husband, 'Going through the supermarket, she keeps taking things down off the shelves like a toddler, and people stare.'

Says a daughter, 'Every time we try to give Mother a bath she opens the window and shouts for help. What are we to tell the neighbours?'

Such experiences *are* embarrassing, although much of your embarrassment may fade as you share your experiences with other families. In such groups families often find they laugh over things like this.

Explaining to neighbours usually helps gain their understanding. You might give them copies of the 'handouts' about these diseases. There is another reason why this is important. Although these dementing diseases are common, many people still think 'senility' is the natural result of getting older. By explaining the illness to your neighbours you are helping to get these diseases out into the open. Your neighbour may well know someone else with one of these diseases who needs treatment.

Occasionally, some insensitive person will ask a rude question, such as 'Why does he act like that?' or 'Whatever is wrong with her?' Sometimes it may be most effective to say 'Whyever would you ask?'

One courageous husband says, 'I still take my wife out to dinner. I don't like to cook and she likes to go out. I ignore other people's glances. This is something we always enjoyed doing together, and we still do!'

Guilt

It is quite common for family members to feel guilty: for the way they treated the person in the past; for being embarrassed by the person's 'odd' behaviour; for losing their temper with a sick person; for not wanting this responsibility; for considering placing the person in a nursing home; and for many other reasons, some trivial, some enormous. For example,

'My mother's illness ruined my marriage and I can't forgive her for it.'

You may feel guilty about your occasional angry outbursts when you are frustrated with the impaired person.

'I lost my temper with Dick and slapped him. Yet I know he is ill and can't help himself.'

You may feel guilty about spending time with your friends away from the person you love, especially when the person is your spouse and you have been accustomed to doing most things together.

You may feel vaguely guilty without knowing why. Sometimes people feel that the person with a dementing illness *makes* them feel guilty. 'Promise me you will never put me in a nursing home,' or 'You wouldn't treat me that way if you loved me' is something the confused person may say that can make you feel guilty.

Sometimes we feel guilty when a person close to us, whom we have always disliked, develops a dementing disease:

'I've never liked my mother and now she has this terrible disease. If only I had been closer to her when I could.'

Families sometimes ask if something they did or failed to do caused the illness. Sometimes the care giver feels responsible when the person gets worse. You may feel that if only you had taken more time with her or kept her more active she would not have become worse. You may feel that a hospital admission for a surgical operation or for medical reasons 'caused' this condition.

The trouble with feelings of guilt is that, when they are not recognised for what they are, they can keep you from making clear-headed decisions about the future and doing what is right for the sick person and the rest of the family. Once such feelings are recognised, they are not surprising or hard to manage.

The first step is to admit that feelings of guilt *are* a problem. They become a problem when they affect your decisions. If you are being influenced by guilt feelings, you must make a decision. Are you going to go around in a circle with one foot caught in the trap of guilt, or are you going to say 'What is done is done' and go on from there? Often, when we look realistically at the situation there is no way to remedy the fact that you never liked your mother or that you slapped a sick person, for example. However, guilt feelings tend to keep us looking for ways to remedy the past instead of letting us accept the fact that you can stop trying to make up for your guilt feelings and instead make decisions and plans based on what is best now. For example,

Mrs Dempsey had never liked her mother. As soon as she could she had moved away from home and telephoned her mother only on special occasions. When her mother developed a dementing illness, she brought her mother to live with her. The confused woman disrupted the family, kept everyone up at night, upset the children, and left Mrs Dempsey exhausted. When the doctor recommended that her mother enter a nursing home, Mrs Dempsey only became more upset. She could not bring herself to put her mother in a nursing home even though this clearly would be better for everyone.

When the feelings of guilt in such a relationship are not acknowledged, they can destructively affect how you act. Perhaps being faced with a chronic illness is a good time to be honest with yourself about not liking someone. You can then choose whether to give a person care and respect without being influenced by not liking her. We have little control over whom we like or love. Some people are not very likeable, but we do have control over how we act toward them. When Mrs Dempsey was able to face the fact that she did not like her mother and that she felt guilty about that, she was able to go ahead and arrange for her mother to get good nursing home care.

When the person with a dementing illness says things like 'Promise you won't put me in a nursing home,' it is helpful to remember that sometimes the person with a dementing illness *cannot* make responsible decisions and that you must make the decisions, acting not on the basis of guilt but on the basis of your responsibility.

Not all feelings of guilt are over major issues or keep you from making good decisions. Sometimes you may feel guilty about little things—being cross with the confused person or snapping at her when you are tired. Saying 'I'm sorry' often clears the air and makes you both feel better. Often the confused person, because he is forgetful, will have forgotten the incident long before you have.

If you worry that you have caused this illness or made it worse, it is helpful to learn all you can about the disease and to talk over the person's illness with her doctor.

In general, Alzheimer's disease is a progressive illness. Neither you nor your doctor can prevent this progression. It may not be possible to stop or reverse a multi-infarct dementia either. Keeping a person active will not stop the progress of such a disease, but it can help the person use her remaining abilities.

A person's condition may first become apparent after an illness or hospital admission, but often, upon close examination, the beginning stages of the illness occurred months or years earlier. At present, earlier identification of Alzheimer's disease does not help to slow or reverse its progression.

If you don't feel right about doing things for yourself and by yourself, remember that it is important for the confused person's well-being that your life have meaning and fulfillment outside of caring for her. Rest and the companionship of friends will do much to keep you going.

When guilt feelings are keeping you from making clear-headed decisions, you may find it helpful to talk the whole thing out with an understanding counsellor, a minister, or other families so that you can go on more easily. Learning that most people do similar things helps to put little nagging guilt feelings in their proper perspective.

Laughter, love, and joy

A dementing illness does not suddenly end a person's capacity to experience love or joy, nor does it end her ability to laugh. And although your life may often seem filled with fatigue, frustration, or grief, your capacity for these emotions is not gone either. Happiness may seem out of place in the face of trouble, but in fact it crops up unexpectedly. The words of a song written by Sister Miriam Theresa Winter of the Medical Mission Sisters reflect this:

I saw raindrops on my window
Joy is like the rain.
Laughter runs across my pain,
slips away and comes again.
Joy is like the rain.

Laughter might be called a gift to help our sanity in the face of trouble. There is no reason to feel badly if you laugh about the mistakes a confused person makes. She may share the laughter even if she is not sure what is funny.

Fortunately love is not dependent upon intellectual abilities. Focus on the ways you and others still share expressions of affection with the impaired person.

Grief

As the person's illness progresses and the person changes, you may experience the loss of a companion and a relationship that was important to you. You may grieve for the 'way she used to be'. You may find yourself feeling sad or discouraged. Sometimes little things may sadden you or can start you crying. You may feel that tearfulness or sadness is welling up inside you. Often such feelings come and go, so that you alternate between feeling sad and feeling hopeful. Feelings of sadness are often mixed with feelings of depression or fatigue. Such feelings are a normal part of grieving.

We usually think of grief as an emotional experience that follows a death. However, grief actually is an emotional response to loss and so is a normal experience for people who love a person with a chronic illness.

Grief associated with a death may be an overwhelming grief in the beginning, and gradually lessen. Grief associated with a chronic illness seems to go on and on. Your feelings may shift back and forth between hope that the person will get better and anger and sadness over an irreversible condition. Just when you think you have 'adjusted' the person may change and you will go through the grieving experience over again. Whether it is the grief that follows a death or that which comes with being with a person with a dementing illness, grief is a feeling associated with losing those qualities of a person who was important to you.

Families often say that their own sadness at losing a loved one is made worse because they must watch the suffering of the person as her illness progresses.

Says Mrs Owens, 'Sometimes I wish he would die so it would be over. It seems as if he is dying a bit at a time, day after day. When something new happens I think I can't stand it. Then I get used to it, and something else happens. And I keep hoping—for a new doctor, a new treatment, maybe a miracle. It seems as though I'm on an emotional treadmill going around and around and it's slowly wearing me down.'

There are certain changes that come with a chronic dementing illness which seem especially hard to bear. Particular characteristics of the people we love symbolise for us who that person is: 'He was always the one who made decisions' or 'She was always such a friendly person'. When these things change, they may precipitate feelings of sadness which are sometimes not understood by people less close to the situation. For example, when a person is unable to talk or understand clearly, her family may feel acutely the loss of her companionship.

A husband or wife has lost the spouse he or she used to have but is not a single person. This creates a special set of problems, which we will discuss below, in the section, 'You as a Spouse Alone'.

Another problem is that the grief that follows a death is understood and accepted by society, while the grief that comes with a chronic illness is often misunderstood by friends and neighbours, especially when the ill person looks well. Your loss then is not as visible as it is in a death. 'Be grateful you still have your husband,' or 'Keep a stiff upper lip,' people may say.

There are no easy antidotes for grief. Perhaps you will find, as others have, that it is eased somewhat when it is shared with other people who are also living with the unique tragedy of a dementing illness. You may feel that you should keep feelings of sadness and grief to yourself and not burden others with your troubles. However, sharing these feelings can be comforting and give you the strength you need to continue to care for a declining person.

Depression

Depression is a feeling of sadness and discouragement. It is often difficult to distinguish between depression and grief, or between depression and anger, or depression and worry. Families of the chronically ill often feel sad, depressed, discouraged, or low, day after day, week after week. Sometimes they feel apathetic or listless. Depressed people may also feel anxious, nervous, or irritable. Sometimes they don't have much appetite and have trouble sleeping at night. The experience of being depressed is painful; we feel miserable and wish for relief from our sad feelings.

A chronic dementing illness takes its toll on our emotions and provides a real reason for feeling low. Sometimes counselling helps reduce the depression you experience, but counselling cannot cure the situation that has made you depressed; it can only help you deal with it. Many families find that it helps to share experiences and emotions with other families in support groups. Others find that it helps to get away from the sick person and spend time with hobbies or people they enjoy. When you are unable to get enough rest, your fatigue may make your feelings of discouragement worse. Getting help so that you can rest may cheer you up. Still, the feelings of discouragement and depression may stick with you—understandably.

For a few people depression goes beyond—or is different from—the understandable feelings of discouragement caused by this illness. Then it is important to consult a doctor. He can help significantly with this sort of depression. If any or several of the things listed on p. 159 are happening, to you or to someone else in the family, it is important to find a doctor who can help you or who can refer you to a counsellor.

Isolation; feeling alone

Sometimes a family member feels that he is facing this alone. 'Despair', one wife said to us. 'Write about that feeling of being alone with this.' You may feel very much alone when the one person with whom you could share everything has changed. You may feel that you must face his illness all alone.

This is a miserable feeling. We are all individuals and no one else can truly understand what we are going through. The feeling of being alone is not uncommon when people are facing a dementing illness. Remaining involved with others—your family, your friends, other people with ill relatives—can help you feel less alone. Sharing experiences with them will help you to realise that others have similar feelings of aloneness. While you may feel that you can never replace the relationship you had with the confused person, you will gradually find that friends and family are offering love and support.

Worry

Who doesn't worry? We could fill many pages with things families worry about, but you already know them. They are real worries, serious concerns. Worry combines with depression and fatigue and is a fact of life for families. Each person has his own way of coping with worries: some people seem to shrug off serious problems, others seem to fret interminably over trivia, most of us fall somewhere in between. Most of us have also discovered that the kind of worrying we do when we lie awake at night does not solve the problem but it does make us tired. Some of this kind of worrying is often inevitable, but if you are doing a lot of it, you may want to take yourself in hand and look for other ways to manage your problems.

A woman who faces some real and terrible possibilities in her life tries this approach to worry: 'I ask myself what is the worst thing that could happen. We could run out of money and lose our home. But I know people wouldn't let us starve or go homeless. It seems as though I don't worry as much once I've faced what the worst could be.'

Being hopeful and being realistic

As you struggle with a dementing disease, you may find yourself sometimes following up every possible hope for a cure and at other times feeling discouraged and defeated. You may find yourself unable to accept the bad news the doctors have given you. Instead, you may seek second, third, and even more medical opinions at great expense to yourself and the sick person. You may find yourself refusing to believe that anything is wrong. You may even find yourself giggling or acting in a silly manner when you really don't have anything to laugh about. Such feelings are normal and are usually a part of our mind's efforts to come to terms with something we don't want to happen.

Sometimes, of course, ignoring the problem can endanger the sick person (for example, if she is driving or living alone when she cannot do so safely). Seeking many medical opinions can be futile, exhausting, and expensive, but sometimes seeking a second opinion may be wise. A second opinion can be obtained, free, through the NHS.

This experience of a mixture of hope and discouragement is common to many families. The problem is complicated when professionals give conflicting information about dementing illnesses.

Most families find reasonable peace in a compromise between hope and realism. How do you know what to do?

Know that we may be a long way from a major research breakthrough or we may be close. Miracles do happen, and yet not often.

Ask yourself if you are going from doctor to doctor or if your reaction is making things more difficult or even risky for the confused person. If you are ignoring her impairments, is she endangering herself by driving, cooking, or continuing to live alone?

Put the sick person in the care of a doctor whom you trust. Avoid quack 'cures'.

Keep yourself informed about the progress of legitimate research. Join the Alzheimer's Disease Society and local groups to keep abreast of new knowledge.

Physical reactions

Fatigue

Fatigue often comes with depression. It is difficult to know which comes first. People who care for a person with a dementing illness are often tired simply because they aren't getting enough rest. However, being tired adds to the feelings of depression. At the same time, being depressed may make you feel more tired. Always feeling tired is a problem for many people who care for a person with a dementing illness.

Do what you can in little ways to help yourself be less exhausted. For example,

> *Mrs Levin says, 'He gets up in the night and puts his hat on and sits on the sofa. I used to wear myself out trying to get him back to bed. Now I just let him sit there. If he wants to wear his hat with his pyjamas, it's OK. I don't worry about it. I used to think I had to clean my windows twice a year and my kitchen floor every week. Now I don't. I have to spend my energy on other things.'*

It is important for your health that the person sleeps at night or at least is safe at night if she is awake. (We discuss this problem in more detail in Chapter 7: 'Sleep Disturbances'.) If you are regularly up in the night and still caring for the person all day, your body is paying a price in exhaustion, and you will not be able to keep up such a routine indefinitely. We know that you cannot always get enough rest. However, it is important that you know your own limits. We have made suggestions throughout this book which will help you find ways to avoid complete exhaustion.

Illness

Illness is a camp follower of depression and fatigue. It often seems that people who are discouraged and tired are sick more frequently than others. And people who aren't feeling well are more tired and discouraged. When someone else is dependent on you for care, your sickness can become a serious problem. Who takes care of the confused person when you have the flu? You, probably. You may feel that you have no choice but to keep on dragging yourself around and hope you don't wear out.

Our bodies and our minds are not separate entities; neither is one the slave of the other. They are both parts that make up a whole person, and that whole person can be made less vulnerable—but not invulnerable—to disease.

Do what you can to reduce fatigue and to get enough rest. Eat a well-balanced diet. Get enough exercise.

Arrange to take a holiday or to have some time away from your duties as care-giver.

Avoid abusing yourself with alcohol, drugs, or overeating. Ask your GP to check you routinely for hidden problems such as high blood pressure or anaemia and chronic low-grade infections.

Few of us do all that we can to maintain good health even when we have no other serious problems. When you are caring for a chronically ill person, there is often not enough time, energy, or money to go around, and it is yourself that most often goes without. However, for your sake, and, very importantly, for the sick person's sake, you must do what you can to maintain your health.

Sexuality

It can seem insensitive to think about your own sexuality when there are so many pressing worries—a chronic illness, financial concerns, and so forth. However, people have a life-long need to be loved and touched, and sexuality is a part of our adulthood. It deserves to be considered. Sometimes sex becomes a problem in a dementing illness, but sometimes it remains one of the good things a couple still enjoys. This section is for those couples for whom it has become a problem. Do not read this *expecting* a problem to develop.

If your spouse is impaired

Despite the so-called sexual revolution, most people, including many doctors, are uncomfortable talking about sex, especially when it involves older people or handicapped people. This embarrassment, combined with misconceptions about human sexuality, can leave the spouse or companion of a person with a dementing illness alone in silence. Many articles on sex are no help; the subject often cannot be discussed with one's friends, and, if one gets up the courage to ask the doctor, he may quickly change the subject.

At the same time, sexual problems, like many other problems, are often easier to face when they can be acknowledged and talked over with an understanding person.

The spouse of a brain-impaired person may find it impossible to enjoy a sexual relationship when so many other aspects of the relationship have changed so drastically. For many people their sexual relationship can only be good when the whole relationship is good. You may be unable to make love with a person with whom you can no longer enjoy sharing conversation, for example. It may not seem 'right' to enjoy sex with a person who has changed so much.

When you are feeling overwhelmed by the tasks of caring for a sick person, when you are tired and depressed, you may be totally uninterested in sex. Sometimes the person with the dementing illness is depressed or moody and loses interest in sex. If this happens early, before the correct diagnosis has been made, it can be misinterpreted as trouble in the relationship.

Sometimes the sexual behaviour of a person with a brain disorder may change in ways that are hard for his partner to accept or manage. When the impaired person cannot remember things for more than a few minutes, she may still be able to make love, and want to make love, but will almost immediately forget when it is over, leaving her spouse or partner heartbroken and alone. A few such experiences can make you want to end this aspect of life forever.

Sometimes the person you have cared for all day may say, 'Who are you? What are you doing in my bed?' Such things can be heartbreaking.

Memory loss sometimes causes a formerly gentle and considerate person to forget the happy preliminaries to sex. This, too, can be discouraging for the partner.

Occasionally a brain injury or brain disease will cause a person to become sexually demanding. It can be devastating to a spouse when a person who needs so much care in other ways makes frequent demands for sex. When the sexual behaviour of a person with a dementing illness changes, this very likely relates to the brain injury or brain damage and is something the person cannot help, rather than being a purposeful affront to your relationship.

Often what people miss most is not the act of sexual intercourse but the touching, holding, and affection that exist between two people. Sometimes, for practical reasons, the well spouse chooses to sleep in a separate room. Sometimes a formerly affectionate person will no longer accept affection when he becomes ill.

Mr Bishop says, 'We always used to touch each other in our sleep. Now if I put an arm across her she jerks away.'

What can you do about problems of sexuality? Like many of the other problems, there are no easy answers.

It is important that you understand from your spouse's doctor the nature of her brain damage and how it affects this and all other aspects of behaviour. If you seek help with this problem, be sure that the counsellor is qualified. Since sexuality is such a sensitive issue, some counsellors are not comfortable discussing it or they give inappropriate advice. The counsellor should have experience addressing the sexual concerns of handicapped people and should clearly understand the nature of a dementing illness. He should be aware of his own feelings about sexual activity in elderly or handicapped people. There are excellent counsellors who have talked about sexuality with many families and who will not be shocked or surprised at what you say. There are also some insensitive people posing as sex counsellors whom you will want to avoid. SPOD, Sexual and Personal Relationships of the Disabled, 286 Camden Road, London N7 (tel. 01 607 8851/2) will give advice on these matters.

If your impaired parent lives with you

So far we have discussed the problems of the spouse of a person with a dementing illness. However, if your ill parent has come to live with you, the sexual aspect of your marriage can be badly disrupted, and this can affect other areas of your relationship. You may be too tired to make love, or you may have stopped going out together in the evening and thus lost the romance that precedes love making. Your confused parent may wander around the house at night, banging things, knocking on your door, or shouting. The least little noise may rouse the parent you tried so hard to get to sleep. Love making can turn into hurried sex when you are too tired to care, or it can cease altogether.

Relationships are enriched by all of the parts of a relationship: talking together, working together, facing trouble together, making love together. A strong relationship can survive having things put aside for a while but not for a long time. It is important that you find the time and energy to sustain a good relationship. Carefully review the discussion in Chapter 13. Make yourself find ways to create the romance and privacy you need at times when neither of you is exhausted.

The future

It is important that you plan for the future. The future will bring changes for the person with a dementing illness and many of these changes will be less painful if you are prepared for them.

Some husbands and wives discuss the future while both of them are well. If you can do this, you will feel more comfortable going on by yourself, knowing what your partner wished for you. If she wishes to do so, the forgetful person may talk about the future when she is unable to care for herself or after her death. Planning how she will dispose of her possessions sometimes helps a person to feel that this is her life, and that she has some control over the end of her life. Other people will not want to think about these things and should not be pressured to do so.

Members of the family may also want to discuss what the future will bring, talking it over, perhaps a little at a time. Sometimes, thinking about the future is too painful for some members of the family. If this happens, you may have to plan alone.

Here are some of the things you will want to consider. (We have discussed each of these concerns elsewhere in this book.)

What will the ill person be like as his illness progresses and as he becomes increasingly physically disabled?
What kind of care will he need?
How much will you honestly be able to continue to give to this person?
At what point will your own emotional resources be exhausted?
What other responsibilities do you have that must be considered?
Do you have a spouse, children, or a job that also demands your time and energies?
What effect will this added burden have on your marriage, on growing children, or on your career?
Where can you turn for help?
How much help will the rest of the family give you?
What financial resources are available for this person's care?
What will be left for you to live on after you have met the expenses of care? It is important to make financial plans for the future even if you and the ill person have only a limited income. The care of a severely ill person can be expensive (see Chapter 15).
What legal provisions have been made for this person's care?
Will the physical environment make it difficult for you to care for an invalid?

Do you live in a house with stairs that the person will eventually be unable to manage? Do you live in a big house that may be difficult to maintain? Do you live a long way from the shops? Do you live in an area where crime is a problem?

As time passes, you, the care-giver, may change. In some ways you may not be the same person you were before this illness. You may have given up friends and hobbies because of this illness, or you may have changed your philosophy or your ideas in the process of learning to accept this chronic illness. What will your future be like? What should you do to prepare for it?

You as a spouse alone

This was a difficult section of this book for us to write. We know that husbands and wives think about their futures but we have no 'right' answers to give you. Each person is unique. What is right for one person is not right for another, and only you can make those decisions. However, as you think through these things, there are several factors you will want to consider.

Your status changes. Sometimes a spouse feels that she is neither part of a couple (because they cannot still do things together, still talk together, and still rely on each other in the same ways) nor a widow.

Couples sometimes find that friends drift away from them. This is a particularly difficult problem for the well partner. 'Couple' friends often drift away simply because the friendship was based on the relationship among four people which has now changed. Establishing new friendships can be difficult when you can no longer include your spouse and yet you still have the responsibility for his care. You may not want to make new friends alone.

You may face a future without the ill person. Statistics indicate that dementing illnesses shorten the life of the victim. It is probable that she will die before you do or that she will become so ill that she needs hospital or nursing home care.

It is important that when the time comes and you are alone, you have friends and interests of your own.

A husband told of trying to write an account of what it is like to live with a person suffering from a dementing illness. He said, 'I realised that I was telling the story of my own deterioration. I gave up my job to take care of her, then I had no time for my hobbies, and gradually we stopped seeing our friends.'

As the illness progresses and the person needs more and more care, you may find yourself giving up more and more of your own life in order to care for her. Friends do drift away, there is no time for hobbies, and you find yourself alone with an invalid.

What then happens to you after she has become so ill that she must be placed in a nursing home or hospital or after she dies? Will you have 'deteriorated'—become isolated, without other interests, lonely, used up? You need your friends and your hobbies through the long illness to give yourself support and a change of pace from the job of care giver. You are going to need them very much after you are left alone.

The marital relationship between husband and wife changes. The problems of being alone but not single are real. However, the relationship usually continues to have meaning. For some this means a continuing commitment to a changed relationship. For some it means establishing a new relationship with another person.

One husband said, 'I will always take care of her but I've started going out with other women again. She is no longer the person I married.'

A wife says, 'It was a terribly difficult decision. For me, the guilt was the hardest part.'

Another husband said, 'For me, caring for her, keeping my promise, is most important. It is true that she is not the same, but this too is a part of our marriage. I try to see it as a challenge.'

Sometimes it happens that a person falls in love again while he is still caring for his ill spouse. If this happens to you, you face difficult decisions about your own beliefs and values. Perhaps you will want to talk this over with other people close to you. Perhaps the 'right' decision is the decision that is 'right' for you.

Not all marriages have been happy. When a marriage was so unhappy that a spouse was already considering divorce when the person became ill, the illness can make the decision more difficult. A good counsellor can help you sort out your mixed feelings.

In any event, should you be faced with questions about new relationships, divorce, or remarriage, you are not alone. Many others have also faced—and resolved—these things.

13 Caring for yourself

The sick person's well-being depends directly on your well-being. *It is essential that you find ways to care for yourself so that you will not exhaust your own emotional and physical resources.*

When you care for a person who has a dementing illness, you may feel sad, discouraged, frustrated, or trapped. You may be tired or overburdened. While there are many reasons for feeling fatigued, the most common is not getting enough rest. You may put aside your own needs for rest, friends, and time alone in order to care for the sick person.

Throughout this book we have offered suggestions for ways to modify annoying behaviour. While modifying the person's behaviour will help considerably, it is often not possible to eliminate some forms of behaviour and they may continue to get on your nerves. In order to continue to cope, you will need to get enough rest and sometimes to get away from the ill person.

It is not unusual for family members to feel alone in their struggle with a chronic illness. Friends drift away and one doesn't know about other people with similar problems. It may seem impossible to get out of the house, and life narrows down to a tight circle of lonely misery. Feelings of sadness and grief seem more painful when you also feel alone with your problem.

For all of these reasons you need to take care of yourself. You need enough rest, time away from the sick person, and friends to enjoy, to share your problems with, and to laugh with. You may find that you need additionally to cope with your feelings of discouragement or to sort out the disagreements in the family. You may decide that it will help you to join other families to exchange concerns, to make new friends, and to advocate better resources for people with dementing illnesses.

Take time off

'If only I could get away from "Alzheimer's disease,"' Mrs Murray said. 'If only I could go somewhere I didn't have to think about "Alzheimer's disease" for a little while.'

It is absolutely essential—both for you and for the person with a dementing illness—that you have regular times to 'get away' from twenty-four-hour care of the chronically ill person. You must have some time to rest and to be able to do some things *just for yourself*. This might be sitting down uninterrupted to watch TV or it might be sleeping through the night. It may mean going out once a week or taking a holiday. We cannot overemphasise the importance of this. The continued care of a person with a dementing illness can be an exhausting and emotionally draining job. It is quite possible to collapse under the load.

It is important that you have other people to help you, to talk with, and to share your problems. We know that it can be difficult to find ways to care for yourself. You may not have understanding friends, your family may not be willing to help, and it may seem impossible to get time away from the sick person. The confused person may refuse to stay with anyone else, or you may not be able to afford help. Finding ways to meet your own needs often takes effort and ingenuity. However, it is so important that it must be done.

If resources to give you time off are difficult to find, perhaps you can piece together a respite plan. For example,

Mr Cooke was under considerable stress as he was caring for his wife seven days a week. He thought there was no help available until he discussed the problem first with his GP and then with a social worker. The latter arranged for Mrs Cooke to attend an Age Concern day centre one day a week and for a Crossroads Care Attendant to take over caring for Mrs Cooke every Friday afternoon.

You may also have to compromise and accept a plan that is not as good as you would like. The care others give may not be the same as the care you try to give. The confused person may be upset by the changes. Family members may complain about being asked to help. Paying for care may mean small financial sacrifices, for example there is often a charge for transport to day centres and charges for Crossroads Care. But be persistent in your search for help, and be willing to piece things together and to make compromises.

Taking time off, away from the care of the confused person, is one of the single most important things that you can do to make it possible for you to continue to care for someone with a dementing illness.

Mrs Murray went on, 'We had planned for a long time to go to France when he retired. When I knew he would never be able to go, I went alone. I left him with my son. I was scared to go alone, so I went with a tour group. He would have wanted me to, and when I came back I was rested—ready to face whatever came next.'

Give yourself a present

Could you do with a 'lift' once in a while? An occasional self-indulgence is another way to help yourself cope. Some people may buy themselves 'presents'—a magazine or a new dress. Listen to a record, stand outside and watch the sunset, order your favourite restaurant meal as a take away.

Friends

Friends are often marvellously comforting, supportive, and helpful. The support of good friends will do much to keep you going through the hardest times. Remember that it is important for you to continue to have friends and social contacts. Try not to feel guilty about maintaining or establishing friendships on your own.

Sometimes friends and neighbours find it hard to accept that a person is ill when he *looks* fine. Sometimes, too, people shy away from 'mental' illnesses. Many people do not know how to act around a person who is forgetful or whose behaviour changes. You may want to explain that this is an organic disease that causes gradual deterioration of the mind. The person cannot help his behaviour and he is not 'crazy' or 'psychotic'. There is no evidence that the disease is contagious. It is a disease condition and not the inevitable result of old age.

Even if the person can talk quite reasonably, and a casual observer cannot see any sign of mental deterioration, he may still not remember names or really follow conversations. It is important to explain to friends that forgetfulness is not bad manners but something the person cannot avoid.

It can be painful to tell old friends what is happening, especially those who do not live nearby and have not seen the gradual changes a dementing disease causes. Some families have solved this problem by composing a Christmas letter, lovingly and honestly sharing this illness with distant friends.

Avoid isolation

What can you do if you find yourself becoming isolated? It take energy and effort to make new friends at a time when you may be feeling tired and discouraged. But this is so important that you must make the necessary effort. Start by finding one small resource for yourself. Little things will give you the guidance and energy to find others. Join a carers' group or get one going yourself. Renew ties with your church, or other religious group. Your rabbi, priest or minister can offer you comfort and support. Friendships within the church can develop, and some churches have resources to provide practical help for you.

As you find time for yourself away from the person you are caring for, use that time to do things with other people: pursue a hobby or attend discussion groups, New friends are most easily made when you are involved in activities you have in common with other people.

We know that it is difficult to find the time or energy to do anything beyond the necessary care of the sick person. Some activities can be put to one side while you are burdened with care, but they must not be completely discontinued. This is important. When the time comes that you no longer have the care of this person, you will need friends and activities.

> *'I used to be a leading member of the Women's Institute but can no longer attend regularly. I still make the occasional cake for bazaars and keep in touch . . . later I hope to become a more active member.'*

'I play the violin. I can't play with the quartet anymore, but I keep in touch with them and I still practice a little. When I have more time, there will be a place for me in the local symphony orchestra.'

You may also become involved in new activities, such as joining a local branch of the Alzheimer's Disease Society or Association of Carers. Some spouses have deliberately sought out new activities.

'My wife became unwell just about the same time as I retired. All I was doing was taking care of her. I thought I should get some exercise, so I joined a senior citizens' exercise group. I take my wife to the day centre on the day I go to that group.'

Find additional help if you need it

Mrs Scott says, 'I worry that I am drinking too much. John and I used to have a drink when he got home in the evening. Now, of course, he doesn't drink, but I find I have to have that sherry and another one at bedtime.'

Fatigue, discouragement, anger, grief, despair, guilt, and ambivalence are all normal feelings that may come with caring for a chronically ill person. Such feelings may seem overwhelming and almost constant. The burden you carry can be staggering. Sometimes one's coping skills are overwhelmed and things can drift out of control. You may want to seek professional help if this happens.

Recognise the warning signs

Each individual is different and each person has his own ways of responding to problems. A healthy response for one person may be unhealthy for another. Ask yourself the following questions: Do I feel so sad or depressed that I am not functioning as I should? Am I often lying awake at night worrying? Am I losing weight? Do I feel overwhelmed most of the time? Do I feel terribly isolated and alone with my problem? While depression and discouragement are common feelings for families of people with chronic diseases, if you are often lying awake at night worrying, if you are losing weight, or if you usually feel isolated, alone with your problem, or overwhelmed, perhaps you need some help to keep your feelings manageable.

Am I drinking too much? Definitions of alcohol abuse vary widely. The amount of alcohol that is too much for one person may not be too much for another. Ask yourself: Is my drinking interfering with how I function with my family, or my job, or in other ways? If it is, you are drinking too much. Are you ever drinking too much to care properly for the sick person? Are others—your co-workers, for example—having to 'cover' for you? Alcoholics Anonymous (listed in the telephone directory) is a good self-help organisation. Call them, explain your special circumstances, and ask for their assistance.

Am I using pills to get me through each day? Tranquillisers and sleeping pills should be used only under the careful supervision of a doctor and only for a short time. If you are already using tranquillisers or sleeping pills on a regular basis, ask a doctor to help you give them up. Some of these drugs create a drug dependency. Abrupt withdrawal can be life-threatening and must be supervised by a doctor.

Let's imagine you are abusing alcohol or medications. You have joined the ranks of thousands of other ordinary people. There is no reason to be ashamed. There *is* a reason to get help *now*.

Am I drinking too much coffee each day? While not nearly as serious as dependency on stimulant drugs, such as amphetamines, excessive caffeine use can be hard on your body and can reduce your ability to manage stress. (Caffeine is also found in tea and most soft drinks.)

Am I screaming or crying too much? Am I often losing my temper with the impaired person? Am I hitting him? Do I find myself more angry and frustrated after I talk with my friends or family about these problems? Do I find that I am getting irritable with a lot of people—friends, my family, the doctors, my co-workers—more than just one or two people in my life?

How much screaming or crying is too much? One person may feel that any crying is too much, while another feels that crying is a good way to 'get things out of my system'. You probably know already if your moods are exceeding what is normal for you.

Anger and frustration are normal responses to caring for a person whose behaviour is difficult. However, when your anger begins to spill over into many relationships or when you take your anger out on the sick person, it may be helpful to find ways to manage your frustrations so that it does not drive people away from you or make the impaired person's behaviour worse.

Am I thinking about suicide?

Mr Cameron said, 'There was a time when I considered giving my wife an overdose, and then killing myself.'

The thought of suicide can come when a person is feeling overwhelmed, helpless, and alone. When someone feels that he cannot escape an impossible situation or feels that he has irrevocably lost the things that make life worth living, he may consider suicide. Suicide may be considered if someone feels that the situation he faces is hopeless, that there is nothing either he or anyone else can do. The present can seem intolerable, and the future appears bleak, dark, empty, and meaningless.

One family member who attempted suicide said, 'Looking back, I don't know why I felt that way. Things have been hard, but I'm glad I didn't die. My perceptions must have been all mixed up.'

This consideration—that one's perception is that things are hopeless—is important. If you are feeling this way, it is imperative to find another person (a counsellor or social worker) whose perception of the situation may be different and with whom you can talk.

Do I feel that I am out of control of my situation or at the end of my tether? Is my body telling me I am under too much stress? Do I often feel panicky, nervous, or frightened? Would it help just to talk the whole thing over with someone who understands? If the answer to some of these questions is yes, it may be that you are carrying too heavy a burden without enough help.

Counselling

It may be that all you need is more time away from a seemingly demanding, difficult person or more help in caring for him. But perhaps you see no way to find more help or more time for yourself. Perhaps you see yourself trapped by your situation. We feel that talking these problems over with a trained person is one good way to help you to feel less pressured. You and he can sort out the problems you face a bit at a time. Since he is not as caught up in the problem as you are, he may be able to see workable alternatives you had not thought of. At the same time you will know that you have a life line in this person that you can turn to when you begin to feel desperate. Family or friends can be of help as well, but if they are too close to the situation they may not be able to see things objectively.

Should you get counselling? Do you need 'help'? Most people are not 'sick', 'crazy' or 'neurotic'. Most people are healthy individuals who sometimes have trouble coping with real problems. They may feel overwhelmed or discouraged, or find that they are thinking in circles. Such a person may find that talking over feelings and problems helps to clarify them.

We believe that most people most of the time do not need counselling. However, we know that counselling is sometimes a great help to families struggling with a dementing illness. Such help may come from discussion groups, clergy, an objective friend, or a social worker, nurse, psychologist, or doctor.

The first step in seeking outside help is often the hardest. One's reasoning sometimes goes around and around in circles.

> *'I can't get out of the house because I can't get a sitter. He's terrible to anyone in the house but me. I can't have counselling because I can't leave the house and a counsellor couldn't help me with that anyway.'*

This kind of circular thinking is partly the product of your situation and partly the way you, in your discouragement, see the problem. A good counsellor can help you objectively separate the problem into more manageable parts, and together you can begin to make changes a little at a time.

Sometimes people feel that it is a sign of their own weakness or inadequacy to go to a counsellor. With the burden you carry in coping with a dementing illness, you can use all the help you can get, and this is not a reflection on your strength.

People sometimes avoid counselling because they think that the therapist will delve into their childhood and 'analyse' them. Many therapists begin directly by helping you in a matter-of-fact way to cope with 'here and now' concerns. Find out in advance what approach the therapist you select prefers. If you decide to seek counselling, the kind of counsellor you choose may be influenced by who is available, and who is knowledgeable about dementing illnesses.

Psychiatrists are doctors and they are able to prescribe drugs to treat mental illness. They have a good understanding of physical problems that accompany psychological problems. Psychologists, social workers, psychiatric nurses, clergy, and some other professionals can have excellent therapeutic or counselling skills. If they do, they may be an excellent choice for counselling. You will want to select a person who is knowledgeable about dementing illnesses, and with whom you feel comfortable.

You have a responsibility to discuss with the counsellor your concerns about your relationship with him. If you have a private counsellor and are worried about your bill, or if you don't like his approach or if you wonder if he is telling your family what you have said, *ask* him.

There are several ways to find a counsellor. If you have an established relationship with a GP with whom you feel comfortable, ask if he can counsel you or can refer you to someone he feels is a good counsellor. Ask a health visitor. If you have friends who have had counselling, ask them if they liked the person they consulted. If there is an active carers' group in your area, ask if there is someone other members have consulted. Ask your GP if you can see a specialist.

Not all counsellors are equally good, nor are they all knowledgeable about dementia. Select a counsellor as carefully as you would any other service you seek.

Joining with other carers: a step beyond

Many carers feel alone with this illness, unable to find doctors, other professionals, or friends who understand, and unable to get information. To meet this need for communication, carers and support groups in many areas have established volunteer organisations. These groups are involved in helping each other, sharing solutions to management problems, exchanging information, supporting needed legislation and research, and educating the community. These organisations welcome members who are concerned about all of the dementing illnesses, of which Alzheimer's disease is the most common. Over and over, all over the country, carers tell us how important it is to know others who are faced with these problems. The number of carers' support groups is growing rapidly. These groups offer friendship, information about the diseases, and information about resources and doctors in your area, and they give their members the opportunity to exchange ideas about how to manage.

While there is a number of independent local carers' groups, many have been set up in association with or are supported by national organisations which can put you in touch with local contacts and groups. The Alzheimer's Disease Society specialises in the needs of carers looking after people with all kinds of dementia. The Association of Carers and the National Council for Carers and their Elderly Dependants both cater for carers of all sorts of dependants, including dementia sufferers. Some Age Concern groups run carers' support groups. The national addresses are listed in Appendix 2. Many groups provide mutual support in the format of a forum for the discussion of common problems and also practical help such as sitting services and advice.

Some organisations publish newsletters that may be helpful to you even if you live too far away to attend meetings. Newsletters give ideas on how to cope, notices of changes in legal policies and insurance coverage, and news about new research.

It is through organisation that legislative attention will be focused on the needs of families and patients.

Setting up an organisation or support group

If no group exists near you, consider forming one yourself. Start out by finding three or four other families and perhaps a helpful professional (social worker, or community psychiatric nurse). It is not hard to find other families. Word of mouth will probably turn up three or four. Local ministers, nursing homes, district nurses, social workers, and Age Concern groups can put you in touch with others.

Your group can begin by writing for information from other groups and by informally exchanging ideas. The national organisations listed above may be able to help you form a carers' group. Here, however, are some particular suggestions:

1 At the first meeting, establish specific time limits for meetings and stick to them. Meetings that run late may become a burden. For the same reason, if refreshments are served, agree to keep them simple.
2 Set simple, specific objectives for each meeting. These could be 'informal discussion of problems' or 'electing officers', but objectives will help keep the group on target.
3 Avoid tackling too much at a time. A few concrete, attainable goals are less likely to overwhelm people already under pressure in their private lives.
4 Be informed. Find out what other groups are doing.

5 Discuss the members' responsibility to maintain confidentiality about personal information shared in the group.
6 Different people have different ways of reacting to crisis. Make it clear from the start that members will not be judgmental.
7 Agree to let each person have time to talk, so that no one person dominates the conversation.

Family members who are caring for a sick person at home may have little energy left over for the work of organising a group. Some families whose loved one has entered a nursing home or has died are happy to participate and will be a resource to the group. Also, professionals who work with the elderly may wish to join the group and can lend their skills to help keep the group going. Local community psychiatric services, voluntary organisations, Social Services Departments and churches may be willing to sponsor a group. They may also have staff with expertise in setting up the organisation.

Sharing groups

Many organisations and hospitals have established discussion groups for carers. These are small sharing groups led by a trained therapist. Families find these groups helpful. Such groups can be set up by anyone with skills in group therapy.

Peer support groups

Lay support groups sometimes operate without professional guidance. Such groups should have goals of mutual encouragement and not be used as therapy groups. They should consist of four to ten people. One way to organise the leadership is to meet each time at a different home. The discussion leader for that meeting is the host, thus rotating leadership through the group. It is often helpful for members to make a commitment to regular participation for a certain set number of meetings. At the first meeting, discuss items 1, 5, 6 and 7 listed previously under 'Setting Up a Group'. In addition, remember that this is not a therapy group; it is a group for mutual exchange and support. Give each person present an opportunity to talk. One or two people should not monopolise the discussion. Good group members avoid giving each other advice. Instead, they listen with interest and concern and give information.

Advocacy and activism

Throughout this book we have emphasised the need for resources to help you. However, the unfortunate fact is that resources you need may not be available, doctors and other professionals are often not well informed about dementing illnesses, and funding for patient care and research may not be available. It has been estimated that ¾ million people in the UK are impaired with a dementing illness and in addition, many may suffer from mild cognitive impairment. Clearly, the prevailing lack of interest in these diseases and the assumption that 'senility' is not even a disease is unfounded and unjust and leads to a lack of services.

Only when the public and the policy makers recognise that dementias are diseases and become aware of the needs of the patients and families will new resources and adequate funding be made available. You may want to do what you can to urge that new or better resources be developed, or that unjust policies be changed. You may want to help to educate those who are not informed about dementia. Here are some ways in which to make your efforts most effective.

1 Discuss your opinion with your MP and local councillors and ask what you can do to support change. Give them your specific concerns in writing.
2 Act as a pressure group with other carers of people with dementing illnesses. Contact the Alzheimer's Disease Society and Association of Carers.
3 Give written information or bibliographies about these problems to the people, including doctors, with whom you have contact.

14 For children and teenagers

This chapter is written especially for the young people who live with or know a person with a dementing illness. Most young people will be able to read and understand the rest of the book as well.

It is important that you understand what is wrong with the person and why he acts as he does. When you understand why the person does certain things, it is easier not to be angry with him. Also, it is important that you understand that he acts as he does because he is sick, not because he wants to or because of you. The person has a disease that destroys part of the brain. With a larger number of brain cells lost, the brain cannot work as it should. That is why the person forgets names, is clumsy, or can't talk properly. Parts of the brain that knew how to do these things have been damaged.

Sometimes these people get upset over little things. That is because the brain can no longer understand what is going on (even when you explain it to the person). The parts of the brain that make us behave as we should are also damaged, so the person cannot control his actions. He cannot help himself. Sometimes people with dementing illnesses don't look ill or act in a strange way, but they may criticise you or correct you too much. The person may not be able to help this because his illness makes him forget things.

You may worry about what will happen to the person or about whether something you do might make him worse, especially when you are not sure what is happening. Most likely nothing you can do will make the person worse. You can make him temporarily more upset, but this does not make his condition worse.

If you worry about things, ask questions. Read other parts of the book. You may want to go back to it from time to time. Read any other material you can find on these diseases also. Ask your parents or the doctor treating the person what you want to know. You will get the best results if you bring the subject up when there are not a lot of other things going on and when the adults are not too tired. However, sometimes adults try to keep bad news from young people.

When you read or talk about these diseases, what you find out may be discouraging. The person may not get well. You may react by feeling bad about the whole thing. If there are things you really don't want to know, don't feel that you are expected to ask about them. Many people have mixed feelings—you may feel sorry for the sick person but also angry that he has to live in your house. Your moods may change a lot too. Sometimes you may put the whole thing out of your mind and not even be able to think about it. Most of these reactions are the normal result of facing problems.

Even under the best circumstances, living with an illness like this is hard. Here are some of the things that young people have told us are problems.

'No privacy: Grandad walks into my room whenever he wants.'
'Having to be quiet. Not being able to play the stereo. As soon as I come in the door I have to be quiet or Grandad gets excited.'
'The way he eats makes me feel sick.'
'I can't bring my friends over because they upset Grandad. Also, I don't want to bring them over because he acts in such strange ways.'
'Having to give up my room.'
'Everybody depends on me more. I have to take a lot of responsibility.'
'Everybody is so busy with Grandad and so tired, we never do anything enjoyable as a family anymore.'
'I'm afraid of what he will do.'
'I'm afraid he will die.'
'I just feel discouraged all the time.'
'My parents become angry with me more than they used to.'

You may have some of the same concerns as these. You may be stuck with some problems, like having to be quiet or having to give up your room. Some things are easier when you understand what is wrong with the person. You can't cope with some things alone and you may need to get an adult to help you. Sometimes it is helpful to pick out the one thing that bothers you the most and ask your family to help you change that. Often, together you can come up with compromises that will help. For example, you might be able to put a lock on your door or get earphones for your stereo. If you have given up your room, perhaps you and your friends can fix up a place in the garage or garden shed where you can get away from the sick person.

Some young people tell us that it is not the sick person's behaviour that is the worst problem, but it is how their parents or the sick person's husband or wife acts that is the worst problem.

'I don't mind Grandad, but Grandmother moved in too, and she wants me to do everything just like she did when she was young.'
'It isn't Grandad, it's my mother always fighting with my grandmother.'

These may be real problems for you. The person who is your grandparent is also a wife or husband of a sick person and is probably upset. Even when a person doesn't get upset he may be feeling sad or unhappy, and this may make that person cross or impatient or hard to live with. Probably the best you can do is to be understanding, since you know that grief and worry are the causes of the trouble. When a grandparent is setting strict standards for you or nagging you, ask your parents to tell you how they want you to manage this. If things get too difficult, find an adult who is not tired and upset—perhaps somebody outside your family—whom you can talk it over with.

Most of what we have written has been for people whose grandparent is ill, because usually people's children are grown before they develop a dementing illness. However, sometimes this illness strikes one's own parents. If it is your father or mother who is ill, life is probably really difficult. We hope this book will help you. However, no book can solve problems that are happening in *your* house with *your* family.

It is important for you and your well parent to talk about what is happening and the problems you are having. In addition, it may be helpful for you, your well parent, and any other children in the family to find someone with whom you can all talk from time to time. If your well parent is unable to seek help, you may have to ask the doctor or your teachers to help you. No one with a parent who has a dementing illness should have to cope by himself.

Belonging to a scout troop, a youth club, an athletic team, or some other group such as a class for learning guitar playing, will give you a chance to get away from the troubles at home and to get your mind on having fun with other young people.

Things are not all bad when a person has a dementing illness. Young people often have clever ideas about how to solve problems that the rest of the family may not have thought of. Also, perhaps because not too long ago you were little, you probably have a lot of understanding for the person who is confused. You will probably do a lot of growing up during this time and you may look back on it with pride.

It is important to remember, when you are caught in a situation you cannot control, that you *do* have control over how you react to it. You decide how a bad situation affects your life.

If your marks at school drop, or if you are fighting with your parents a lot or opting out most of the time, you need to talk the problem over with someone. Often you can talk things over with your parents, other adult friends, or teachers. Some people are easy to talk to and some are not. Sometimes a counsellor is a good person to talk with. If you cannot talk to your parents, your teachers can usually help you find a counsellor. Some people feel funny about talking to a counsellor. It isn't because there is something 'wrong' with you that you want counselling. Here are some of the things that happen with a good counsellor or someone else who is a good listener.

You can find out what's going on.
You can let off steam.
You can talk to your parents with the counsellor helping so that you don't fight with them.
You can find out what your parents are thinking.
You can say all you want about your side of the problem.
You can ask about things that worry you—such as whether the sick person will die—in private.

None of these things may solve the problem, but they will make living with the problem easier.

You might like to contact the National Association of Young People's Counselling and Advisory Services, National Youth Bureau, 17–23 Albion Street, Leicester LE1 6GD.

15 Financial and legal issues

To discuss in detail the financial and legal issues that may arise around the care of a person with a dementing illness is beyond the purpose and scope of this book. However, we have outlined some of the key factors for you to consider. You may need to seek professional financial and legal advice.

Your financial assessment

Providing care for the person with a chronic illness can be costly. In addition, the older person may be living on a fixed income and inflation can be expected to continue to eat into that income. It is important that you assess both available financial resources and potentially increasing costs of care, and make plans for the impaired person's financial future. If you are a spouse, your own financial future may well be affected by decisions and plans you make now. Many factors must be considered in assessing your financial future, including the nature of the illness and your individual expectations.

Begin by assessing the potential costs of care both now and as the person becomes more severely impaired and assessing her available resources. Whether the ill person has little income or is affluent, it is most important that you plan ahead for her financial future.

Potential Expenses

Potential lost income:
Will the impaired person have to give up her job?
Will someone who would otherwise be employed have to stay at home to care for the person?
Will their pension rights be affected?
Will the real purchasing power of a fixed income decline as inflation rises?

Potential housing costs:
Will you or the impaired person have to move to a home that is without stairs, closer to services, or easier to maintain?
Will you move a parent into your home? This may mean expenses of renovating a room for her.
Will the person enter a residential or nursing home, long stay hospital or sheltered housing?
Will you have to make modifications to your home (new locks, grab rails, safety devices, wheel chair ramps)?

Potential medical costs:
Will you need:

private medical care?
appliances (bath aids and other adaptations)?

Potential cost of help or respite care:
Will you need
someone to help in the home?
someone to stay with the person?
someone to help with care?
day care?

Potential food costs:
Will there be costs of having meals prepared or of eating out?

Transportation costs: someone to drive if you cannot; taxis.

Taxes.

Legal fees.

Miscellaneous costs:
Easy-to-use clothing, incontinence supplies, laundry service, various devices for safety or convenience may be listed here.

Nursing home costs.

Potential resources

The impaired person's resources

You will want to look first at the sick person's own assets and financial resources. Consider occupational and state pensions, savings accounts, property, cars, and any other potential sources of income or capital.

Occasionally, an impaired person become secretive about her finances. At the end of this chapter we list some of the possible available resources and where to look for them.

Resources from the state

If the impaired person is below state retirement age, and is unable to continue work, there may be an entitlement to sickness benefit for up to 28 weeks. After that there is automatic entitlement to invalidity benefit which is paid up to state retirement age or up to the age of 70 (65 women)—for more information see Social Security leaflet N16 (Sickness Benefit) and N1 16A (Invalidity Benefit). If the person first became incapable more than 5 years before state retirement age there may be an additional entitlement to an invalidity allowance.

For those who are not entitled to an invalidity benefit, there was a non-contributory invalidity pension instead. It has now been replaced by a Severe Disablement Allowance which is available for the first time to those under 65 (men) and 60 (women). They must have been incapable of work for at least 2 weeks. If they are over 20 when the incapacity begins, they must be assessed as being over 75 per cent disabled.

If the impaired person's income is not sufficient to cover basic living costs, additional help may be forthcoming from a supplementary benefit which will assess her needs against resources. If the impaired person is a man of 60 or more he may be able to get the long-term rate of supplementary benefit. If he is under 60, he may receive this if he has been on invalidity benefit for a year. Leaflet 56 from the Social Security Office will give more information. On top of a basic needs allowance which is higher for the long-term rate of supplementary benefit, regular support can also be given towards water rates, heating, ground rent, insurance and repairs, interest payments on a mortgage and laundry for incontinence. Single payments are also available for special needs for essential items. They are hard to obtain but Social Security leaflet SB16 gives further information. Help can also be achieved towards housing costs through the Housing Benefit scheme which covers general rates and rent for private, housing association or council tenants. It is administered by London Borough, Metropolitan Borough and District Councils in the counties. Ask at your local council office for information.

If the impaired person has needed the attention of another person by day or by night for at least six months, an Attendance Allowance is available. This is paid at a lower rate for day or night supervision and a higher rate for someone who needs 24 hour attention. There is a claim form for this (DS2 attached to an explanatory leaflet N1 205) available at the local Social Security Office. If the impaired person has a physical handicap they may be eligible for a Mobility Allowance. This is paid to people who become unable or virtually unable to walk before their 65th birthday. It can be claimed until the age of 66. Claim form MY1 is attached to explanatory leaflet NI211 and is also available from the Social Security office.

Where the person is being cared for by someone who cannot work because they spend at least 35 hours a week in caring, they may be able to claim the Invalid Care Allowance. This is not available for married or cohabiting women. Claim form DS 700 attached to explanatory leaflet NI 212 can also be obtained from the local Social Security office. When the carer has to stop work, contributions to the basic state pension can be protected under the Home Responsibilities Protection Scheme (leaflet NP 27).

Resources of the impaired person's spouse, children, and other relatives

(Also see Chapter 11.)

There are no legal requirements on children and other relatives to give financial support but there are laws relating to the financial responsibility of the spouse. If the impaired person is left without income or insufficient for her needs, Social Security will have regard to the income of the spouse in calculating any means tested benefit. This can be complicated and not all social workers or lawyers are completely familiar with them (also read pp. 191–2 on financing nursing home care).

In some cases (such as with state pensions) a divorced wife may be entitled to benefits from a former husband. It is important to know about laws that may affect a well spouse if the ill spouse may eventually need expensive care. Advance planning may protect the spouse financially. This is important for families of modest means as well as for more affluent families.

Resources from a pension

Where a person is forced to leave work before retirement age, there may be income from an occupational pension. It will be necessary to consult with the employer, personnel officer or trade union to see what rights the pension fund will give.

A state retirement pension is paid to those who have paid enough national insurance contributions or to wives on their husbands' contributions. It cannot be paid before the age of 65 for a man and 60 for a woman in her own right, although her husband could receive a dependant's allowance if she is below that age and he is over 65. If the impaired person leaves work early, the local Social Security office will be able to tell her how much her pension will be when she reaches retirement age. Other forms of benefit will be available before that time, based on national insurance contributions that have been made or through means tested benefits.

Resources from insurance

If a private health insurance policy is held it may cover active medical treatment but health insurance policies often contain exclusions that affect payment for dementing or chronic illnesses. You need to know exactly what your insurance covers. Find out what life insurance policies the person has and whether these can be a resource. Some insurance policies waive the premiums if the insured person becomes disabled. This is a saving for her.

Legal matters

(Also see Chapter 9.)

The time may come when a person with a dementing illness cannot continue to take legal or financial responsibility for herself. This may mean that she can no longer balance a cheque book or that she has forgotten what financial assets or debts she has. It may mean that she is unable to decide responsibly what to do with property or to give permission for needed medical care.

Often these abilities are not all lost at once. A person who is unable to manage her cheque book may still be able to make a will or accept medical care. However, as her impairment increases, she may gradually reach the point where she cannot make any decisions for herself, and someone else will have to assume legal responsibility for her.

The most efficient way to prepare for this eventual disability (which could happen to any of us) is for the person to make plans for herself before she reaches the time when she cannot do so. A person should make a will while she is still considered legally competent to do so. This is called *testamentary capacity*. It means that the person knows without prompting that she is making a will, the names of and her relationship to the people who will receive her property, and the nature and extent of the property.

A person who is still able to manage her own affairs (by the above definition) may sign a *power of attorney*, which gives a spouse, child, or any other person who has reached legal age authority to manage her property. A power of attorney can give broad authority to the specified person or it can be limited. A limited power of attorney only gives the person authority to do specific things (sell a house or review income tax records, for example).

Since a power of attorney authorises someone to act on another person's behalf, the person giving such power must be sure that the one selected will, in fact, act in her best interests. Someone who holds a power of attorney is legally responsible to act in the other person's best interests, but once in a while someone abuses this responsibility.

We believe that it is important to discuss with a lawyer what plans you should make, so that he can advise you on how best to protect the confused person and what type of powers should be transferred, and so that you can be sure that whatever papers are drawn up are legally valid.

At the present moment once the person is unable to handle their own affairs the power of attorney becomes invalid, but a new Act of Parliament has established an enduring power of attorney which will continue to operate when the person is no longer able to handle their own affairs. This should become operative in 1986.

Some people are unwilling to sign a power of attorney, have no one that they trust to do this, or may already be too impaired to do so. If this is the case, you will need the help of a solicitor. Ask a friend or family member to recommend one. If you do not know a solicitor, you can call the Law Society, 113 Chancery Lane, London WC1 (tel. 01 242 1222), and they can give you the names of lawyers near you. Lists should be available also in your local library. Lawyers may specialise in different areas of the law (criminal law, corporate law, divorce law, civil law), just as doctors specialise in different areas of medicine. You have a right to know what you can expect from the lawyer and what his fees are. Misunderstandings can be avoided by discussing with him what he charges and what services you will get for that fee. Find out if he practices this sort of law and is knowledgeable about it.

If the person is currently unable to manage her property and affairs effectively because of her disability, it is usually necessary to apply to the Court of Protection, 25 Store Street, London WC1E 7BP (tel. 01 636 6877) for an order appointing someone to act on behalf of a 'patient' to receive the income and administer the property under the direction of the court. Such a person is called a Receiver and is often a relative or close friend. If there is no relation or friend able or willing to act or because there is a family disagreement, the Court can order an official of the Court to be appointed as Receiver. In certain small cases, the appointment of a Receiver may not be necessary, the matter being dealt with by a simple order authorising the relative or friend to use the patient's means sensibly without a Receiver having been appointed. Details of this are on leaflet PN1 from the Court.

Application to the Court may be made by any person (but preferably by a near relative) either by instructing a solicitor to carry through the application in which case the solicitor will prepare the necessary forms or alternatively, an application can be made with the assistance of the Personal Application Branch of the Court. Unless an estate is a small one, fees are payable to cover the cost of administration but the Court can postpone or waive the fees in cases of hardship. Leaflets are available from the Court on its procedures as is a booklet on the duties and responsibilities of a Receiver.

In many cases neither a power of attorney nor powers under the Court of Protection are sought. It may be possible to provide for the impaired person's needs out of income which can be utilised by simpler procedures. For example, Social Security Benefits or pensions can be managed by an agent; that is the holder of the pension book signs on the front of the order book and on the back it states that a named person can collect the account and sign the order form. Where this is happening regularly, the Department of Health and Social Security may issue a card stating that the named person is authorised to collect the money on behalf of the book holder. Another procedure allows benefits and pensions to be managed by an appointee on her behalf (Form BF56 from the Social Security Office). Some occupational pensions are handled in the same manner; inquiries should be made to the employer, personnel officer or trade union for further information. If this income is sufficient there may be no need to use capital assets such as savings which can remain lodged in a safe place. However, when circumstances change radically there may be need to seek legal powers of action, for instance the home may need to be sold for the person's benefit.

If a home is owned jointly by a husband and wife, and one of them becomes impaired, the well spouse will need a power of attorney or power gained through the Court of Protection in order to sell the home.

Sometimes a disabled person is unable to care for her daily needs and must have medical care or nursing home care. She may refuse to consent to this or may be unable to make such decisions. Often a hospital or nursing home will accept the consent of the next of kin: a husband or wife, or a son or daughter. Sometimes, however, application will have to be made to the hospital managers under Section 3 of the 1983 Mental Health Act by either the nearest relative or an approved social worker supported by two medical recommendations that the person should be compulsorily admitted to hospital. Application might also be made to the local authority for guardianship by the same procedure under Sections 7 and 8 of the Act, which will require the person to live at a certain place, attend for medical treatment or allow access where the patient is residing for treatment.

Where to look for the forgetful person's resources

Sometimes an impaired person forgets what financial resources she has or what debts she owes. People may be private about their resources or disorganised in recording them. Sometimes suspiciousness is a part of the illness and the individual hides what she has. Families may not know what resources a person has that could be used to provide for her care. Finding out what resources a person has can be difficult, especially when things are in disarray or are hidden.

Debts usually turn up on their own, often in the post. Most businesses will be understanding if a debt or bill is not paid on time. When you do find a bill, ring the company, explain the circumstances, and arrange with them how and when the bill will be paid. If the confused person is losing the post you may be able to have it held for you at the post office.

Assets may be harder to find. Review recent post. Look in the obvious places such as a desk, an office, clothing, and other places where papers are kept. Look under the bed, in shoe boxes, in pockets of clothes, in old purses, in kettles or other kitchen items, under rugs, and in jewellery boxes.

One wife asked the grandchildren to join her in a 'treasure hunt'. The children thought of obscure places to look. Look for: bank statements, cancelled cheques, bank books, savings books, pass-books, or cheque books; keys; address books; insurance policies; receipts; business or legal correspondence. The Inland Revenue will help with queries on Income Tax if the person enquiring has a power of attorney or powers under the Court of Protection.

There are many kinds of assets:

Bank accounts. Look for bank books, bank statements, cheque books, savings books, pass-books, statements of interest paid, joint accounts held with others. Most banks will not release information about accounts, loans, or investments to anyone whose name is not on the account. However, they may give limited information (such as whether there is an account in an individual's name) if you send a letter to the bank from your doctor or lawyer explaining the nature of the person's disability and the reason you need the information. Banks will release information about the amount in an account or about current transactions only to a properly authorised person. However often you can piece together what you need to know from papers you can find.

Share certificates, bonds, savings certificates and account, building society accounts. Look for the actual bonds, pass-books, notices of payments due, notices of dividends paid, earnings claimed on income tax, regular amount paid out from bank account receipts. Look for cancelled cheques, correspondence, or receipts from a broker. Look for record of purchases or sale.

Insurance policies (life insurance, disability insurance, health insurance). These are among the most frequently overlooked assets. Life insurance policies and health insurance policies may pay lump sum or other benefits. Look for premium notices, policies, or cancelled cheques that give you the name of the insurer. Contact him for full information about the policy. Some insurers will release this information upon receipt of a letter from a doctor or solicitor; others will need proof of your legal right to information.

Safe deposit boxes. Look for a key, bill, or receipt. You will need a court order to be permitted to open the box.

Property (houses, land, businesses, rental property, joint ownership or partial ownership of the above). Look for regular payments into or from a current account, gains or losses declared on income tax, keys, fire insurance premiums (on houses, businesses and other property). The insurance agent may be able to help you. Look for rating notices on properties. Ownership of property is a matter of public record. The Land Registry may be able to help you locate properties, if you are a properly authorised person.

Retirement or disability benefits. These are also often overlooked. You must apply for Social Security. Spouses and divorced spouses may also be eligible for benefits. Special benefits may be available from past employment, union membership and military service. Check into retirement or disability benefits from all past employers. Look for an old curriculum vitae which will list previous jobs. Look for benefit letters.

Collections, gold, jewellery, cash, loose gems, cars, antiques, art, boats, camera equipment, furniture, other negotiable property. In addition to looking for such items, look for valuable items listed on property insurance policies. Some of these items are small enough to be easily hidden. Others may be in plain sight and so familiar as to be overlooked.

Wills. If the individual has made a will, it should list her assets. Wills, if not hidden, are often kept in a safe deposit box, recorded by the court, or kept by one's solicitor.

Trust accounts. Look for statements of interest paid.

Personal loans. Look for withdrawals, payments, correspondence, maintenance payments (occasionally divorce settlements provide for payment of maintenance should the wife become disabled).

Foreign bank accounts. Look for statements of interest paid, bank statements.

Inheritance. Find out whether the impaired person is someone else's heir.

Cemetery plot. Look for evidence of purchase.

16 Residential and other long stay provision

A time may come when it is no longer sensible or realistic for someone who is suffering from dementia to continue living on their own or with a caring relative or friend. When that occasion arises several forms of accommodation might be considered but the main options are a residential home, a nursing home, or long stay hospital provision. The decision that your relative should go and live in a home or hospital is not one to be taken lightly, particularly as such a step may be seen by your relative as finally giving up her last independence, although this need not be the case. For both the well being of the elderly person and for your own peace of mind it is therefore advisable to consider whether it really is necessary for your dependant to leave her present home.

Making a decision about long stay care

Remember that with *adequate* support it is possible for very confused elderly people to remain in their own homes. The range of support services which may be available have already been described and imaginative schemes which provide care to dementing people between the early hours of the morning when they get up and late at night when they go to bed do exist. It is therefore worth checking to see that there is no provision which you have overlooked which may enable your relative to 'stay put'. Do not be afraid to admit your lack of knowledge and ask for help. Research conducted among carers of demented relatives in Glasgow found an alarmingly high level of ignorance of what support existed as no one, including GPs, had thought to give them the necessary information.

Services for confused elderly people are often overstretched and it is important to consider whether they really are *adequate* for your needs and those of your relative. Comprehensive care, from 7 o'clock in the morning until 11 o'clock in the evening, and tailored to meet the precise needs of the individual, may be sufficient. Such support, however, is the exception rather than the rule and the limited range of services which are likely to be offered—Meals-on-Wheels, home help, day care, and community nurses —may not be enough when the elderly person is very confused and perhaps also physically frail, incontinent, and generally difficult to look after. The appropriateness and extent of support services is thus one important factor to consider when deciding whether your relative should enter residential care. It may well be the case that you could cope with looking after your mother if she attended a day centre two days a week, but if there is no day centre or no places available and you are already under a considerable strain, it may well be appropriate to look for a residential or nursing home, or hospital bed.

Other indications that residential care is necessary could include:

A deterioration in the physical and mental health of your elderly dependant. You may find that you can cope with dementia but the onset of incontinence or the habit of constant and repetitive questioning may prove a last straw.

You not being able to control your relative wandering from home and getting lost. This is particularly worrying at night.

Your own health suffering as a result of the strain of caring. If you become unwell you can neither properly look after your elderly dependant nor any other dependants such as a spouse or children.

The health and well being of other members of the family suffering. They may rightly or wrongly feel that you are neglecting them or be disturbed by constant sleepless nights. This could, for example, be important when children are studying for exams.

There may be other considerations to bear in mind, particularly as each person's circumstances are different, and at the end of the day it will be your decision that your relative should go into a home or hospital. Nevertheless, if you think about things calmly you can confidently proceed on the basis that what you have decided is right for you, your dependant, and your family.

If a stage has been reached when you feel you can no longer carry on caring, try and take a break so that you can reflect on the situation. A relative or close friend might come and stay in your home to look after your dependant while you go away for a few days. It may be possible for your dependant to go into hospital, or a residential or nursing home for a week or two to enable you to have some relief. Similarly, some local authorities and voluntary organisations organise family placement or fostering schemes whereby an elderly person can go and stay in the home of someone paid to look after her. Ask your doctor or a social worker if there are any such opportunities for respite in your area. Having had a break you may decide that you want to continue looking after your relative. On the other hand, you may now believe that long stay care for your confused relative is in everyone's best interest. Unfortunately, not all carers will have access to short stay or respite accommodation but in any case you should consider matters carefully and consult widely.

The views of other members of the family should be sought. If you have brothers and sisters they may feel they have a right to be consulted on your mother's future. They may wish to take over the caring role. They may have some ideas about how to deal with the present situation. They may not want your parent to go into a home and may subsequently raise objections. There may be financial implications which unfortunately can often cause deep resentments within families as some members see their 'inheritance' disappearing as residential home fees are paid. For all these reasons it is important that all interested parties are given an opportunity to have their say in the matter. Everyone should have the full facts and a chance to ask questions so it may be easiest to call a 'family conference' to which you could invite your dependant's family doctor or social worker who can explain the situation and describe the options available. If the family is in full agreement so much the better but if at the end of the day there is disagreement on how to proceed and nobody else is prepared to look after the dementing relative you will have to make your own decision about what to do, assured in the knowledge that you have consulted everyone affected.

Often friends know better than your family so it may be helpful and comforting to discuss the situation with them. They may know what homes exist locally if they have looked after an elderly parent. The value of carers' support groups is discussed elsewhere in this book and if you belong to one it is obviously appropriate to discuss questions about long stay care with other members of the group. The Association of Carers and the Alzheimer's Disease Society will give you the names and addresses of their local contacts who may be able to advise you.

In addition to discussing the matter with other members of the family, you should also be advised by relevant professional staff: the GP and a social worker or, if your relative has them, the community psychiatric nurse, community nurse, geriatrician or psychogeriatrician. Each will be able to advise you on what they think is the best form of care or refer you to a more specialist opinion. They will explain the options. If you find your GP is unsympathetic you may find it helpful to talk to a health visitor or community psychiatric nurse who you will be able to reach through your doctor's surgery. When you are contemplating placing your relative in long stay care, it is always advisable to have her medical needs properly assessed by either a doctor or a specialist.

In your discussions with the family and outside agencies do not forget the need to consult with the confused relative whose future you are deciding. It is a good idea to involve her as much as possible and to ask her what she thinks. This will make her less likely to resist any changes which you see as unavoidable. People with dementia may fear change and they may function less effectively in unfamiliar surroundings. That is why it may be helpful if your relative has visited a home with you several tirnes before she goes there to live permanently or if she has attended a day centre which is run in that home. If, however, your relative is so confused that she cannot understand, you may find it less distressing if you make the arrangements on your own.

As with so many things, the need to 'be prepared' applies to finding long stay care. In many areas there are shortages of such accommodation and once you have decided that your relative needs this care it can be very frustrating to find there are no places available and that you face a long waiting list. Hindsight is of little comfort so if you think you are ever likely to need long stay care for your relative it is advisable to gather as much information as well in advance as possible.

Conversely, however, many elderly people enter hospital and other forms of long term care in emergency or crisis situations, perhaps following a fall, medical complication, or unexpected breakdown in the system of care. Such emergency admissions can be very bewildering, disruptive and alarming for a confused elderly person and it is therefore expedient to try to make preparations for these admissions, in so far as it is possible to plan for crisis situations. You could, for example, discuss the possibility of going into hospital or a home with your dependant and point out the advantages.

Types of care

Confused elderly people are found in several different forms of long stay care, rather suggesting that no one type of care is necessarily the most appropriate form for this client group. Research conducted in the early 1980s showed that 50 per cent of residents in old people's homes, 65 per cent of patients in geriatric hospitals, and 90 per cent of residents in psychogeriatric hospitals wards were confused. While in theory distinctions may be drawn between the different forms of care and for whom it caters, in practice these differences are often blurred.

There are three main categories of long stay care for confused elderly people:

1 Residential Care Homes, which are run by local authorities, voluntary agencies, and private organisations.
2 Nursing Homes which, with the exception of the three experimental NHS nursing homes, are run by private and voluntary organisations.
3 Long stay hospital provision which may be in geriatric wards or in psychogeriatric wards which are part of a psychiatric hospital.

A further form of care which often seems attractive, perhaps because it seems less 'institutional' to caring relatives, is sheltered housing. This is fairly independent, self-contained accommodation in two or three rooms and each resident has her own front door. Often there is a warden on site who has the job of keeping a watchful eye on residents to ensure that they are all right and managing. The warden is not expected to provide any form of care or nursing but will alert other agencies when help is needed. Most sheltered housing schemes have alarm systems which the resident can operate in emergency situations. Occupants of sheltered housing, while they may receive the services provided to other elderly people in their own homes—Meals-on-Wheels, home help and district nursing—are expected to look after themselves and be fairly independent. For this reason sheltered accommodation is not really an option for confused elderly people who might not, for example, be able to operate an alarm or be able to alert the warden. They may also wander off, leave stoves alight, and be more confused than if they were in their own home. Unless there is a special sheltered housing complex catering for confused and dementing elderly people in your locality—and there are few such schemes in existence—sheltered housing is not really worth exploring in any depth.

An early inquiry to your local social services department or Age Concern group will inform you of any such special schemes in your area.

Local authority homes

The Social Services Department of each local council runs residential homes for frail elderly people. They can have a variety of different names but are often called 'Part III homes' after the part of the National Assistance Act 1948 which empowered local authorities to make such provision. It is left to each local authority to decide how many homes and places it provides and consequently there are quite marked variations throughout the country. In recent years moreover there has been a tendency to stop building or opening new council homes and also to provide more short-term care in existing homes. As a result of these factors there are usually long waiting lists for places in Part III homes.

Many local authority homes are staffed by sensitive, caring people who provide a high standard of care. While you would expect a uniform level of care in all council run homes, staff shortages and a lack of resources can lead to some homes justifiably having poor reputations. Guidance on assessing a home is given below, but if you have any doubts, you could ask your local Age Concern group or Community Health Council what they think about a particular home.

Whether a Part III home will take a confused elderly person sometimes depends upon the degree of mental impairment. Some local authorities may have a policy that it is not fair on the mentally alert residents to provide care to large numbers of very confused and disruptive people since this may disturb them and destroy the homely atmosphere of a residence. Others argue that such an environment can be maintained if no more than 25–30 per cent of the residents are confused. In practice, the proportion of confused residents in many homes may be much greater and this may be a factor you may wish to consider in choosing a home—you might inquire if there are sufficient staff to meet the needs of all the confused and alert residents.

Problems in balancing the needs of lucid against confused elderly people has led some local authorities to open specialist homes for mentally infirm people. With only around seventy specialist homes being run by about forty local authorities in England, this sort of provision is not widespread and indeed its desirability has been questioned. Such homes can be difficult to staff and pose tremendous problems in providing a normal lifestyle for residents. Nevertheless, these difficulties are not insurmountable and high quality care is provided in some of these homes run by local authorities, sometimes in association with the local psychogeriatric service.

Places in local authority homes are centrally allocated and applications should be made not to an individual home but to the Social Services Department. If you have already been allocated a social worker who is supporting you and your dependant, contact him or her and say that you wish to apply for a place in a council home. In other circumstances you should make a similar request in writing and send your letter to the 'Residential Care Services Section' at the main office of your local authority's Social Services Department. The address will be in the telephone directory but you can also obtain it from the library, local Citizens' Advice Bureau or Age Concern group.

After the initial application, a social worker will visit you to assess the needs of your relative. You will be given a form to complete usually seeking details of your relative's physical and mental condition, degree of independence, present circumstances, and financial position. On the basis of this information your relative will be placed on a waiting list. Support from your GP may lead to your case being given priority but usually there is a long wait. The social worker may be able to give you some idea of waiting times and if they prove to be lengthy it is always advisable to remind the Social Services Department every four to six months or so that you are still interested. Be prepared for a long wait and if your circumstances do not allow this, consider other sources of care.

When a place in a home is offered you will usually be required to accept or reject it within a few days. If you are not familiar with the home, arrange to visit it and discuss the needs of your relative with the staff. A place in another home may not be available for a very long time, so consider this offer very carefully. It may be possible for your relative to have a trial stay in the home, particularly if she is not too confused, and this should be requested. Once however you have decided to accept the offer, your relative will be expected to take up residence fairly quickly.

Private and voluntary homes

Until quite recently, local authorities provided most of the available residential care. In the past few years, however, there has been a large expansion in the number of private residential homes which, apart from some inner city districts, are now found in nearly all parts of the country and not just in the traditional south coast and retirement areas. Private homes are run for profit by private organisations and individual proprietors and while this sector is tremendously varied, it contains examples of both the best and the worst quality of care provided anywhere.

Voluntary homes are non-profit making and are run by charities and religious organisations. Sometimes such homes are open only to particular groups, followers of a certain faith or denomination or people with special needs, illnesses or other common characteristics. Some voluntary homes may, for example, cater just for retired teachers, lawyers, actors, or ex-members of forces. Residents and their relatives may feel reassured by the fact that a voluntary home is being sponsored by a recognised charity to which redress may be sought if there is ever cause for complaint.

These homes vary in size and may be quite small, perhaps taking no more than 8–12 residents, in comparison with the 30 or more often cared for in local authority homes. Voluntary homes are likely to have a waiting list for places, as may private homes although the recent expansion of the private sector has meant that places are more easy to find. Both sorts of homes can choose to whom they offer accommodation and a number of private and voluntary homes provide care to confused elderly people. Nevertheless, some may shy away from what they see as a difficult and demanding client group.

In recent months the legislation and regulations controlling private and voluntary homes have been strengthened in an effort to achieve uniformity throughout the country, promote high quality care, and safeguard the rights of residents. Any home providing personal care to four or more elderly and dependent people is required by law to register with and be inspected at least annually by the local authority. It is a punishable offence to operate an unregistered home and it is most unwise to place a relative in a home which is not registered. Registration should only be granted if the people owning and running the home are suitable, if adequate services and facilities are provided, and if the building is suitable. The local authority will specify on the certificate of registration the number and type of residents a home may accommodate. By law residential care homes are required to display the certificate of registration 'in a conspicuous place' and to maintain certain records. The Department of Health and Social Security maintains a national list of people whose registration has been cancelled.

The type of care provided in a private or voluntary home can be an area of contention and it is sensible to ascertain this right from the start. These homes are not expected to provide nursing care but are expected to provide a level of care which is equivalent to that which might be given by a competent and caring relative who is able to respond to both physical and emotional needs. This need not prevent a *confused* person being cared for in a residential home—she may not need nursing—and in any case she would still be able to receive general practitioner services, community nursing, including night nursing, as though she were in her own home. Nevertheless, if a person does need continuous nursing, a nursing home would be more appropriate than a residential home. It is illegal for a residential home to act as a nursing home.

Applications for places in private and voluntary homes should usually be made to the home in question which will provide you with details of charges and conditions. If you know of a home which you like or one which has been recommended by friends so much the better. Often, however, members of the public are unsure of how to find a private home. All private and voluntary homes are required to register and so each local authority will have a list of non-statutory homes in its area. You could ask the Registration Officer for Private Homes, based in the local Social Services Department, to see a copy of the list. Social workers may also be able to provide you with details of private homes and while they cannot recommend a particular home they may be able to advise you on 'the appropriateness' of certain homes for meeting the needs of your relative.

Other agencies which might help you find a home include the local Age Concern group, the Community Health Council and local branches of the National Confederation of Registered Rest Homes Association. Visits are made to private homes in the Greater London area by Counsel and Care for the Elderly which will recommend homes in the metropolis and provide general advice on seeking private residential accommodation. As the private market expands it is likely that a number of private agencies will be set up to help the public locate homes. GRACE (Mrs Gould's Residential Advisory Services for the Elderly) is one such agency which offers detailed information on private homes in Southern England and while a small booking fee is charged, this will be waived in exceptional circumstances.

Nursing homes

The three experimental National Health Service nursing homes in Sheffield, Fleetwood and Portsmouth will be inaccessible to most people and in any case can provide care to fewer than a hundred patients. While some nursing homes are provided by voluntary organisations, the majority are run by private organisations. As their title suggests, nursing homes provide nursing care by qualified nurses to people suffering from sickness, injury, or infirmity. It is the provision of nursing, as opposed to simply care, which differentiates them from residential homes.

Any home providing nursing care to more than one person has to be registered with the District Health Authority and inspected by it at least twice a year. By law the person in charge must be either a registered medical practitioner or a qualified nurse and there should be adequate staff on duty throughout the day so that each patient can have efficient nursing care from suitably qualified staff 24 hours a day. The certificate of registration, which must be displayed in a conspicuous place, will state the maximum number of people for whom the nursing home can care. The District Health Authority will also issue a notice specifying the required qualifications of the nursing staff which will have been determined in the context of such factors as the number and type of patients in the home.

As with private residential homes, the legislation and regulations governing private nursing homes were strengthened in 1984 in an effort to improve the standard of provision. Health authorities have been instructed to visit and inspect any unregistered premises thought to be acting as a nursing home and a national list of cancelled registrations is being compiled. It is also now an offence to describe a premises as a nursing or mental nursing home if it has not been registered with the District Health Authority. It is hoped that this provision will now give the public an assurance that any home advertised as a nursing home has been registered and inspected by the District Health Authority.

Personal recommendation from people with relatives who have experienced a stay in a private nursing home is the best way to find a suitable home for your dependant. Failing that you could contact the District Nursing Officer of your local District Health Authority who has responsibility for registering nursing homes and she may be able to provide you with a list of homes in the area. The local Social Services Department, Community Health Council, Age Concern group, Citizens' Advice Bureau, or Council of Voluntary Service may also be able to provide you with a list or make recommendations. Counsel and Care for the Elderly visits and provides information on homes in the Greater London area and the Registered Nursing Homes Association publishes a national directory of its members, thereby providing the addresses of a number of homes throughout the country.

Dual registered homes

The category of 'dual registered home' was created in legislation passed in 1984 and while there are probably only a few such homes in existence brief details are given here so that readers will have some knowledge should they encounter them. A worry sometimes expressed about residential homes, which may be more real in theory than in practice, is that because they can only provide residential care, if residents become very ill or disabled and so require nursing, they may be forced to leave their present home and then be placed in either a nursing home or a hospital. The new legislation enables a residential home to also register as a nursing home and so provide the two sorts of care either in a resident's own room, in separate parts of the home or in a distinct wing. This avoids the need to transfer very frail or confused residents out of residential homes.

Even though the whole of the home will be dual registered the home is still required to state the maximum number of people to whom each type of care will be provided. This is because the registration will only be granted if a certain number of nurses with specified qualifications are provided. This number is determined by the number and type of patients needing nursing.

Each part of the dual registered home will be subjected to the same regulations, controls and inspections as a residential or nursing home, as outlined above, and will in addition receive joint inspections from the District Health Authority and local authority. As this type of home constitutes a new departure it remains to be seen how effective it is in comparison with the usual residential and nursing homes. Nevertheless, it may be assumed that since dual registered homes are a fresh development, they will be closely scrutinised and monitored to begin with at least.

Which home is best?

It is important to choose the 'right' home since it would be upsetting to both you and your relative if you made a mistake. In addition to the agencies, already listed, which may be able to give you names and addresses of homes and make recommendations, you could also ask your local Age Concern group, Citizens' Advice Bureau or Community Health Council for an opinion on particular homes. One basic rule to remember when thinking about a private home is that you should never consider an unregistered home. Always make inquiries about this and ask to see the certificate of registration. The points which follow apply to all homes, residential and nursing, and statutory, voluntary and private alike.

Problems in finding a home can make it very tempting to accept the first place which has an empty bed. This should be resisted and if you have time it is a good idea to look at several establishments. Because of the recent expansion in the market, vacancies in private homes are now quite common in some areas. Certainly, you should always visit the home, have a good look round and chat to the staff and person in charge. In particular you should observe the residents, speak to them and consider whether they seem contented. Are they sitting round doing nothing or are they involved in activities? Is there a homely, warm and busy environment? Do the staff seem interested and caring? How long have they been in post and is the staff turnover high? Do you think your relative would fit in?

It is a good sign if the home publishes a *brochure* outlining what it provides, the philosophy of the home, and the charges. Make sure, however, that the reality of the home matches how it is portrayed in the brochure and check that you know all the charges, including those for any extra services. There may be some, for example, for additional laundry costs for residents who are incontinent. Aim to collect the fullest information possible on the prospective home for your relative and then make a decision. You will know the sorts of things which please and upset you and your relative and which are important to you both so find out if these individual needs will be met. There will be an endless list of questions you will probably want to ask but some points which are worth considering include:

Do the residents share or have their own single rooms?
Are they encouraged to bring personal possessions with them, such as photographs, ornaments, and small items of furniture?
What are the meals like?
Is the home clean and safe? Check the bathroom and kitchen.
Are there aids in the bathroom and toilet?
What are the fire drills and when was the last practice?
Are there free visiting hours and is there provision for residents to speak to their visitors in private?
What activities go on in the home and are residents encouraged to continue their hobbies?

Do residents keep their own general practitioner?
How are medicines administered and what records are kept?
What is the complaints procedure?
Under what conditions would a resident be asked to leave?

All these questions relate to the quality of life in the home and are vitally important. Other issues to bear in mind are listed in *Home Life: A Code of Practice for Residential Care* published by the Centre for Policy on Ageing and which is intended for *staff* running private and voluntary residential homes, although it could equally apply to local authority homes. The Code seeks to promote the highest quality of care possible. A similar code for nursing homes has been published by the National Association of Health Authorities. The codes will give you some idea of the ideal standards to which homes should be striving and they should be available from good libraries.

Many homes allow residents to have a trial stay for a few days or for several weeks and it is wise to take advantage of this provision if your circumstances allow. The actual experience of your relative living in a particular home will enable you both to judge how happy you both are with its arrangements. You will probably find that it will not take you long to 'get the feel' of the place and know if it will provide a satisfactory standard of care. Hopefully it will.

Long stay hospital care

If you believe that your relative now needs long stay hospital care the first person to approach is your family doctor who, if he agrees with you, will refer your dependant to a specialist or consultant. The sort of specialist who will be seen depends on the local service provided and the nature of your relative's illness. If your relative has a number of problems as well as a mental infirmity she may be seen by a consultant geriatrician who specialises in the general diseases of the elderly. When the dementia or confusion is the prime illness a consultant psychogeriatrician, who specialises in mental illness in old age, or a general psychiatrist may be called in. The specialist will make quite a detailed assessment of your relative's needs and often will make a home visit. Your relative may, however, be given an appointment with the consultant at an assessment unit in the hospital and you should go along to both support your dependant and also to ask and answer questions.

The consultant will conduct various tests and may keep your relative in an assessment ward for a short period for detailed examinations which may be carried out by both a geriatrician and a psychogeriatrician. The aim at this stage is to make an accurate diagnosis of what is wrong and to see whether your relative's condition can be improved. The consultant may decide that quite lengthy treatment or permanent long stay hospital care is needed and your relative may be sent home while the necessary arrangements are made. If a bed is immediately available your relative may be sent directly to the ward either for treatment and rehabilitation if her condition can be improved or for permanent care.

Often the hospital will treat your relative's condition and it will be suggested that she does not need hospital care but should be looked after in a residential or nursing home. The hospital may also propose that you continue looking after her at home. Unless you want to do so, you should resist this suggestion and argue that an alternative—either hospital care or a home—should be found. Unfortunately, it will often be left to you to find a suitable home and the hospital may try to discharge her to your home while you do so. If this happens you will need to speak firmly to the consultant and explain that you cannot look after your mother, are looking for a home, and want her to stay in the hospital until you have found one. A social worker, if you have one, may support your case.

If it is decided that your relative does need long stay hospital care you will probably feel a combination of different emotions—often sadness, grief and guilt. These feelings are quite usual but you should talk about them with your family, friends, a social worker, your doctor, or a relatives' support group. You can be assured that hospital care is what your relative needs. Moreover you should try and prepare her for going into hospital. You may have several days or weeks to do so while a bed is being found or while she is in the assessment ward. During that time find out what possessions and clothes should be taken into the hospital and check that they are clearly labelled with your relative's name. Also, if you can, spend some time explaining to your relative what is going to happen, that it is for the best, and that you, the family and friends will visit her in hospital.

The type of hospital and ward in which your relative will be placed will vary from area to area, depending on the type of service provided and what is available. She may be cared for in a geriatric ward or psychogeriatric ward of a general hospital, in a dementia unit, or in a ward for mentally ill elderly people in a psychiatric hospital. If your relative suffers from a severe degree of dementia and shows extreme behaviour disorders she is likely to be placed under the care of a psychogeriatrician in a psychiatric hospital. If she is mildly to moderately confused, with other medical problems, immobility and/or is doubly incontinent, she may be placed in a geriatric ward with elderly patients who although frail are quite alert.

In some districts the long stay wards are not located in the same hospital as the assessment and rehabilitation wards but are in a building several miles away. Unfortunately, it is also all too often the case that such wards are in old, Victorian buildings which may seem unfriendly and imposing. Many people are calling for the closure of such outmoded and dilapidated buildings and for their replacement with new purpose built wards. You may like to join in such a campaign, if one exists, and your local Age Concern group or Community Health Council will be able to give you details.

It is important to remember, however, that more important than the buildings is the quality of the care provided. Most hospital staff are very committed people who work in very difficult, sometimes understaffed, conditions. Occasionally things can go wrong and when you see this happening draw it to the attention of the hospital administration so that hopefully it will not happen again. Hospital administrators welcome comments on the services provided.

The standard of care provided in long stay wards is improving all the time and there is some very imaginative and exciting work being carried out with confused elderly patients. Some schemes involve volunteers from the local community who, working alongside hospital staff, spend much time improving the quality of the patients' lives. While the patient's dementia cannot be reversed it is claimed that with careful support the decline is sometimes arrested or slowed down. Do not look upon long stay hospital care as the end of the road for your relative but view it positively as the most appropriate form of care available. You will also find that since you no longer have the responsibility and tremendous stress of caring for your relative, you can now relate more favourably to her and be in a position to recall the happier times you have shared together.

Charges and financial implications

There is no charge for anyone who lives in a National Health Service Hospital (including NHS Nursing Homes) but those who stay in for a time will have part of their basic National Insurance Pension withdrawn. After the first 8 weeks the pension is partly reduced and after one year it is completely reduced to allow the patient only a personal spending allowance unless they have dependants outside hospital. Anyone holding a supplementary pension must notify Social Security immediately as some part of that pension may be withdrawn. The Attendance Allowance, if held, will be stopped after four weeks and the Invalid Care Allowance could be stopped immediately or may go on for twelve weeks. Leaflet NI9 on 'Going into Hospital' from your local DHSS office will give fuller details and current figures on the withdrawal of pensions.

No account is taken of other state pensions, that is the graduated and additional pensions, nor of other income from an occupational pension or of any savings. For anyone who had more income than the basic pensions it costs less to live in a NHS hospital than in a residential or nursing home.

Most people will not have sufficient income to enable them to pay for care in a home indefinitely; it is important therefore to look at the financial aspects of the situation a long time in advance.

Local authorities may charge for their residential home places, and must charge a minimum figure which relates to the level of the basic state pension leaving the resident a few pounds personal spending allowance, known as 'pocket money'. A cost figure is set for the place at the home and residents are then assessed to pay above the minimum in relation to their income based on a sliding scale which takes into account income and assets including in some circumstances the value of a family home and a contribution from the spouse outside the residential home. No contribution is required from other members of the family.

A similar procedure exists when a local authority sponsors someone in a private or voluntary residential home. As the situation is subject to change, you should consult your local Social Services Department and obtain a copy of the Fact Sheet 'Charges for elderly people in residential accommodation' from the Information Department at Age Concern England. This explains how the system works and the other avenues to financial support through the Department of Health and Social Security.

Social Security will help to pay for people in residential and nursing homes providing their income is not sufficient to pay for a place outright and their capital is below a certain limit. Capital assets will include a home and in certain circumstances spouses outside might be required to pay something towards care, although this will not be the normal circumstance. As with local authority support other members of the family are not expected to contribute to the cost of care.

If all resources are not sufficient to cover costs, advice on alternative financing can be obtained from Counsel and Care who may be able to indicate charitable help to top up income or tide over until statutory payments are arranged.

Sexual issues in residential homes, nursing homes and hospital

Some confused people in residential homes, nursing homes and hospitals, undress themselves in public, masturbate or make advances to staff or other residents. Sexual behaviour in these long-term care facilities differs in significant ways from such behaviour at home: it is no longer a private matter, but in one way or another has an impact on staff, other residents and the families of residents; and it raises the ethical issue of whether a person who is impaired can or should retain the right to make sexual decisions for himself.

While our culture seems to be saturated with talk about sex, it is the sexuality of the young and beautiful that is being discussed. Most of us are uncomfortable considering the sexuality of the old, the unattractive, the handicapped or the demented. Residential home, nursing home and hospital staff also often feel uncomfortable.

If the staff reports inappropriate behaviour to you, remember that much of the behaviour that at first seems sexual is really behaviour of disorientation and confusion. You and the staff can work together to help the person know where he is, where he can use the toilet, and where he can undress. Often all that is needed is to say 'It isn't time to go to bed yet. We'll put your pyjamas on later.' Distractions such as offering a glass of fruit squash or a cup of tea are helpful.

Confused persons may become close friends with another resident, often without a sexual relationship. Friendship is a universal need that does not stop when one becomes demented. Occasionally one hears stories about people getting in bed with other residents. This is not hard to understand when we consider that most of us have shared a bed with someone for many years and have enjoyed the closeness this sharing brings. The confused person may not realise where he is or whom he is with. He may not realise he is not in his own bed. He may feel that he is with his spouse. Remember that living in a home or hospital can be lonely, and there may not be much opportunity for the confused person to be held and loved. How you respond to such an incident depends on your attitudes and values and on the response of the staff.

Some residents will masturbate. The staff usually ignores such behaviour which is usually done in private. If it occurs in public the person should be quietly returned to his room or taken back to his bedside.

Some men make overtures to the staff. The irony of this is that many men have always enjoyed flirting with the ladies without offending anyone. When the staff matter-of-factly and kindly set limits, this behaviour seldom becomes a problem.

Carrying on caring

A feeling of relief may be the immediate reaction you will experience when your relative has been taken into long-term care. This is an entirely appropriate response as you will have spent considerable time and energy in the task of caring and probably received no thanks or recognition. You will have earned a rest. Often, however, feelings of guilt, regret, and anger quickly follow. You may think you are the only person who can properly care for your relative and wrongly see yourself as having 'dumped' your dependant in a home. Guilt arises because you are no longer caring and because you remember quarrels and outburst of temper which may have arisen in the past. You might regret that you are no longer caring despite the fact that to do so would be an impossible task. You may feel angry at the lack of services which meant you were unable to look after your relative at home. You may grieve an apparently lost relationship.

All these feelings are quite usual and should pass. If they persist, however, you should discuss them with your doctor, a social worker, perhaps the hospital social worker or possibly the carers' support group. Many carers continue to attend a group after their dependant has gone into a home or hospital. It will take time for you to adjust to a new life in which you do not have prime responsibility for caring for a mentally confused elderly person. Soon, however, you will pick up the threads of the life you led before you started having to provide 24 hour care and you will be able to do the things that you always promised yourself. You can plan and go on holiday, for example, start going out for meals, invite friends into your home, take up old hobbies, decorate the home, and generally and gradually adapt to having more free time on your hands.

It will, however, also take time for your relative to adjust to her new lifestyle and surroundings and it will be no easier for her than it is for you.

While it may be distressing for you at first, you can help your relative adapt to her new home and you may find it helps relieve feelings of guilt and regret to do so. As you are the person who knows your relative best of all, it will help, particulaly if she is very confused, if you can orientate her around the home or hospital, show her the toilet, bathroom and dining rooms, and explain who the different people are.

Remember that the person you once nursed is still a member of the family no matter how demented she is, and try to visit her as often as possible. Encourage other members of the family and friends to do so too, but first explain what they are likely to see. If you have a dog or cat which your relative liked when she lived with you, ask the hospital or caring staff if you can bring it into the hospital or home. Make sure the family continues to be important to your relative by showing and giving her photographs of other relations, giving her news of what grandchildren, nieces and other members of the family are doing, and remind her of birthdays and anniversaries. You may eventually be able to take her on outings and home overnight but discuss such ideas with the appropriate staff first and before you tell your relative as such activities may not be beneficial. Her routine may be disrupted too much and she may become very distressed when she returns to the hospital or home. On the other hand she may benefit from a change of environment and a short break.

There may also be opportunities for you to become more actively involved in looking after your relative, perhaps by helping to wash and dress her and assisting at meal times. There may be special projects—arts and crafts, reminiscence, music, cookery, and gardening, for example—with which you could help. Schemes of this nature can be very beneficial to the patients or residents but often the full time staff do not have the time to run them. The nursing and caring staff often like to see such activities going on as they make for a happier, interesting and creative home or hospital.

As well as your relative, the staff of the hospital or home will enjoy your visits. They like to see other people taking an interest in the patients and residents. Use your visits as an opportunity to talk to the staff and tell them about your relative and her past. This information is welcomed since, particularly if your relative is very demented, it enables them to relate to her more as an individual who has lived an interesting life, perhaps once held an important job, visited unusual places or whatever else she may have achieved—and everyone has achieved or contributed something to life. If the nursing and caring staff can think of your relative in these terms they will be better able to provide her with the sort of care and attention which you quite rightly think she deserves. The staff will derive greater satisfaction from this, your relative will be better off and you will find the long stay care which she is receiving less institutional and much more acceptable.

17 Brain disorders and the causes of dementia

Sometimes the brain does not work as it should. Such problems may be called retardation, dyslexia, dementia, or psychosis. They may be caused by an injury to the brain, a genetic condition, chemicals in the environment which are damaging to the brain, or many other things. In this chapter we will explain how dementia differs from other problems of the brain and describe some of the most common causes of dementia.

Dementia

Doctors and scientists group the different things that can go wrong with the brain by their symptoms. Just as fever, coughing, vomiting, and dizziness are symptoms of several different diseases, memory loss, confusion, personality change, and problems with speaking are also symptoms of several diseases.

Dementia is the medical term for a group of symptoms. It describes a global decline in intellectual ability sufficiently severe to interfere with a person's daily functioning, which occurs in a person who is awake and alert (not drowsy, intoxicated, or unable to pay attention). This decline in intellectual functioning means a loss of several kinds of mental processes that may include mathematical ability, vocabulary, abstract thinking, judgment, speaking, or coordination. It may include changes in personality. 'Not feeling quite as sharp as you used to' does not mean that one is developing a dementia. The person's ability must decline from what was normal for him. This is different from mental retardation, in which a person has been impaired since infancy.

These symptoms of dementia can be caused by many diseases. Some of the diseases are treatable; some are not. In some, the dementia can be stopped; in some it can be reversed; in others the primary condition cannot be changed. Some of these diseases are rare. Other diseases are not rare, but the people who have them do not usually become demented. Do not assume that a dementia is the inevitable result of having these diseases. A *partial* list of the conditions that can cause dementia follows:

Metabolic disorders:
- Thyroid, parathyroid, or adrenal gland dysfunction
- Liver or kidney dysfunction
- Certain vitamin deficiencies, such as Vitamin B-12 deficiency

Structural problems of the brain:
- Normal pressure hydrocephalus (abnormal flow of spinal fluid)
- Brain tumours
- Subdural haematoma (bleeding beneath the skull which results in collections of blood which press on the brain)

Trauma (injuries to the brain)
Hypoxia and anoxia (insufficient oxygen)

Infections:
Tuberculosis
Syphilis
Fungal, bacterial, and viral infections of the brain, such as meningitis or encephalitis

Toxins (poisons):
Carbon monoxide
Drugs
Metal poisoning
Alcohol (scientists disagree about whether alcohol can cause dementia)

Degenerative diseases (causes generally unknown):
Alzheimer's disease
Friedreich's ataxia
Huntington's chorea
Parkinson's disease
Pick's disease
Progressive supranuclear palsy
Wilson's disease

Vascular (blood vessel) disease:
Stroke or multi-infarct disease

Autoimmune diseases:
Temporal arteritis
Lupus erythematosus

Psychiatric diseases:
Depression
Schizophrenia

Multiple sclerosis

Korsakoff's syndrome causes an impairment only in memory and not in other mental functions. It looks like a dementing illness but, because it affects only one area of mental function, it is not a true dementia.

Most research indicates that about 50 per cent of the cases of dementia are caused by Alzheimer's disease, 20 per cent are caused by multi-infarct disease, and 20 per cent are caused by a combination of Alzheimer's disease and multi-infarct disease. About 10 per cent of the cases of dementia are caused by one or other of all the remaining conditions.

Alzheimer's disease

Alzheimer's disease was first described by a German physician, Alois Alzheimer, in 1907, and the condition was named after him. The disease Alzheimer originally described occurred in a woman in her fifties and was called *presenile dementia*. Neurologists now agree that the dementia that occurs in the elderly is the same as or similar to the presenile condition. It is usually called senile dementia of the Alzheimer's type (*SDAT*).

The symptoms of the disease usually are a gradual though sometimes imperceptible decline in many areas of intellectual abilities and an accompanying physical decline. Early in the illness only memory may be noticeably impaired. The person is more than a little forgetful. She may have difficulty learning new skills or difficulty with tasks that require abstract reasoning or calculation, such as maths. She may have trouble with her job or she may not enjoy reading as much as she used to. Her personality may change or she may become depressed.

Later, impairment in both language and motor abilities are seen. At first the person will be unable to find the right word for things or will use the wrong word, but she will gradually become unable to express herself. She will also have increasing trouble understanding explanations. She may give up reading or stop watching television. She may have increasing difficulty doing tasks that once were easy for her. Her handwriting may change or she may walk with a stoop or shuffle or become clumsy. She may get lost easily, forget that she has turned on the cooker, misunderstand what is going on, show poor judgment. She may have changes in her personality or uncharacteristic outbursts of anger. She will be unable to plan responsibly for herself. Families often do not notice the beginnings of language and motor problems, but as the disease progresses all of these symptoms will become apparent.

Late in the illness the person becomes severely impaired, incontinent, and unable to walk or may fall frequently. She may be unable to say more than one or two words, and may not recognise anyone or only one or two people. She will need nursing care from you or from professionals. She will be physically disabled as well as intellectually impaired.

Alzheimer's disease usually leads to death in about seven to ten years, but it can progress more quickly (three to four years) or more slowly (as much as fifteen years).

Under a microscope, changes can be seen in the structure of the brain of a person who suffered from Alzheimer's disease. These include abnormally large numbers of structures called neuritic plaques and neurofibrillary tangles (see Chapter 18). This is clearly an injury to the brain itself. A diagnosis of Alzheimer's disease can be made on the basis of the type of symptoms, the way the symptoms progress over time, the absence of any other cause for the condition, and a compatible CAT scan. However, a final diagnosis of Alzheimer's disease rests on the presence of these specific abnormal structures (neuritic plaques and neurofibrillary tangles) in the brain tissue. A brain biopsy is the only way of making this determination. The biopsy is done by removing a piece of skull bone and taking out a small piece of brain tissue. The removal of this small amount of tissue has no effect on mental function. Brain biopsies are not routinely done at present because no treatment is available even if a diagnosis is made. This may change as research in dementia progresses.

Multi-infarct dementia

In the past, dementing illnesses of old age were thought to be caused by *hardening of the arteries* of the brain. We now know that this is not the case. In multi-infarct dementia, repeated strokes within the brain destroy small areas of the brain. The cumulative effect of this damage leads to a dementia.

Multi-infarct dementias affect several functions, such as memory, coordination, or speech, but the symptoms differ somewhat depending on which areas of the brain are being damaged.

Multi-infarct dementias generally progress in a step-like way. You may be able to look back and recall that the person was worse after a specific time (instead of the gradual, imperceptible decline in Alzheimer's disease). Then she may not seem to get worse for a period, or she may even appear to get a little better. Some multi-infarct dementias progress as time passes; others may not get any worse for years. Some multi-infarct dementias may be stopped by preventing further strokes; in others the progression cannot be stopped.

Some people may have both Alzheimer's disease and multi-infarct disease.

Depression

Depression is a treatable cause of dementia. In a study of patients seen at The Johns Hopkins Hospital, about one-quarter of those who had symptoms of dementia were depressed. Eighty-two per cent of these got better when the patient received treatment for the depression. That depression can cause dementia has been widely accepted only recently and occasionally a doctor may not recognise dementia caused by depression. However, the symptoms of the depression are usually easily recognisable.

Whenever a person with a memory problem is depressed, she should be assessed to determine whether the depression is the cause of her dementia or vice versa. Her depression should be treated whether or not she has an irreversible dementia. Do not allow a doctor to dismiss depression. However, keep in mind that the person's depression may improve but not his memory problems.

Other brain disorders

There are several other mental conditions that are not dementias.

Delirium

The term *delirium* describes another *set of symptoms* that can have various causes. Delirium is often confused with dementia. Like the demented patient, the delirious patient may be forgetful or disoriented. Unlike a demented person, *the delirious person shows a reduced level of consciousness*. She may have a reduced ability to shift attention, focus attention, or sustain attention. Other symptoms of delirium may include misinterpretation of reality, false ideas, or hallucinations; incoherent speech; either sleepiness in the daytime or wakefulness at night; and increased or decreased physical (motor) activity. Symptoms of delirium often develop over a few hours or days. They tend to vary through the day.

Older people who do not have dementing illness may show symptoms—often intermittent—of impaired alertness, confusion, or memory problems. This may be a delirium caused by some other illness or medication. Such a delirium should be regarded as a symptom, and the causative disease should be identified and treated, if possible.

People with dementing illnesses are vulnerable to developing a delirium in addition to their dementia. You may observe a sudden worsening in a person who also has other problems, such as constipation, the flu, an infection, or even a slight cold. It is important to treat any such problem, because even very minor problems can seriously affect a person with a dementing illness.

Senility, chronic organic brain syndrome, acute or reversible organic brain syndromes

The word *senile* merely means 'old'. Thus, senility does not describe a disease and is considered by many people to be derogatory or prejudicial.

Chronic organic brain syndrome and *acute* or *reversible organic brain syndromes* are terms used by some to refer to those dementias that could not be treated (chronic) and to deliriums that respond to treatment (acute), respectively. These terms are no longer used because they are not specific and because they include implications of prognosis. We hope that in time there will be no 'chronic' brain syndromes.

TIA

TIA stands for transient ischemic attack. This is a temporary impairment due to an insufficient supply of blood to part of the brain. The person may be unable to speak, or may have slurred speech. She may be weak or paralysed, dizzy or nauseated. These symptoms usually last only a few minutes or hours before the person recovers. This is in contrast to a stroke which may have the same symptoms but after which some deficit remains. Very small deficits may not be noticeable. TIAs should be regarded as warnings of stroke and should be reported to your doctor.

Localised brain injuries

Damage can happen to the brain or head which temporarily or permanently affects either small or greater parts of the brain. This can be caused by brain tumours, strokes, or head injuries. Unlike dementia, such injuries may not be global, although they may affect more than one mental function. The symptoms can tell a neurologist just where the damage is. This is called a focal (localised) brain lesion (injury). When the damage is widespread the symptoms may be those of dementia.

Major *stroke*, which causes such things as sudden paralysis of one side of the body, drooping of one side of the face, or speech problems, is an injury to part of the brain. Strokes can be caused by a blood clot blocking vessels in the brain or by a blood vessel bursting and causing bleeding in the brain. Often the brain cells are injured or impaired by swelling but can recover when the swelling goes down. It may be that other parts of the brain can gradually learn to do the jobs of damaged sections of the brain. People who have had a stroke may get better. Rehabilitation training is important for people who have had a stroke. The chance of having another stroke can be reduced by good medical management.

Head injuries

Head injuries can destroy brain tissue directly or can cause bleeding within the brain. Sometimes blood collects between the skull and the brain, forming a pool of blood. This puts pressure on the brain cells and damages them. It is called a *subdural haematoma*. Even mild falls can cause such bleeding.

People with dementing diseases are vulnerable to falls and may not be able to tell you about them. If you suspect that a person has banged her head, she should be seen promptly by a doctor because treatment can prevent permanent damage. The bleeding beneath the skull may not occur in the same place as the head was hit.

18 Research in dementia

We have reached an exciting point in research into dementia. Not too long ago, most people assumed that dementia was the natural result of ageing and only a few pioneers were interested in studying it. In the last ten years that has changed. It is now known that:

1 dementia is not the natural result of ageing,
2 it is caused by specific, identifiable diseases,
3 diagnosis is important to identify treatable conditions,
4 a proper assessment is important in the management of contributing diseases that at present are not curable.

Today an increasing amount of research is focusing on the dementing illnesses. With new tools for study we can get a much clearer look at what goes on in the brain. Because of better public understanding, there is a growing demand for solutions. These factors acting together have attracted talented men and women to the study of dementia and we hope they will encourage allocation of more research money.

Understanding research

Understanding and interpreting *what* the research data mean is sometimes difficult for scientists and families alike. Here are some things you need to know about research to help you understand what you read.

It is essential that studies carefully define their terms. For example, some researchers have studied people with 'organic brain syndrome'. Data from such a study can be misleading because we do not know whether the people had Alzheimer's disease or other illnesses.

There is a difference between a relationship between two things and proof that one thing causes the other. We may find both A and B in the brains of dementia patients, but this does not mean that A caused B. A and B might both have been caused by an unknown factor, C.

It is essential that studies eliminate the influence of other factors. Sometimes when a new technique or drug is tried, the patient gets better. The hopes of the doctor, the patient, and the family, the additional attention, or some other factor may affect his improvement. This is called the *placebo effect* and it is quite common. Good studies of drugs, for example, are carefully designed to eliminate the possibility that other factors cause improvement. When you hear that several people got better on a certain drug, it may be because either they did not have the same illness or the placebo effect caused temporary improvement.

It is important to know what studies of laboratory animals mean.

Researchers who work with animals take into account in which ways the animals' reactions are similar to human reactions and in which ways they are not. Giving enormous doses of a chemical to an animal with a short life span magnifies the chances of seeing a relationship between the chemical and a disease, if one exists.

Epidemiology is the study of the distribution of diseases in large groups of people. The epidemiology of dementing illnesses may eventually show scientists a link between a dementing illness and something else as yet unknown—for example, a hereditary factor, diet in childhood, or use of a medicine many years ago. If you have participated in research programmes, you may have been asked many questions that don't seem in any way related to your problem, but which give researchers important epidemiologic information.

The increased public awareness of Alzheimer's disease has been accompanied by increased advertising of 'cures'. Some of these are expensive, dangerous, ineffective, or unfairly raise hopes. The Alzheimer's Disease Society can tell you which treatments are generally believed by doctors to be of no value.

Following is a summary of some of the research you may have read or heard about.

Research in multi-infarct dementia and stroke

Scientists are seeking to determine what effect hypertension, obesity, diet, smoking, heart disease, and other factors have on a person's vulnerability to stroke or multi-infarct disease. They are studying which areas of the brain are most likely to be damaged and the changes in brain chemistry that take place after a stroke. They are looking at how, when, and to what extent rehabilitative training helps a person. They are examining the effect of drugs on preventing stroke, on dilating blood vessels, on increasing the oxygen supply to the brain, and on preventing clotting.

Research in Alzheimer's disease

Neurotransmitters

Researchers have discovered that chemicals in the brain called *neurotransmitters* are necessary for messages to pass from one nerve cell to the next. They have learned that in some diseases there is less than the normal amount of a certain neurotransmitter. For example, a patient with Parkinson's disease can take L-Dopa, which increases the amount of the deficient neurotransmitter dopamine and alleviates the symptoms.

Scientists know that people with Alzheimer's disease have a deficiency of the enzyme *choline acetyltransferase*, which is necessary to produce the neurotransmitter *acetylcholine*. Thus, acetylcholine is presumed to be deficient in the brain of people with Alzheimer's disease. Research is in progress to find a way to increase the amount of acetylcholine in the brain or to find a drug that mimics it. Other neurotransmitters, such as somatostatin, may also be deficient.

Researchers have recently learned that a small area of the brain, the Nucleus Basalis of Meynert, shows cell loss in patients with Alzheimer's disease. Moreover, it now appears that this area is the site from which the brain's acetylcholine originates. It may be that the plaques and tangles are remaining fragments of the cells which contained acetylcholine.

Structural brain changes

It has long been known that there are microscopic changes in the brain of people with Alzheimer's disease called neuritic senile plaques and neurofibrillary tangles. These are found in much smaller quantities in the brain of normal older people. Scientists are analysing their structure and chemistry for clues to their formation and what their role in the disease may be.

Abnormal protein synthesis

The discovery of abnormally low levels of RNA in the brain cells of victims of Alzheimer's disease has given researchers a key to the way this disease affects the basic building blocks of brain cells.

In the normal brain RNA directs the production of protein necessary to the life of the cell. The amount of RNA present in the brain is limited by an enzyme, ribonuclease, which in turn is controlled by an inhibitor. Together they provide a proper chemical balance for the synthesis of protein needed for normal brain cell function.

In the brains of Alzheimer's disease victims scientists found far less than the normal amount of RNA. They found that ribonuclease was not controlled by its inhibitor but was freely destroying RNA and thereby limiting protein production.

While the cause of this abnormality has not been found, it offers valuable clues to diagnosis and potential treatments.

Nutrition

Lecithin and choline, substances occurring in many foods, are known to be used by the body to make acetylcholine. Studies have been done in which lecithin has been given to groups of demented people. The results are disappointing but many issues need to be looked at more closely. More needs to be known about why acetylcholine appears to be in short supply in some brains. Families often try giving people lecithin bought from a health food store, but there is no evidence that this can improve memory, mood, or behaviour.

Metals

Aluminium has been found in larger than expected amounts in the brains of some people with Alzheimer's disease. Other metals, such as manganese, are known to be associated with other forms of dementia. It now seems most likely that the presence of aluminium is a result of whatever is causing the dementia rather than itself a cause of the dementia. People sometimes wonder if they should stop taking antacids or cooking with aluminium pans or using deodorants (all sources of aluminium). There is no evidence that their use is a cause of dementia. Studies of people who have been exposed to much larger amounts of aluminium indicate that exposure does not lead to dementia. Some studies of drugs that assist in the elimination of aluminium from the body are being conducted.

Viruses

Some tentative research led scientists to suspect that a viral disease could be causing Alzheimer's disease. You may read about Creutzfeldt-Jacob disease or Kuru. Both of these rare diseases have been studied because they appear to be transmitted by a viruslike agent. There is no direct evidence at present to support the hypothesis that Alzheimer's disease is caused by a slow virus, but research is actively going on to determine this.

Drugs

Researchers are studying many compounds for the effects on memory. From time to time various drugs are proposed to treat people who have dementing illnesses. So far, however, none of them has been found to be effective when it is carefully tested in the laboratory, in spite of initial reports of people who improved. New drugs continue to be tested. You may hear about many of them. Some of these will lead to new treatments. Others will not be used after careful studies indicate that they are not effective.

Immunological defects

The immune system is the body's defence against infection. Studies of some of the proteins that the body uses to fight infection show abnormal levels in patients with Alzheimer's disease.

Scientists suspect that sometimes the body's defence system, which is designed to attack outside cells such as disease organisms, goes awry and attacks cells in the body. One theory is that this is what is happening in Alzheimer's disease. Numerous studies are being done approaching the problem from this angle.

Neuropsychology

Neuropsychology is the study of the relationship between brain structure and behaviour. Neuropsychologists are developing more sophisticated ways to diagnose Alzheimer's disease and to determine exactly which parts of the brain are being affected.

Other approaches

Other researchers are studying blood flow to the brain, genetic background, and the histories of demented patients. Perhaps from such studies some clue will emerge that will point to a cause of the disease. So far no such clues have been conclusive. One new and exciting tool is positron emission transaxial tomography (PETT), which will enable scientists to see just which parts of the brain are active when the brain does specific things. Comparing the results of normal and sick people should give us clues to what is not working in the brains of people with dementing illnesses.

The role of heredity

Families often ask if this disease is inherited or if later generations are likely to get Alzheimer's disease. An adult's chances of developing Alzheimer's disease are about 1 or 2 in 100 at age sixty-five but the odds increase fourfold if a close relative has the disease. These data, plus evidence that the disease may be related to other diseases such as Down's syndrome (Mongolism) known to be caused by defects in chromosomes, lead investigators to suspect that there may be a genetic factor in Alzheimer's disease. A genetic factor may mean a person has inherited a *tendency* to be more vulnerable to the disease but not that he will necessarily develop the disease.

Some investigators believe that women are more prone to Alzheimer's disease than men, but that men are more prone to multi-infarct dementia. This may be simply because men are more likely to develop vascular disease, while women tend to live longer and the incidence of Alzheimer's disease increases with age. Scientists are looking for clues as to whether this is so.

Keeping active

People often wonder if keeping mentally alert and involved or maintaining physical exercise will prevent a person from developing a dementing illness. As far as is known, neither physical exercise nor keeping mentally active will prevent or alter the course of Alzheimer's disease. Activity will help to maintain general health and improve the quality of life. Some studies that did not differentiate among causes of dementia have produced misleading results about the effect of activity on dementia. Sometimes people seem to develop a dementia after they retire. Upon close examination, however, it usually appears that the early stages of a dementia were developing before the person retired and that this early, unidentified dementia may have been a factor in the person's decision to retire.

The effect of acute illness on dementia

Sometimes people appear to develop a dementia after a serious illness, an admission to hospital, or surgery. Again, as far as is known, these things do not affect or alter the course of Alzheimer's dementia. Upon close examination it is often clear that the dementing illness had begun before the person had surgery or developed another disease. The stress of the acute illness and the tendency of people with a dementia to develop a delirium make the person worse, so his dementia is noticeable for the first time. Then his brain impairment will make it more difficult for him to adjust after his illness and he will *seem* more demented.

Studies of management of dementia

Scientists are now focusing on Alzheimer's disease, multi-infarct disease, and stroke. In time, we will learn to prevent or treat each disease. In the interim, the good news is what we have learned about caring for people with dementing illnesses. Much can be done to make life better for the impaired person and his family. This book is one step in disseminating our growing understanding of ways to improve the quality of life in the presence of illness.

Appendix 1: Further reading

References for professionals:

ARIE, T. (Ed.) 1981. *Health Care of the Elderly*. Beckenham: Croom Helm.

DHSS 1972. HM(72)71. *Services for Mental Illness Related to Old Age*. London: HMSO.

HOLDEN, U. P. & WOODS, R. T. 1982. *Reality Orientation. Psychological Approaches to the Confused Elderly*. Edinburgh: Churchill Livingstone.

ISAACS, A. D. Post F. 1979. *Studies in Geriatric Psychiatry*. Chichester: Wiley.

LEVY, R. Post F. (Ed). 1982. *The Psychiatry of Later Life*. Oxford: Blackwell.

PITT, B. 1982. *Psychogeriatrics*. Edinburgh: Churchill Livingstone.

REISBERG, B. (Ed.) 1984. *Alzheimer's Disease: The Standard Reference*. West Drayton, Middx: Free Press/Collier Macmillan.

WHITEHEAD, J. M. 1978. *Psychiatric Disorders in Old Age*. London: Harvey Miller.

WILCOCK, G. K. & MUIR GRAY, J. A. 1981. *Our Elders*. Oxford: Oxford University Press.

References for relatives:

AGE CONCERN. *Forgetfulness in Elderly Persons-Advice for Carers*. Age Concern Publication. Available from Age Concern Greater London, 54 Knatchbull Road, London SE5 3Q7 (£0.35p). A short practical booklet for carers of patients with early Alzheimer's disease.

ALZHEIMER'S DISEASE SOCIETY. 1984. *Caring for the Person with Dementia: A Guide for Families and Other Carers*.

GILLEARD, C. & WATT, G. 1983. *Coping with Ageing Parents*. London: Macdonald.

GRAY, J. M. & MCKENZIE, H. 1980. *Take Care of Your Elderly Relative*. London: Allen and Unwin.

HALE, G. 1983. *Source Book for the Disabled*. London: Heinemann.

HOLDEN, UNA *et al. 24hr Approach to the Problems of Confusion in Elderly People*. Winslow Press. Available from Winslow Press, 23 Horn Street, Winslow Bucks MK18 3AP. £0.35p. The booklet explains some basic principles of communication and orientation for people suffering from dementia.

KUBLER ROSS E. 1970. *On Death and Dying*. New York: MacMillan.

LODGE, B. 1981. *Coping with Caring—A Guide to Identifying and Supporting an Elderly Person with Dementia*. MIND Publication. Available from MIND Bookshop, 155/157 Woodhouse Lane, Leeds LS2 3EF (£1.60). This booklet includes a great deal of useful information on how to support and help the elderly confused and their relatives.

NORMAN, ALISON J. 1980. *Rights and Risk: A Discussion Document on Civil Liberty in Old Age*. National Corporation for the Care of Old People, London. Available from Bailey Bros. & Swinfen Ltd., Warner House, Folkestone, Kent CT19 6PH. £2.00. 30pp. A report of importance for those dealing with elderly both for professionals and carers.

Video References:

Communication in Dementia. A three-part (2 hour) video teaching guide made by Alzheimer's Disease Society Scotland for training courses.

Suffer the Carers. An Alzheimer's Disease Society—Sidhartha Films videotape which illustrates how the self-help group can support the sufferer and carer.

Where Is the Key. An hour-long authorised BBC videotape of a TV drama which depicts the many problems facing both sufferer and carer.

All videos (VHS System) are available for loan or hire from ADS London Office.

Appendix 2: Organisations

Age Concern England, Bernard Sunley House, 60 Pitcairn Road, Mitcham, Surrey CR4 3LL. Tel: (01) 640 5431.

Alzheimer's Disease Society, 3rd floor, Bank Building, Fulham Broadway, London SW6 1EP. Tel: (01) 381 3177.

Arthritis Care, 6 Grosvenor Crescent, London SW1X 7ER. Tel: (01) 235 0902.

Association of Carers, Lilac House, Medway Homes, Balfour Road, Rochester, Kent, ME4 6QU. Tel: Chatham (0634) 813981/2.

Association of Crossroads Care Attendant Schemes, 11 Whitehall Road, Rugby, Warwickshire. Tel: Rugby (0788) 61536.

British Association for Service of the Elderly, c/o Mrs C. Wyld, 3 Keele Farm House, Keele, Staffordshire.

British Association of the Hard of Hearing, 7/11 Armstrong Road, London W3 7JL. Tel: (01) 743 1110/1353.

British Pensioners and Trade Unions Action Association, 97 Kings Drive, Gravesend, Kent. Tel: Gravesend (0474) 61802.

British Red Cross Society, 9 Grosvenor Crescent, London SW1X 7EJ. Tel: (01) 235 5454.

Chest, Heart and Stroke Association, Tavistock House North, Tavistock Square, London WC1H 9JE. Tel: (01) 387 3012.

Contact, 15 Henrietta Street, London WC2E 8QH. Tel: (01) 240 0630.

Counsel and Care for the Elderly, 131 Middlesex Street, London E1 7JF. Tel: (01) 621 1624.

Cruse (National Organisation for the Widowed and their Children), Cruse House, 126 Sheen Road, Richmond, Surrey, TW9 1UR. Tel: (01) 940 4818/9047.

Disability Alliance, 25 Denmark Street, London WC2 8NJ. Tel: (01) 240 0806.

Disabled Living Foundation, 380/4 Harrow Road, London W9 2HU. Tel: (01) 289 6111.

Disablement Income Group, Attlee House, 28 Commercial Street, London E1 6LR. Tel: (01) 247 2128.

Distressed Gentlefolk's Aid Association, Vicarage Gate House, Vicarage Gate, London W8 4AQ. Tel: (01) 229 9341.

Extend (Exercise Training for the Elderly and Disabled), 5 Conway Road, Sheringham, Norfolk NR26 8DD. Tel: (0263) 822479.

Family Welfare Association, 501/5 Kingsland Road, London E8 4AU. Tel: (01) 254 6251.

Friends of the Elderly and Gentlefolk's Help, 42 Ebury Street, London SW1W OLZ. Tel: (01) 730 8263.

GRACE (Mrs Gould's Residential Advisory Centre for the Elderly), PO Box 71, Cobham, Surrey. Tel: Cobham (09326) 2928/5765.

Holiday Care Service, 2 Old Bank Chambers, Station Road, Horley, Surrey. Tel: Horley (02937) 74535.

Jewish Welfare Board, Lionel Cohen House, 315/17 Ballards Lane, London N12 8LP. Tel: (01) 446 1499.

Medic Alert Foundation, 11/13 Clifton Terrace, London N4 3JP. Tel: (01) 263 8597.

MIND (National Association for Mental Health), 22 Harley Street, London W1N 2ED. Tel: (01) 637 0741.

National Association of Citizens Advice Bureaux, Myddelton House, 115/123 Pentonville Road, London N1 9LZ. Tel: (01) 833 2181.

National Association of Widows, Stafford and District Voluntary Service Centre, Chell Road, Stafford ST16 2QA. Tel: Stafford (0785) 45465.

National Confederation of Registered Rest Homes Association, 74 London Road, St Leonards-on-Sea, East Sussex.

National Council for Carers and their Elderly Dependants, 29 Chilworth Mews, London W2 3RG. Tel: (01) 262 1451/2.

Partially Sighted Society, 40 Wordsworth Street, Hove, East Sussex BN3 5BH. Tel: Hove (0273) 736053.

Patients Association, Room 33, 18 Charing Cross Road, London WC2H OHR. Tel: (01) 240 0671.

Pensioners' Link, 17 Balfe Street, London N1 9EB. Tel: (01) 278 5501.

Pensioners' Voice (National Federation of Old Age Pension Associations), Melling House, 91 Preston New Road, Blackburn, Lancs BB2 6BO. Tel: Blackburn (0254) 52606.

RADAR (Royal Association for Disability and Rehabilitation), 25 Mortimer Street, London W1N 8AB. Tel: (01) 637 5400.

Registered Nursing Homes Association, 75 Portland Place, London W1N 4AN. Tel: (01) 631 1524.

Royal British Legion, 48 Pall Mall, London SW1Y 5JY. Tel: (01) 930 8131.

Royal National Institute for the Blind, 224 Great Portland Street, London W1N 6AA. Tel: (01) 388 1266.

Royal National Institute for the Deaf, 105 Gower Street, London WC1E 6AH. Tel: (01) 387 8033.

St Johns' Ambulance, 1 Grosvenor Crescent, London SW1H 7EF. Tel: (01) 235 5231.

Samaritans, 17 Uxbridge Road, Slough, Berks SO1 1SN. Tel: Slough (0753) 32713/4.

Soldiers, Sailors, and Airmen's Families Association, 27 Queen Anne's Gate, London SW1H 9BZ. Tel: (01) 222 9221.

Women's Royal Voluntary Service, 17 Old Park Lane, London W1Y 4AJ. Tel: (01) 499 6040.

Appendix 3: Where to loan or buy supplies

Incontinence supplies, eating aids, bathroom aids, wheelchairs, geriatric chairs, etc: You can obtain or loan much of this equipment from local Social Services and Home Nursing supplies, or some local voluntary organisations.

You can also purchase equipment from various manufacturers and suppliers. Information on these can be obtained from:

The Information Service
Disabled Living Foundation
380–4 Harrow Road
London W9 2HU
Tel: (01) 289 6111

Appendix 4: Codes of Practice

The United Kingdom does not have a 'bill of rights' for patients in hospitals and nursing homes, as does the United States. However, under the *Registered Homes Act 1984*, a Code of Practice has been published as part of the Government's measures to regulate the establishment and conduct of private and voluntary residential care homes. This has been published in *Home Life: A Code of Practice for Residential Care*, Report of a Working Party sponsored by the Department of Health and Social Security and convened by the Centre for Policy on Ageing under the chairmanship of Kina, Lady Avebury. Centre for Policy on Ageing, London, 1984, available (price £2.50) from Bailey Brothers and Swinfen Limited, Warner House, Folkestone, Kent CT19 6PH. Reprinted below as a checklist is a summary of their recommendations, reproduced by permission of the Centre for Policy on Ageing. The National Association of Health Authorities in England and Wales has issued in January 1985 a handbook for health authorities, *Registration and Inspection of Nursing Homes*. It is obtainable from NAHA, Garth House, 47 Edgbaston Park Road, Birmingham B15 2RS.

Summary of recommendations—a check list

In order to clarify the status of items in this check list, the word 'must' has been reserved for legal requirements. The legal basis of these requirements lies outside the Code.

Social care

Admission procedures

1 All homes should produce a brochure setting out the aims of the establishment and the facilities which it intends to provide.
2 Intending residents should be able to visit a home prior to admission and to be visited by someone from the home in the place where they are living.
3 The admission of residents on a short-term basis into a home should not disrupt or diminish the quality of life of longer term residents.
4 The first two months after a resident enters a home on a long-term basis should be agreed by both parties as a recognised trial period.
5 At the end of the trial period, the ability of the home to meet the needs of the resident should be fully considered by the resident, the proprietor and any key supporters.
6 Subsequent regular reviews should take place, in order to plan future health and social care for the resident.
7 The resident and key supporter should normally be present during the reviews.
8 Residents should be encouraged to bring personal possessions, including furniture, into a home.
9 Residents' personal possessions should be treated with respect, and any valuable items noted. Unobtrusive procedures for the recording of major additions and deletions should be established.

10 Residents should be helped to buy their own clothing and should never be supplied with clothing from a communal pool.

Terms and conditions of residence

11 All residents, and where necessary their sponsor as well, should be given in writing a clear statement of the terms under which the accommodation is offered.

12 Homes should be made aware of health factors affecting the type of care required. These should include the prospective resident's current medical condition and prognosis, together with any relevant social circumstances.

13 Information of this nature should be provided with the consent of the resident, and treated in the strictest confidence.

General administration

14 Records which the home is required to keep must be kept in a secure place and treated as confidential. Such records must be available for inspection by the registration authority.

15 Domestic routines in the home should aim to meet the needs and preferences of the resident rather than administrative convenience.

16 Rules relating to residents should be kept to a minimum.

17 Residents should be encouraged to maintain their independence within the home, recognising that this may involve a degree of responsible risk-taking.

18 Residents should be involved as much as possible in making decisions concerning the way in which the home is run.

19 Residents should be addressed in the manner they have chosen.

20 Professional advice and guidance from the registration authority should be sought when a resident's ability to make decisions or exercise choice appears to be in doubt.

21 All complaints should be treated seriously and recorded.

22 Residents should be made aware that they have the right to refer any unresolved complaint to the registration authority.

23 Any infringement of this Code of Practice should constitute grounds for a complaint.

24 Residents should normally have access to their personal records maintained by the home.

25 When information is provided about, or derived from, a third party it should not be disclosed to a resident without the consent of that third party.

26 Information about a child should not be given to parents or guardians without the child's consent, unless the child is precluded by age or mental impairment from giving informed consent.

27 Information may be withheld from the resident only in exceptional circumstances and after most careful assessment. Such a decision should be made at senior level within the home, and the resident may appeal to the registration authority.

Security of tenure

28 If there is any doubt about security of tenure, residents should be referred to a local Citizens Advice Bureau or the local Law Society.

Privacy and personal autonomy

29 It is recommended that residents in long-term care should have their own room, unless they prefer otherwise.
30 The right to privacy in residents' own rooms should be respected.
31 Where rooms are shared, personal space for each resident should be provided and privacy ensured by the use of room dividers and other furniture.
32 Bedroom and sitting room temperatures should be maintained at similar levels.
33 Residents should be able to meet whom they wish in private, either in their own room, or in other comfortable accommodation.
34 Residents should be encouraged to pursue existing interests and acquire new ones.
35 Residents' mobility should be maintained by encouraging walks, outside visits and social activity.
36 All residents should be enabled to make use of community facilities.
37 Involvement in political and religious activities should be respected, provided it does not interfere unduly with others.
38 Visitors should be welcome at all reasonable times.
39 A resident's right to refuse to see a visitor should be respected.
40 If a proprietor decides to exclude a resident's visitor, he should record the fact, and be able to justify this action to the registration authority.
41 The involvement of suitable volunteers to befriend isolated residents is to be encouraged.

Financial affairs

42 Adults who are likely to be permanent residents should be encouraged to make a will prior to admission to the home.
43 Proprietors or staff should not normally act as witnesses to any resident's will. In no circumstances should the proprietor or any member of staff become an executor of any resident's will.
44 If a resident's incompetence to make a will is confirmed by a medical practitioner, consideration should be given to contacting the Court of Protection.
45 It should be the publicly-known practice of a home to decline all personal gifts from residents, except for small token presents. If a resident insists, independent advice, if possible from the registration authority, should be sought.
46 The acceptance of gratuities by staff should not be permitted.
47 Residents should be made aware of their responsibility for the safe-keeping of money and valuables, and of any insurance provided by the home which covers this. They should be advised to take out any further insurance which may be needed.
48 The home must have a secure facility, with limited access by a responsible person, for the storage of residents' valuables. Receipts should be given to depositors.
49 The home should also keep a permanent register of deposits and withdrawals.

50 In the case of temporary or permanent incapacity of a resident to safeguard his possessions, the agent acting on his behalf should undertake the responsibility (see 51–54).

51 A resident may appoint a relative, friend or someone over 18 in the community to act as his agent in the handling of his finances.

52 In the absence of someone known to the resident, the registration authority should be asked to recommend someone to act as agent. References for agents should be sought, and all names of individuals and organisations acting as agents should be lodged with the registration authority. Only in exceptional circumstances should the proprietor or manager assume the role of agent.

53 A resident wishing to delegate more extensive powers to act on his behalf may execute a power of attorney. No one connected with the home should be appointed an attorney.

54 When a qualified medical practitioner has assessed a resident as mentally unable to manage his financial affairs, and the value of assets warrants it, careful consideration should be given to placing the resident under the jurisdiction of the Court of Protection.

55 In the case of children, guidance and education in the handling of personal money is good practice.

56 Proprietors and staff should not become involved in the handling and management of residents' monies. They should be able to draw the attention of the registration authority to any concern they may have about particular problems of a resident's finances.

Health care

57 **All residents have the right of access to health and remedial services provided in the community.**

58 **Homes have the right of access to community health resources for their residents.**

59 **No medical treatment must be given to a resident without his valid consent except where the law permits in cases of life-threatening emergencies, or under the terms of the Mental Health Act 1983.**

60 **When a resident's ability to give valid consent is restricted by inability to understand the language, every effort must be made to explain the nature of the treatment and to gain consent through the use of an interpreter.**

61 **Children under 16 may be able to consent to or refuse treatment. Where they cannot do so by reason of age or mental impairment, parents or those *in loco parentis* may do so, subject to the Court's powers to take action in the child's best interests.**

62 **Only household remedies should be given without a doctor's prescription.**

63 **Residents who are deemed able to retain and administer their own medication should be encouraged to do so, and have a secure place to keep it in.**

64 **Drugs for which the proprietor is responsible must be kept in a secure place, be individually labelled, and administered only by the trained responsible person authorised by the proprietor. A record must be kept of drugs received and administered by the home.**

65 **A resident's failure to take prescribed drugs which are held by the proprietor should be reported to the resident's medical practitioner.**

66 The proprietor should take responsibility for ensuring that staff are trained in the administration of drugs.

67 Medication must never be administered as a means of social control.

Dying and death

68 When a home has admitted a resident with an assurance of 'care till death', the use of external sources of care, such as the community nursing, or hospice nursing service, is strongly recommended.

69 Intensive or terminal care should be given in a resident's own room and not in any special unit.

70 If a resident is aware he is dying, he should be consulted about his wishes on terminal care and funeral or cremation arrangements.

71 Contact should be made, if the resident wishes it, with the appropriate minister of religion.

72 When a resident is dying, the need for support to relatives, staff, and other residents should be recognised and met.

73 Local, cultural and religious customs surrounding the death of a resident should be observed.

74 Proprietors should ascertain at an early stage who will take responsibility for a resident's property pending the proving of a will.

Physical features

75 When considering whether there is reasonable and appropriate accommodation and space, the registration authority will refer to the appropriate Building Notes. In the case of adapted premises, these should be flexibly interpreted.

76 Registering authorities should ensure that the location and surrounding environment are suited to the aims of a home, in the case of new applications.

77 The availability of local amenities, accessibility, health services and public transport should be considerations in granting registration.

78 The physical size of the building and the total number of residents in each social grouping within it shall be important considerations in deciding whether to grant registration.

79 The stated aims of the establishment should determine what is meant by reasonable accommodation and space and such accommodation should conform to the relevant Building Notes for particular client groups.

80 Communal rooms in a home should be arranged to allow residents to follow their chosen hobbies or interests. Where there are children there should be room for homework to be done.

81 The home should be decorated and furnished in a non-institutional manner.

82 Storage space for residents' luggage should be provided.

83 All residents' rooms should have at least one armchair, chest of drawers, wardrobe facilities and table. There should be one lockable piece of furniture.

84 In rooms for adults and older children, there should be accessible power and light sockets. For younger children these must not be easily accessible.

85 Residents should be allowed a choice of bedding, and it should be ensured that such bedding is flame- and smoulder-proof.
86 Floors in residents' rooms should be covered in non-slip materials.
87 Residents should be able to have their names outside their doors, if wished, and where possible letter boxes and locks should be provided on the doors.
88 There should be a private washbasin within each bedroom.
89 Washing areas in bedrooms should be screened to provide privacy.
90 There should be an overall ratio of one toilet to four residents.
91 One bathroom to eight residents should be the minimum provided.
92 The ratios of toilets and bathrooms to residents should not include those exclusively for staff use.
93 The location and fittings of bathrooms and toilets should be planned to minimise the effects of disability of residents.
94 Equipment should be provided for residents who so wish to launder their personal clothing.

Diet and food preparation

95 Meals must be varied, properly served and nutritious, and should provide choice.
96 Ready-plated meals should be avoided.
97 The timing of meals should be flexible and provision made for residents to prepare snacks and drinks for themselves.
98 Attention to residents with eating difficulties should be given discreetly.
99 Homes should be prepared to cater for special diets, whether these are medically advised, of cultural, religious or philosophical significance or the result of strong preference.
100 Residents should never be deceived into eating foods they would not otherwise take.
101 Staff training should include the cultural and social importance of meals, their content and preparation.
102 Proprietors should ascertain residents' dietary needs on admission, seeking advice from the community dietician or religious advisers where necessary in order to meet these needs.

Client groups

103 Irrespective of the client group, homes should understand the importance of recognising and responding to the needs of the individual residents and enabling them to achieve their maximum potential.

Disabled people

104 Disabled people should have normal opportunities to make informed choices and take risks.
105 The intimate personal needs of handicapped people should be met sensitively, always enabling them to retain autonomy and dignity.

106 Staff should be trained to understand the communication needs and difficulties of residents suffering from sensory handicaps and speech disorders.
107 Accommodation should be adapted and aids provided to reduce the effects of disability.
108 The disabled person should be consulted about his needs and management of his disability.

Mentally ill people

109 Signs of institutionalisation in former long stay hospital patients should be recognised and their special needs identified in making appropriate placements.
110 Staff should have the support and advice of relevant professions in the community.
111 Where a therapeutic regime limits autonomy, the resident should first be given a full explanation and agree to accept such limitations.
112 Provision of positive day-time activity is essential and may be met either in the home or community. The resources of specialist voluntary agencies should be considered.
113 In the case of a placement from hospital the registration authority should ensure that arrangements are agreed to cover after-care of the resident.

Mentally handicapped people

114 The home should create an enabling environment for mentally handicapped people, encouraging choice.
115 A full assessment of educational and social potential, and physical and emotional needs, should be available on admission.
116 Mentally handicapped residents should have access to a social worker or other suitable person to provide personal support.
117 Appropriate day-time occupation and education in the case of a child must be arranged and activities for adults should be provided.
118 Opportunities for suitable employment should be considered at regular reviews.

Children and young people

119 Proprietors and staff should be aware of reactions and behaviour patterns of child residents.
120 Staff should have an understanding of the significance of personal relationships between a child and care staff.
121 Children should be helped to understand the reality of their situation and their need to be in the home.
122 The recording of past events in a 'life story book' will be of major importance to most children.
123 Long-term goal planning should involve the child. Plans should not make unrealistic demands upon the child.

124 Controls and sanctions should not undermine the self-respect of children.
125 Intervention should be positive rather than negative, based on reward rather than punishment.
126 Restriction of contact with parents, food deprivation and other unacceptable sanctions should not be used.
127 All sanctions used to control bad behaviour must be recorded and this record must be available for inspection by authorised persons.
128 Parents should share and be responsible for decisions affecting the child whenever possible.
129 Care staff should be able to offer understanding and reassurance to parents.
130 Handicapped children have the same needs as other children and should have the same opportunities to develop their full potential.
131 Proprietors and staff should be made aware of specialist help available for handicapped children.
132 The child's legal status should be clearly identified on admission. Explanations should be given to the resident and staff of the effect of the legal status of a child resident and of restrictions imposed by orders of the court.
133 Proprietors must make suitable arrangements for the education of all children present.

Elderly people

134 The right of elderly residents to autonomy and choice should always be recognised.
135 The layout, decor and furnishing of the home should be designed to minimise confusion.
136 Staff should be trained to understand the needs of mentally and physically frail old people.
137 Community support and treatment services should be consulted in the care of mentally ill elderly people.
138 Physical restraint and control by sedation should not be used.

Drug addiction, alcohol and solvent abuse

139 Before admission the potential resident should have a full explanation of the regime and any rules which modify his freedom.
140 Admission should be subject to a contractual agreement.
141 Residents should be encouraged to participate in the day-to-day running of the home or hostel.
142 Within the limits of the regime, opportunities and space for privacy should be safeguarded.
143 In-service training should be provided for all staff.
144 Staff with a personal history of addiction should have undertaken training or have been employed elsewhere for at least one year after completing rehabilitation.
145 A clearly defined management structure should be agreed. Health, social services and probation service representatives should act as advisers or members of the management committee.

146 Where appropriate, the proprietor should retain the service of a consultant psychiatrist.

147 Where residents are subject to a supervision or probation order, arrangements for regular access to clients by probation officers must be agreed.

Staff

148 Staff qualities should include responsiveness to and respect for the needs of the individual.

149 Staff skills should match the residents' needs as identified in the objectives of the home.

150 Staff should have the ability to give competent and tactful care, whilst enabling residents to retain dignity and self-determination.

151 In the selection of staff at least two references should be taken up, where possible from previous employers.

152 Applicants' curriculum vitae should be checked and for this purpose employers should give warning that convictions otherwise spent should be disclosed.

153 Proprietors should consider residents' needs in relation to all categories of staff when drawing up staffing proposals.

154 Job descriptions will be required for all posts and staff should be provided with relevant job descriptions on appointment.

155 In small homes where staff carry a range of responsibilities, these must be clearly understood by staff.

156 Any change of role or duty should be made clear to the member of staff in writing.

157 Minimum staff cover should be designed to cope with residents' anticipated problems at any time.

158 Staff deployment should take account of periods of high demand.

159 Where residents require lifting at least two members of staff should be on duty at all times.

160 Where married couples are employed, rotas should allow for shared time off.

161 Night staff should be experienced and trained. Where night staff are insufficiently experienced it is necessary for senior staff to be on call on the premises.

162 The potential therapeutic role of ancillary staff should be recognised.

163 Staff involved in meal planning and preparation should receive appropriate training.

164 Residents' clothing should be well treated, and laundering and needlework should be done with care, whether staff or residents carry out these tasks.

165 Good maintenance of the building and garden is important for the comfort of residents and should not be neglected.

166 Clerical staff should be employed to ensure that records and administration are kept up-to-date without using senior management time inappropriately.

167 Proprietors should demonstrate that they have considered the range of specialist services residents may require.

168 Where specialists are not available through statutory agencies, proprietors must show how such services will be provided and how the cost will be met.

169 Management structure should allow for senior staff to be effectively deployed and available at all times.

170 Staff induction and training and individual supervision should be carefully considered and planned in detail.

171 Proprietors should demonstrate that they are able to provide support for staff to the degree required by the complexity and stress involved in the work, and to enable, through supervision, maximum career development.

172 The responsible person in day-to-day charge should have at least one year's experience at senior level in a residential home and/or a qualification recognised by the registration authority as appropriate for the stated aim of the home.

173 The proprietor or responsible person in charge should be able to demonstrate an ability to administer and manage the home on a successful business level.

174 Staff deployment should allow for, and the registration authority assist in, the provision of 'in-house' training.

175 Staff should be encouraged to undertake appropriate further training.

176 The cost of training should be considered when the level of residents' fees is assessed.

177 Voluntary workers should be aware of the aims and objectives of the home.

178 The role of voluntary workers should be clearly described.

179 Staff should be made aware of the expected contribution of voluntary workers.

Responsibilities of registration authorities

180 The registration authority should ensure that the care given in the home matches the stated objectives.

181 The officer responsible for registration should have experience and ability commensurate with the responsibilities of the job. Other departmental duties should be kept to a minimum.

182 The registration authority should provide written guidance on legislation and local conditions to initial enquirers.

183 Prospective proprietors should receive counselling and advice on the financial implications and responsibilities of residential care homes.

184 The registration authority policy on sponsorship of residents should be explained.

185 Prospective proprietors should be informed of the role and responsibilities of other statutory services/agencies.

186 The responsibility of residents in connection with their own financial affairs should be clarified.

187 A prospective proprietor should demonstrate to the registration authority competence and understanding in business matters.

188 The registration authority should ensure that a check is made on the DHSS list of former proprietors who have been deregistered, before granting registration.

189 Registration authorities should consider setting up, in conjunction with other agencies, introduction courses to assist prospective proprietors prepare for this task.

190 Registration authorities should ensure that actual and legal divisions of responsibility in voluntary organisations are clearly defined.

191 It should be recognised that management bodies may need professional advice on training, costings and staff appointments.

192 Progress and preparation for opening a new home should be monitored by the registration authority.

193 The need for advice in the early stages should be recognised, to ensure that registration requirements are understood and implemented.

194 When residents are placed by social services departments the role of the social worker should be explained.

195 Care should be given to explaining the needs of special client groups and those who may be subject to additional legal requirements.

196 Information on available community specialist services should be provided to proprietors.

197 Managers and staff of homes should have access to training opportunities in the public sector.

198 Registration authorities should provide information on alternative training resources.

199 Prospective proprietors/managers should be reminded that they may not operate until a certificate of registration is issued. They should be informed of the penalties for operating unregistered homes.

200 Registration authorities should issue certificates of registration as soon as is practicable.

201 Proprietors should inform the registration authority of any intended change of ownership.

202 Residents should be fully informed of any proposed changes of ownership.

203 The registration authority must be informed of any proposed change of objectives or facilities. Such changes must be mutually agreed for the registration to remain valid.

204 The brochure should be altered when changes in objectives or facilities are agreed.

205 The registration authority should ensure that a visit of inspection is made within three months of registration or where a new manager of a home has been appointed.

206 Registration authorities are required by law to inspect homes not less than once every 12 months. It is advised that visits take place more frequently.

207 Inspections should focus on the quality of life and care of the residents and on the standards of management.

208 A check list should be used as an aid in the formal annual inspection but discussion with the proprietor or person in day-to-day charge is also essential.

209 The officer making the inspection should identify any change of circumstance which might affect the registration.

210 Following the annual review, a written report should be sent to the proprietor.

211 Residents should have access freely and in private to the inspection officer when the inspection is made.

212 Residents must be told on or before admission how to make complaints to the registered person and to the registration authority.

213 Complaints not resolved in the home should be referred to the registration authority in writing for investigation by the authority.

214 The registration authority should arrange to interview all persons relevant to the complaint and state in writing to the proprietor, manager and resident the outcome of the investigation, specifying action to be taken.

215 Where a registration authority is considering deregistering a home, the proprietor should be informed prior to action being taken.

216 Residents, sponsoring agencies and key supporters should be informed that the registration authority intends to take action to deregister the home.

217 Registration authorities must make available for inspection at all reasonable times the registers of residential care homes within their area.

218 Registration authorities should consider providing general advice on financial assistance for residents and also clarify differences between private and voluntary homes and residential care homes and nursing homes.

Index